Consuming Literature

Best Sellers and the Commercialization of Literary Production in Contemporary China

SHUYU KONG

Stanford University Press
Stanford, California
2005

01024344

Stanford University Press
Stanford, California

© 2005 by the Board of Trustees of the
Leland Stanford Junior University.
All rights reserved.

Chapter Six, "Literary Journals: Between a Rock and a Hard Place,"
was originally published as "Between a Rock and a Hard Place:
Chinese Literary Journals in the Cultural Marketplace" in *Modern
Chinese Literature and Culture*, vol. 14, no. 1 (Spring 2002). Reprinted
with permission.

No part of this book may be reproduced or transmitted in any form or
by any means, electronic or mechanical, including photocopying and
recording, or in any information storage or retrieval system without the
prior written permission of Stanford University Press.

Printed in the United States of America
On acid-free, archival-quality paper.

Library of Congress Cataloging-in-Publication Data

Kong, Shuyu.
   Consuming literature : best sellers and the commercialization of
literary production in contemporary China / Shuyu Kong.
      p.   cm.
   Includes bibliographical references and index.
   ISBN 0-8047-4939-6 (alk. paper)—
ISBN 0-8047-4940-X (pbk. : alk. paper)
      1. Publishers and publishing—China.   2. Booksellers and
bookselling—China.   I. Title: Best sellers and the commercialization
of literary production in contemporary China.   II. Title.
Z462.K66   2005
070.5'0951—dc22   2004017604

Original Printing 2005
Last figure below indicates year of this printing:
14   13   12   11   10   09   08   07   06   05

Typeset by Heather Boone in 10.5/12 Bembo

3613646800  *Literature*

University of Stirling Library, FK9 4LA
Tel: 01786 467220

LONG LOAN

Please **RETURN** or **RENEW**
no later than the date on the receipt
Subject to recall if requested

WITHDRAWN
from
STIRLING UNIVERSITY LIBRARY

*To Colin
and my parents
with love*

Contents

Acknowledgments

THIS BOOK IS BASED on the results of several field trips I made to China between 1999 and 2002, which were funded mainly by Support for the Advancement of Scholarship Research Grants from the University of Alberta. I am especially grateful to Dr. Eva Neumaier, the Chair of East Asian Studies, and Dr. Harvey Krahn, Associate Dean of Research, for their encouragement and support for this project during that period.

The following people in China gracefully accepted my interview requests: An Boshun, Bai Bing, Bai Ye, Cai Xuejun, Cao Wenxuan, Chen Liu, Chen Xiaoming, Dai Jinhua, Gu Jianping, Guan Bo, Han Jingqun, Li Chaoquan, Li Dawei, Li Feng, Li Jingze, Lin Bai, Xin Jiping, Xing An, Lu Yuanchang, Miao Hong, Nie Zhenning, Qin Shunxin, Wang Lixing, Wang Shuli, Xu Kun, Zhang Dening, Zhang Xiaoqiang, Zhao Suping, Zhu Xiaofeng, and Zhong Renfa. Without the many fascinating inside stories they related to me, this empirically based study would have been simply impossible. On the Western academic front, Bonnie McDougall, Kirk Denton, Kam Louie, and two anonymous readers provided very helpful suggestions and critiques at various stages on the papers and chapters out of which this book emerged.

Many friends and colleagues, including some outside the academic world, helped me in various ways: Wang Ying, Wang Yuan, Xue Hui, Zhang Xiaoqiang, Zuo Shandan, Cao Wenxuan, Han Jingqun, Zhou Zan, Neng Xiangqun, Yue Daiyun, and Wen Rumin. Some inspired me and extended me moral support and feedback through years of intellectual investigation; others provided practical help during the long and painstaking process of collecting materials in China. Special thanks to the residents and staff of St. John's College at the University of British Columbia, where I stayed for a short few months in 2002 and rekindled my enthusiasm for completing this book.

I am very fortunate to have had Carmen Borbon-Wu as the acquisitions editor and Mariana Raykov as the production editor. I am also grateful to Matthew Kudelka for the excellent job he did copy editing my manuscript.

Their enthusiasm and hard work helped to turn a rough manuscript into a well-polished product.

Lastly, I would like to thank my husband, Colin Hawes, for his generosity and support. Without his constant encouragement, gentle pushing, quiet sacrifices, and practical help, this book would never have come into existence. His confidence and love for me have kept me going through this project, and to him I dedicate this book.

Consuming Literature

Introduction

COMMERCIALIZATION AND
LITERARY BEST SELLERS

THE ECONOMIC REFORMS that have swept through China over the past two decades have created a vibrant cultural marketplace, and the newly established norms of this marketplace have in turn transformed how culture is being produced and consumed in China. Because of its central importance as an ideological tool during the Maoist years, literature can provide us with some of the most striking evidence of these far-reaching changes, which include both institutional and conceptual paradigm shifts. New literary practices that are economically rather than ideologically motivated have eroded and reshaped the existing socialist literary establishment.

Yet in the midst of all this dramatic change, literary and cultural institutions in this transitional society must confront a number of dilemmas. For instance, publishing and media enterprises are still owned and supervised by the state, and thus are impeded by hidebound, socialist-style bureaucracies; but at the same time, they must heed the state's calls to compete in the market, to become financially independent, and (ideally) to manage and operate themselves as if they were private companies. Commercial incentives and market logic have tended to bring literary production more into line with popular culture, and many worry that Chinese literature is suffering "the loss of its humanistic spirit."[1] Yet one could also argue that the tremendous expansion of literary and publishing outlets since the 1990s has opened up space for greater diversity in public discourse and for a kind of cultural pluralism, thereby freeing literature from the recent decades of political and social moralism.[2] Examining the transformations and paradoxes of literary practices in China today will thus help us broaden our understanding of the varied and contradictory forces that are driving social and cultural change in a complex transitional society.

This book originated in a paper I wrote in 1999 on the societal factors underlying the sudden boom in women's writing in China during the mid-1990s. While collecting materials for that paper, I was impressed by the wide availability of daring works that revealed women's innermost experiences and sexual desires; their publication would have been unthinkable even fifteen years earlier.[3]

Further investigation revealed several reasons for this sudden explosion in women's writing: a heightened feminist consciousness among women writers (a result of Western feminist theoretical works being translated into Chinese); and government propaganda praising the achievements of Chinese women, especially before and during the UN World Conference on Women, held in Beijing in 1995. Yet when I looked "behind" the texts to scrutinize the processes of literary production, I began to feel that deeper socioeconomic factors could account for the sudden growth in women's writing and for the particular focus of its subject matter—namely, the major changes taking place in publishing institutions as a result of economic reforms, especially since the early 1990s. Publishers were now much more consumer and market oriented; they were also less restricted by political and party guidelines than they had been even during the 1980s. Indeed, it was clear that the growing commercialization of Chinese culture was driving a whole new approach to publishing, one that had revitalized the book and literature sectors. Guided now by consumers' needs rather than by Communist Party interests, all kinds of new materials once regarded as politically incorrect—or at least insufficiently revolutionary—could now be published openly as long as market demand for them existed. Popular fiction, entertainment books, lifestyle magazines, foreign literature in translation, and a huge variety of other genres had all begun appearing on the flourishing Chinese book market. At the same time, increased competition among commercial publishers was leading to much higher overall quality of both books and magazines. Publishers were becoming keenly aware that they needed to exploit every possible market niche in order to expand their businesses and increase their profits. Contemporary women's writing, with its remarkably explicit reflections on gender and sexuality, became one of the hottest-selling genres, and publishers competed to bring out the works of the most popular, even notorious, women writers.

The 1995 UN World Conference on Women was one of the biggest international events held in China during the 1990s. The Chinese government took advantage of this event to trumpet its achievements in the area of women's liberation; meanwhile, commercial publishers saw the conference as an excellent opportunity to profit from the unprecedented exposure being given to women's issues. Publishers' sudden "enthusiasm" for women's writing during the mid-1990s—in particular, their tendency to narrow the broader concerns of women writers down to marketable themes such as women's private lives and sexuality—thus can be fully explained only with reference to the commercial transformations taking place in the Chinese literary publishing industry as a whole.

Although it was in the area of women's writing that I first explored these ideas (case studies of women's writing are the focus of Chapter 4), the commercialization of publishing in China has affected many other areas of literature in similarly dramatic fashion. It seems to me that in describing any cultural phenomenon in 1990s China, we cannot ignore the constant noise of commercialization in the background and the ever-evolving institutional and conceptual changes that have accompanied economic reforms. Unfortunately, few scholars, be they Chinese or Western, have dealt with these changes systematically. There is a need for a book that will fill the gap in our understanding of contemporary Chinese literature by examining the transformation that economic reform has brought to all stages in the literary production process—from writing to publishing to distribution. I want this to be that book.

During four field trips to China between 1999 and 2002, I spent much time interviewing writers, editors, and publishers, visiting bookstores new and old, and combing through literary newspapers and journals. It steadily became clear to me that notwithstanding frequent complaints by elite writers and critics about the "death of literature" at the hands of commercial forces, the production and consumption of literature is a vital and flourishing fact in China, although admittedly this is to define "literature" somewhat more loosely than before.[4] Chinese writers have become far more aware of their potential readers and of the market's demands, and their writing has become more diverse and entertainment-oriented. Many publishing houses have introduced more efficient operations that are generating profits without completely sacrificing socialist ideals. So-called "second-channel" book agents are running back and forth acting as mediators between state publishing houses and individual writers; sometimes they publish "unofficial" books themselves. And a complex network of private book distribution channels has opened up to augment and challenge the inefficient state-run Xinhua bookstore system.

Changes like these have not always resulted in the publication of higher-quality literature—in the purely aesthetic sense—or in the development of a stable cultural environment. In fact, commercialization has many disturbing features (discussed in later chapters); and we can say that as a result of them, the 1980s ideal of creating an autonomous literature and experimenting with the avant-garde has faded away. This provides another main theme for this book: pure literature has altered its identity now that the market is turning literary works into consumable goods.

Despite these negatives, there is no doubt that Chinese literary production is more vigorous, more diverse, more open, and more ideologically ambivalent than at any time since the Communists took power in 1949. From the chaos and confusion of a society in transition, a Chinese literary industry is emerging based on dynamic commercial principles—principles that are undermining when not transforming the literary institutions that have served the socialist establishment for the past four decades.

While collecting the materials for this study and talking to Chinese writers, publishers, and booksellers, I constantly encountered another term new to Socialist China: best seller (*changxiao shu*).[5] After four decades during which literature was treated as noble spiritual food to nourish the young or as a rigid ideological tool to mobilize the people—something far removed from the dirty and avaricious capitalist world—the Chinese had suddenly discovered that books, even literary works, could be treated as commodities to be mass produced, advertised, and sold for profit. And for most players in the newly transformed world of literary publishing, the overarching goal was to release a best seller.

Indeed, one could almost describe the 1990s in China as the decade of the best seller, since all the major literary events that shook Chinese publishing during that period were associated with best sellers. That is why this book, which aims to investigate the effects of the market economy on literature, is organized around the recurring theme of how best sellers have emerged in literary publishing.

In 1992, Huayi Publishing House (Huayi chubanshe) in Beijing published its four-volume *Wang Shuo wenji* (The Collected Works of Wang Shuo), and paid Wang with royalties instead of a fixed fee. This was virtually the first time in more than four decades that the "value" of a Chinese literary work had been linked directly to its market appeal. As a result of Wang's reputation as a cultural iconoclast and his efforts to help Huayi promote the book, this collection became one of the top best sellers of the 1990s, making Wang a very wealthy man. I discuss this author's entrepreneurial innovations in Chapter 1, contrasting him with popular fiction writers of the 1980s such as "Xue Mili," who became rich but at the expense of their reputations as literary writers. Wang Shuo represents the new era, in which market-savvy writers can produce best-selling works and generate great wealth without being accused of selling out to the lowest-brow tastes.

Although some writers have resisted the temptations of the marketplace, continuing to produce "pure literature" without any expectation of profit, it is clear that most Chinese writers since the 1990s have become much more attuned to the need to make their writing salable. For example, in 1993 the notorious novel *Fei du* (Ruined Capital) by Jia Pingwa sold more than a million copies, becoming one of the highest-grossing books of that year. This novel is a sterling example of an established "serious" writer becoming "popularized." Under the socialist system, Jia had garnered a high reputation but little money. His previous works had focused on Chinese peasant life; his new novel, with its descriptions of social and moral decadence in a provincial Chinese city and its explicit male sexual fantasies, easily lent itself to marketing hype and had obvious appeal for a mass Chinese audience.

Publishers have since managed to persuade many established writers to produce more popular works for a mass audience. In 1994, Chunfeng Art and Literature Publishing House (Chunfeng wenyi chubanshe) established the Cloth Tiger series (Bu laohu congshu) to promote the concept of popular and romantic fiction by established writers. The house soon developed Cloth Tiger into a highly successful literary "brand name" publishing quality products for a well-defined and carefully targeted consumer base. In Chapter 2, on state publishing houses, I discuss Chunfeng's "branding process" in detail, along with the equally successful "best seller machine" of Writers Publishing House (Zuojia chubanshe). I will demonstrate that the most progressive and profitable Chinese publishing houses of the 1990s have transformed their business structures and marketing approaches in order to motivate both their employees and the writers who sign with them to produce best-selling titles. This is in marked contrast to the elitist, state-supported publishing system of the prereform period, during which writers and publishers produced and published books with little hope of profit and for largely political ends.

One of the ten publishing phenomena of 1997, as reported by *Zhongguo tushu shangbao* (Chinese Book Business Review), was the emergence of studios (*gongzuoshi*)—unofficial cultural units that functioned as literary agents, editors, and book marketers.[6] These studios, also known as shadow publishing houses (*yingzi chubanshe*), have become such a force in the Chinese publishing industry that some claim that most of the recent best sellers in China were actually produced by them, not by the state-owned publishers whose names appear on the covers. The Chinese second channel is the subject of Chapter 3.

Critics and official government publications in China hold a generally negative view of the second channel. I do not. Certainly, they have been involved in many dubious practices since the 1980s, such as book piracy and pornography distribution. More recently, however, second-channel publishers and distributors have greatly enriched the literary and cultural book market. Furthermore, it was they that pioneered most of the business innovations that have transformed the publishing industry in China. They have also penetrated deeply into the state-controlled publishing sector through alliances, business partnerships, franchises, and various semilegal methods. This places them in a strong position to take over the book market once further deregulation occurs. Later I will present two detailed examples—Alpha Books, an unofficial publisher, and Xishu Bookstore, a private distributor and retail franchise—and show how they have made available interesting and diverse titles that might never have seen the light of day had they relied on the state-run publishing and distribution system. I will conclude the same chapter by suggesting that government control of publishing through state-run publishing houses and a book license / number system has broken down, with cash-strapped state publishers increasingly happy to sell their licenses and to contract with commercially successful second-channel publishers in order to make a profit. Sooner or later, the book license system will probably be replaced by an open registration system for publishing houses.

The first half of this book deals with the different stages of the publishing process; it begins with the writers, then goes on to the publishers (both official and second-channel), then the distributors and booksellers. The second half shifts the focus to three distinct fields of literary production: women's writing, foreign literature translation, and literary journals. Throughout this book I will show how deeply the commercial ethic and the quest for best sellers have infiltrated the Chinese literary world.

Each of Chapters 4, 5, and 6 focuses on a specific milestone year. For example, 1995 saw the explosion in women's writing that I noted earlier, and this forms the starting point for Chapter 4. Publishers attempted to capitalize on the enormous publicity surrounding the UN World Conference on Women by bringing out many popular works by women writers. Yet as I will demonstrate, the desire of publishers to appeal to a mass audience led some to focus unduly on the sexual aspects of women's literature and on the private lives and attractive appearance of the writers themselves. In the case of some best-selling novels, such as Lin Bai's *Yi ge ren de zhanzheng* (A War with Oneself), the result was distorted publicity and misleading alterations of the writer's work—something that apparently caused great distress to the writer herself. More recent women writers, especially the "babe writers" such as Wei Hui and Mian Mian, have exploited the commercial appeal of their private lives, producing remarkably explicit semiautobiographical fiction that has caused a storm of controversy while simultaneously pumping up sales. In this chapter, I contrast the events surrounding the publication of Wei Hui's *Shanghai baobei* (Shanghai Babe) in 1999–2000 with the treatment and reception of Lin Bai's *A War with Oneself*, in order to show how publishers have consistently exploited the market for women writers and how women writers have adjusted their work and their personas for their own commercial ends.

For Chapter 5, about foreign literature translation, I have chosen 1996 as the milestone year. The Chinese version of *The Bridges of Madison County*, published by People's Literature Publishing House (Renmin wenxue chu-banshe), became a huge best seller, with five reprints and more than 600,000 copies sold in one year. This opened mainstream Chinese publishers' eyes to the relatively untapped potential of the market for foreign popular literature. Actually, by that time some specialist publishers had been introducing foreign literature to China for many years. One publisher in particular, Yilin Press (Yili chubanshe), had since the 1980s been raising the publication of popular foreign works from a shady and illicit second-channel pulp-fiction phenomenon to a respectable and highly successful cultural enterprise. In Chapter 5, I trace the development of Yilin from its beginnings as a literary translation journal, through its successful efforts to found a publishing house for popular best sellers, up to its most recent and successful attempts to market foreign "classics"—notably James Joyce's *Ulysses*—as best sellers.

I argue that the growth of Yilin clearly demonstrates the double-dynamic that has become increasingly common in all areas of Chinese publishing during the 1990s. Publishers have greatly improved the quality of popular literature titles, realizing that these have the greatest sales potential; thus, popular fiction is no longer treated as a dowdy second cousin to "mainstream" and "upscale" pure literature. At the same time, publishers have been using clever new marketing and promotional techniques to repackage elite and classical literary works—works that previously would not have appealed to a large readership—in order to turn them into best sellers, or at least generate a profit from them. This is an example of commercialization at its most powerful, when it creates demand instead of simply responding to demand.

In Chapter 6, I turn to literary journals, the venue where most Chinese writers first publish their literary works. In 1998, most Chinese literary journals were compelled to confront a funding crisis that had been developing for a decade. The government was reducing or abolishing its subsidies to journals, demanding that they become self-supporting; meanwhile, journal subscriptions were dropping to record lows. Readers were seeking more stimulation and were finding it in lifestyle and popular fiction magazines and in other forms of entertainment such as television. Chapter 6 traces the roots of the crisis back to the mid-1980s, a time when journals were refusing to heed the signs that the publishing market was becoming increasingly competitive. I focus on the occasionally ludicrous efforts of one journal in particular, *Beijing wenxue* (Beijing Literature), to seek alternative sources of funding from commercial enterprises and to attract more subscribers by broadening its definition of literature to include journalism or semijournalism on current affairs as well as general-interest features. The problems confronting literary journals, and their stumbling attempts to become more commercially aware, closely reflect changes that were occurring throughout the state-owned literary publishing industry in China during the reform period.

In the conclusion to this book I look to the future. I discuss two of the most hyped Chinese publishing trends at the turn of the new millennium—TV/film literature and Internet literature—and consider how literary production in China is developing into a truly multimedia phenomenon. Writers and literary publishers used to be content to sell their products in a single market—the book or journal market. Now, increasingly, they are trying to develop their literary products in as many different media formats as possible, from books and magazines to TV series, movies, e-texts, and even related merchandise. In this way, they can capitalize to the greatest extent possible on the commercial appeal of a writer's talents. This is perhaps the ultimate exploitation of the commercial potential of literature.

Throughout the case studies in this book, one theme resonates: the revival of literary best sellers through the establishment of a "best-seller industry" in contemporary China. This reflects the first meaning of my title "consuming literature"—namely, the production of literature for the mass consumer market, or the turning of literature into commercial goods. Here I use "consuming" in a broader sense; the focus is not simply on the end product, or on consumption; it includes the entire production and marketing process that leads up to and encourages consumption.

Yet in examining my case studies more closely, I also try to convey another meaning of "consuming literature"—that is, how the commercialization of literature has also led to literature being "consumed" in the negative sense of losing its identity. This includes a tendency for some profit-hungry publishers to produce titles that appeal to the lowest common denominator of taste; a disturbing emphasis on style over substance; the spread of false hype and unscrupulous marketing and promotional techniques; and the stereotyping and channeling of writers and works into narrow marketable categories, with a corresponding reduction in their freedom of expression. My study of individual cases in the publishing, writing, and distribution businesses often brings such problems to light.

Overall, however, I conclude that in the Chinese context, the positive results of commercialization have outweighed the negative ones, since they have led to a much more vibrant and open literary production scene than existed under the socialist system. A narrow, elitist view that sees all commercialization as evil, as leading to the death of "pure" literature, ignores both the serious restrictions on writing and publishing during the socialist era and the obvious vitality and variety of literary production that has emerged in the cultural market today.

Of course, the commercialization of literary production in a dual-track transitional society such as China has followed a trajectory that differs in many respects from that of the West. In this study, I am especially sensitive to the unique Chinese social and historical context behind the "marketization" of literature in the 1990s. For example, even if market forces have now become the dominant element in literary production, lingering government influence is still readily apparent in the various regulations, in the recurrent political campaigns, and in the continuing state ownership of publishing houses and in authors' internalized self-censorship. For ideological reasons, the Chinese government often tries to curtail the independence of writers and publishers working within the new market economy. Often chasms open up between actual practices in the literary field, which are progressive and based largely on market demand, and official government directives, which tend to lag behind.

Currently, the deepest chasm is between the second-channel publishing sector—which is thriving on alliances with state publishers—and the government's continued insistence that all unauthorized publishing remain illegal. In this study I argue that despite its superficial opposition to these "illegal" practices, the government no longer has the authority or the will to stop the market from encroaching on literary and cultural production.

With the market economy increasingly influencing the cultural field, a profound contradiction in the current dual-track system—the "ideologically restricted market"—has become apparent. The government no longer wants to carry the huge financial and administrative burden it inherited from the previous militantly socialist state; for this reason, it is permitting and even urging cultural institutions to transform themselves into financially independent cultural enterprises. Yet it still withholds ownership rights, exerts control over human resources and administration, and often attempts to censor the print media. This has caused many problems, not the least of which is that many inefficient state-run publishers can no longer survive without forming parasitic relationships—that is, unless they sell book licenses to "illegal" second-channel publishers. Yet the market has its own logic: as we can begin to see now, commercialization has already sapped the strength of government regulations. Eventually the government will have to admit that a fully commercialized literary production industry cannot be contained by out-of-date state regulations, which ironically have already been turned into money-making mechanisms. The government will doubtless realize that the benefits of reducing the economic burden on the state outweigh the ideological advantages of controlling publishing—advantages that have in practice largely been lost already. So it is highly likely that the present deregulation process will continue and that government control over the literary publishing industry will steadily recede, as it already has to a great extent for other cultural products such as Chinese films and newspapers.[7]

Although most of my chapters include a brief chronological survey of the topic being covered, my basic approach is to select individual case studies for detailed analysis. I have adopted this approach for practical reasons and because I believe that careful empirical research often reveals more about the human context of an evolving social reality than bare statistics and obscure theory.[8]

I have already given the reasons why I have selected the case studies I will be analyzing, so I will not repeat them here. But several points are worth reiterating. First, this book does not focus on individual best sellers; rather, I simply use the new phenomenon of the best seller as perhaps the clearest indication of the commercializing tendencies in literary production in contemporary China. I will not be closely scrutinizing the content of these best sellers unless it relates to my argument. When choosing the best sellers for analysis and gathering the related statistics, I consulted several sources, including bookstore best seller lists, publishing trade papers and newspaper reviews, and my own observations and interviews, to get an accurate and balanced picture of the best sellers for each specific period and subject area.[9]

Second, although I try to deal with the transformation of literature as a whole under economic reform, I will be focusing mainly on prose works, including fiction, novels, reportage (*jishi wenxue*), and personal essays (*sanwen*). This is simply because most literary best sellers belong to these categories rather than other genres. And because this book is not meant to be a comprehensive study of contemporary Chinese literature, I feel it is better not to disperse my argument over too many genres. True, one could argue that the decline of poetry in the consumer market of the 1990s, and its absence from most best seller lists, reflects the new patterns of literary production and consumption just as much as the prosperity of fictional and general-interest best sellers.[10]

Third, although I focus mainly on the 1990s, which I believe was the transformative period in the commodification of Chinese literature, I will often compare those years with the earlier reform period of the 1980s, and with the socialist regime that began in 1949. Developments during the 1980s prepared the ground for the transformation process of the 1990s. In discussing the socialist literary system prior to the 1980s, I will be showing just how profoundly the market economy has changed cultural institutions over the past two decades. Fortunately, these areas have been covered very well in the work of Perry Link and others; this makes such comparisons relatively straightforward, so that they need not be a focus of this present study.[11]

CHAPTER 1

Breaking Away

WRITERS AS CULTURAL ENTREPRENEURS

1. The Socialist Literary System and Chinese Writers

In Socialist China, writers were often referred to as "cultural workers" (*wenhua gongzuo zhe*). This term in fact precisely defines most writers' self-identity and social function in the literary system that operated during most of the second half of the twentieth century. As one scholar put it, through their writing, writers were able to "liv[e] as salaried company men and shar[e] in the political power."[1] In other words, they were state-controlled artists whose patron and employer was the Communist Party and the socialist state.

The official body that recruited, organized, supported, and regulated writers under socialism was the Chinese Writers Association (Zhongguo zuojia xiehui, commonly abbreviated to "zuoxie"). Established soon after the Communist takeover in 1949, and modeled on the Writers' Union in the former Soviet Union, the Chinese Writers Association was far more than the professional association that its title indicates: it actually functioned as an official cultural bureaucracy mediating between writers and the Communist Party's Department of Propaganda. Since the Chinese political leadership saw literature and art as an important vehicle for building militant socialism and conducting socialist education, the Communist Party over several decades maintained a monopoly over the patronage of writers through the Writers Association and various related official literary institutions at the local and national levels.

The Writers Association had two specific mandates. As Perry Link has noted, it both "provide[d] the Party with a means of monitoring and controlling creative writing and "establish[ed] a clear-cut ladder of success for writers within the socialist literary system."[2] Thus, although it is true that the Communist Party took measures to silence, reform, and regulate "bourgeois" writers by means of various political and literary campaigns, it also acted positively through the Writers Association to build a new and thriving literary system that supported its own socialist ideals and to foster and train a whole new generation of socialist writers.[3]

With its central offices in Beijing and provincial and municipal branches throughout the country, the Writers Association—often in concert with the China Federation of Literary and Art Circles (Zhongguo wenxue yishu jie lianhe hui, or "wenlian")—formed a vast network engaged in cultural and (by extension) political work. The association directly managed virtually all literary newspapers and journals, which were the main venues for literary publication in Mainland China. It also organized various cultural activities, such as training sessions (*jiangxi ban*) and writing seminars (*bi hui*) for young and amateur writers, and established a plethora of literary prizes at all levels to encourage more writing that followed certain aesthetic and moral standards. Also, the association exerted indirect control over writers by establishing a hierarchical system of patronage. The most established writers were appointed to important cultural posts in the association, from which they carried out administrative and ceremonial duties. Many ordinary members were also given paid positions in various cultural bodies as administrators, editors, and so on. A small minority of writers who had proved their talent could even become full-time professional writers (*zhuanye zuojia*), with salaries and benefits paid by the association.[4]

Membership in the Writers Association was a prerequisite for participating in literary lectures and seminars and in official excursions to scenic and cultural sites to broaden members' "life experience." It was also a precondition for applying for creative writing grants and sabbaticals. Perhaps most important, it was required in order to publish works in national and local literary journals. One could therefore say that the Writers Association was for many decades the exclusive "work unit" for Chinese writers.

This literary system efficiently transformed the vast majority of Chinese writers into state employees; inevitably, it also led them to view literature in utilitarian terms, since state-supported writers enjoyed high status in society as well as privileged lifestyles. Especially in the late 1970s and the 1980s, following the Cultural Revolution (1966–76), when the Writers Association system was restored after a ten-year hiatus, the prestige enjoyed by writers inspired many materially deprived but literarily gifted youth to engage in creative writing as a means to better their lives and climb the social ladder. Contrary to the common Western assumption that socialist control over art and literature had only the negative effect of suppressing creativity, most Chinese writers actually viewed the system as an ideal environment in which to fulfill their moral responsibilities toward society while at the same time treading the path to personal success and social status. Because of their close involvement in the political and cultural activities of the state, most Chinese writers prior to the mid-1980s could be seen as part of a "cultural priesthood" whose pulpit was constructed and monitored by the government.[5]

This stable and privileged position of writers as state artists began to be shaken in the 1980s, when economic reforms and emerging market forces started undermining the foundations of the socialist literary system.

First, in the mid-1980s the ideology of militant socialism began giving way to an emphasis on economic reforms, and the government began to withdraw much of its support from the cultural infrastructure. This placed serious financial pressure on literary institutions and in some cases threatened their very survival. This withdrawal was manifested in many ways, most notably through a reduction in financial allocations in real terms to the Writers Association.[6] Hit especially hard were the provincial Writers Associations. For example, in an open letter to Literature Press (*Wenxue bao*), the president of the Henan Writers Association, Zhang Yigong, declared: "I am searching for entrepreneurs (to donate money)." He also complained that the Henan provincial government had given the local Writers Association only sixteen thousand yuan for that year and that it was covering no vocational costs; as a result, the association no longer had the means to support its literary journal or theoretical studies, which had been the backbone of its activities.[7]

Cuts in government subsidies during the 1980s and early 1990s had profound effects on literary production throughout the country. For example, manuscript fees were ridiculously low, and serious writers now found it difficult to have their works published either in journals or as books. A major part of the problem was the crisis facing the literary journals, which had once been fully subsidized. At the end of 1984, the government began requiring all literary journals except for a handful of prominent ones with national circulations to aim for financial independence. Faced with declining subscriptions and shrinking subsidies, many journals either closed down or transformed themselves into trashy popular magazines.[8]

The Writers Association also became less enthusiastic about sponsoring national literary awards. These had once been an important way to reward favored writers and establish literary models. For more than a decade, the annual National Awards for short stories (Quanguo youxiu duanpianxiaoshuo jiang, started in 1979), poetry (1983), novellas (1981), and reportage (1982) had played an active role in developing stylistic trends and promoting new writers. In 1989, during the government's political and cultural purge after the Tian'anmen crackdown, all of these awards stopped, and since that time the Writers Association has never bothered to revive them. After Tian'anmen, the Mao Dun Literary Award (Maodun wenxue jiang) for novels was the only official award to continue until the Lu Xun Literary Awards (Luxun wenxue jiang) were founded in 1998. And the Mao Dun Award was given out in irregular fashion, not every three years as it was supposed to be; only two awards were made in the ten years from 1989 to 1999, with much controversy among writers and critics alike over its unfair judging procedures. The prize-winning works were obviously selected more for their political correctness than for literary merit. As we shall see later, during the 1990s many unofficial literary prizes sponsored by businesses sprang up to replace the official awards; these offered much larger prizes and demanded much less ideological conformity.

The reduction in government support for the Writers Association also broke the "iron rice bowl" of the professional writers' system. As early as the mid-1980s, some branches of the Writers Association had discarded the tenure system and were beginning to pay writers based on short-term contracts; their writers were now called "contract writers" (qianyue zuojia or hetong zuojia), rather than "tenured writers" (zhongshenzhi zuojia). For example, in 1986 the Shanghai Writers Association began contracting professional writers for four-year terms.[9] This new practice was introduced on a much larger scale after 1992, when it was embraced by the associations in Hubei, Hunan, Heilongjiang, and Beijing. By the end of the decade, almost all provincial associations in China had adopted the contract method for recruiting new writers.

Some regional associations took the reforms a step further, recruiting promising writers from other regions to complete single-term contracts instead of going to the effort and expense of nurturing their own writers. For example, the Guangdong Writers Association received generous sponsorship from a local corporation from 1994 onwards, and was thus able to contract ten writers from all over China. During their two-year contracts, these writers could remain at their home bases, as long as the works they produced acknowledged the support of the Guangdong Writers Association and were publicized as such. Other provincial associations even made use of piecework contracts rather than term contracts—for example, the Nanjing Federation of Literary and Art Circles in 1996, and the Guangxi Writers Association the same year.[10]

Some writers debated whether literature should be completely commercialized in this way, or whether writers as "cultural workers" should continue to be fed by the state.[11] In any case, the general trend throughout the 1990s was for the government to push new writers firmly in the direction of the cultural marketplace, while still supporting some older writers who had achieved tenure before the reforms.[12]

In the second half of the 1980s, almost in tandem with the government

cuts, serious literature (*yansu wenxue*) also suffered a sharp decline in readership. This exacerbated the crisis facing the literary system and forced writers
to seek other means of support.

Many factors besides economic reform led to this decline. First, a new
generation of avant-garde writers was turning to modernist experiments
with hermetic personal writing; others were simply ignoring contemporary
issues in favor of exploring their cultural roots. These works certainly had
their own literary and cultural value, and one might argue that through them
contemporary Chinese literature was finally regaining its "artistic autonomy."
Undoubtedly, however, they did not have the same appeal for ordinary readers as works reflecting strong contemporary concerns—that is, the sort published in the years immediately following the Cultural Revolution.

Second, the explosion in mass media and other forms of popular culture
distracted many readers. Video halls, dance clubs, karaoke bars, and popular
music concerts, and of course pirated videos and the growing variety of television channels and programs, offered entire new worlds of entertainment to
"starved" Chinese audiences, and this reduced the time they had for reading
literature, especially if they did not find the works immediately relevant to
their lives.

But perhaps the most serious threat to serious literature came from the
boom in popular reading. Suddenly available were a multitude of fashion,
entertainment, and general-interest magazines, and popular literature or "pulp
fiction."

Popular literature reappeared in China in the 1980s after three decades
away. Its revival was signaled by the reprinting of traditional popular novels
and historical tales (*lishi yanyi*) and by translations of classic foreign enter-
tainments such as Agatha Christie's Hercule Poirot mysteries and Arthur
Conan Doyle's Sherlock Holmes detective stories. Soon after that appeared
more contemporary works, often pirated, imported from the West or from
Hong Kong and Taiwan. By the mid-1980s, a huge market for popular literature had been created, dominated by translations of foreign fiction, from
Sidney Sheldon potboilers to Japanese pop fiction by Watanabe Jyunichi
and Nishimura Toshiyuki. There were also Hong Kong Chinese martial arts
tales by Jin Yong and Liang Yusheng, Taiwanese romances and personal essays by Qiong Yao and San Mao, and pulp fiction filled with sex and violence, either imported or locally produced.[13]

For the first time in several decades, the book market was offering ordinary Chinese readers light entertainment; before this, only serious literary
fiction had been available. Despite their generally crude format and content,
most of these books easily sold millions of copies because they were meeting a strong need for entertainment felt by a population that had suffered
through ten years of Cultural Revolution, when virtually no popular enter-

tainment had been publicly produced and distributed. Another reason for its success was that unlike serious literature, which was still largely produced by state-regulated publishing houses and literary journals, popular literature was from the very beginning dominated by and keenly aware of market forces. Thus, it was in this marginal and even despised area of publishing that market mechanisms first demonstrated their power.

It is true that state-run publishing houses—especially those in the South and in provinces distant from the central government—also published popular best sellers, using these commercially successful books to solve their financial difficulties and to subsidize more serious or academic works. However, the driving force behind the rapid spread of popular literature was the "second channel" (di er qudao)—that is, the unofficial publishing and distribution channels.[14] With their own distribution networks—mainly street vendors and private bookstores and distributors—these books sold much more quickly and efficiently than state-produced titles. And since this sort of publishing was driven solely by the profit motive, book dealers quickly became adept at ascertaining and satisfying the needs of mass-market readers. They had to in order to survive. It is not surprising that with such a huge demand from ordinary readers, and as a result of second-channel business methods of production and distribution, popular literature thrived to an unprecedented extent.

One consequence of popular culture's market success was that writers of "pure" or serious literature now found it difficult to get their works published. Confronted with this new competition on one side and with government cuts on the other, even houses that specialized in serious art and literature were reluctant to publish what was unlikely to sell well. In fact, as a result of the collapse of the state's Xinhua bookstore system and the slow pace of economic reform in state-controlled publishing houses, by the late 1980s and early 1990s even quality literature that might have sold well often remained unpublished. But because of their belief in the established methods of publication, the shaky reputation of popular literature, and the false security of continuing support from the Writers Associations, many Chinese writers still tried to ignore the inevitable effects of the coming market economy. Some even expressed strong disapproval of commercial publication and the notion of earning money from their literary works.

However, as their popularity among ordinary readers waned, some serious writers became dissatisfied with the present literary system and began seeking a way out. As we will see in our discussion of the "Xue Mili" phenomenon, they took on pen names and sneaked through the back door of popular fiction to attain commercial success. However, when unmasked, they suffered an irreparable loss of reputation.

2. *Xue Mili: from Politics to Profits*

In late 1987, a mysterious "Hong Kong female writer" calling herself "Xue Mili" suddenly appeared on the popular literature market, which was just beginning to establish itself. People assumed that "she" was a woman because of the feminine name Xue Mili, and that she was from Hong Kong because this was clearly stated on the jackets of her books. She burst onto the scene with *Nü daijia* (Female Couriers), an international adventure story about two beautiful young women smuggling drugs for Hong Kong gangsters while at the same time collecting information for the international police. Published in October 1987 by Huaxia Publishing House (Huaxia chubanshe) in Beijing, *Female Couriers* sold very quickly, mainly through private bookstores and streetstalls; one million copies were eventually in print.

After this, Xue Mili produced a whole series of best-selling pulp titles, all with "female" in their name, such as *Nü laoban* (Female Boss), *Nü tejing* (Female Secret Police), *Nü qiuzhang* (Female Tribal Chief), and *Nü shaxing* (Femme Fatale). Xue Mili was supplying the market at a remarkable pace, one book every two to three months, and most titles sold more than a hundred thousand copies. The books in the Xue Mili series followed the formula established in *Female Couriers*; all of them cobbled together various pulp-fiction staples such as drugs, crime, sex, international gangs, and beautiful but dangerous women. The plots were full of highly implausible twists and turns. All were set in the exotic but recognizable city of Hong Kong or in other cosmopolitan cities—New York, Rome, Bangkok. All were marketed with crude but colorful covers. Yet even as the books kept coming out at a breakneck pace, Xue Mili remained mysteriously elusive.

The secret identity of Xue Mili was abruptly exposed in the May 3, 1989, issue of *Literature Press*, in the article "Xianggang Xue Mili, yichang fengmi shushi de pianju" (Hong Kong's Xue Mili: A Big Deception in the Book Market), which declared: "This Xue Mili is not a woman and does not hold a Hong Kong passport: 'she' is actually several men from the remote [Chinese] hinterland. Some of these men have previously written respectable literary works on rural mountain life, and some have even won literary awards." The article criticized these promising young writers for abandoning their bright literary future and for writing "filthy" pulp fiction to meet the vulgar demands of the market. It also exposed their "degenerate" approach to writing. They had stolen their plots from pirated crime videos and imported best sellers; descriptions of exotic places that the writers had never visited were borrowed from maps and travel guides of Hong Kong and elsewhere; and worse still, the novels were produced by a kind of assembly line process, with one person conceiving the outline and basic plot, then several others collectively fleshing out the details at the rate of one book per couple of weeks.

The writers never contacted any formal publishing houses, but instead gave their works to a book dealer. As the article put it, "one hand gave the manuscript, and the other passed over the cash" (yishou jiao qian, yi shou jiao huo). Finally, they had created a fake identity—Xue Mili, an imaginary Hong Kong female writer—to increase the exotic appeal of the books and pump up their sales. The article concluded by declaring that these people had completely abandoned their moral obligations as writers and were treating literary creation as simply another moneymaking business.

This article, with its lurid description of a group of "degenerate writers" greedy for profit and lacking any sense of morality, had a huge impact. It triggered a virtual literary crusade, with many further articles and discussions appearing in various prestigious newspapers and journals. Xue Mili became the star attraction in a number of biting attacks on the marketplace, which supposedly was corrupting serious literary undertakings. Many writers and critics expressed their deep bitterness and resentment by calling Xue Mili a literary prostitute (wen chang). All of this was exacerbated when the government temporarily tightened its control over literature and culture after the 1989 students' democracy movement. During the subsequent campaign against pornography and illicit publishing in 1989–90, many politically radical as well as "unhealthy flavored" publications were blocked or confiscated, and all publishing houses were required to reregister in order to receive approval to continue their work. As a result, for several years the works of Xue Mili were turned away by virtually all publishing houses, even those which in the past had profited handsomely from them.[15]

The phenomenon of Xue Mili is in some ways a stereotypical example of selling out for profit, and is not especially unique to China. Yet when we learn more about the background of the writers involved, it also reveals the profound dilemmas facing Chinese writers at the turn of the twenty-first century, following the collapse of the socialist literary system. As Tian Yanning and Tan Li, the two men who created the disguise of Xue Mili, put it in their subsequent book explaining their behavior, they were "driven to join the bandits on the Water Margin [bishang Liangshan]"—in other words, they had no other option if they wished to survive as writers.[16] What follows is a brief summary and analysis of their early careers and their decision to follow the road to commercial success, based on their own account *Tanbai: Xue Mili zhenxiang jiemi* (Confession: The Truth about Xue Mili).

Born in the early to mid-1950s in rural Sichuan province, Tian and Tan were typical of the so-called rustic educated literary youth of their generation. Even though the Cultural Revolution seriously disrupted their education and career opportunities, they developed a strong, almost obsessive, attraction to literature. Literature provided them with spiritual food and consolation; it also offered them a chance to escape from the isolation and poverty into which they had been born.

In 1978, partly owing to their literary talent, Tian and Tan were both accepted by the Normal Teaching College of Da County in Sichuan province. Local teaching colleges were the lowest form of tertiary education, and usually led to dead-end work teaching children in rural schools. Yet during their college years, both Tian and Tan continued to write stories extremely diligently, and both managed to publish their work in provincial literary magazines. As a reward for their productivity, they were given temporary summer jobs as literary editors for *Sichuan wenxue* (Sichuan Literature) in the provincial capital Chengdu, and were invited to attend literary seminars sponsored by the Sichuan Writers Association. Soon they became members of the Sichuan branch of the Writers Association. This helped them land jobs after graduation at the local Art Museum (Yishu guan) and Creative Writing Office (Chuangzuo shi), respectively. Both institutions were under the control of the Cultural Bureau of Da County (Daxian wenhuaju). But if they were going to leave Da County and find work elsewhere, they would need to gain much greater reputations than they had so far attained.

In the first half of the 1980s, Tian and Tan continued publishing their work in literary journals throughout China. They also attended training seminars hosted by the Writers Association and literary journals and won various literary awards. Tian won a National Short Story Award in 1987 for "Niu fanzi shan dao" (The Mountain Road of the Cow Seller). Equally impressive for a local writer, Tan Li's novel *Lan hua bao* (Blue-Spotted Panther) was published in the prestigious national literary journal *Shiyue* (October) and was turned into a television drama series. In 1985, both Tian and Tan became members of the Chinese Writers Association, the national organization.

However, climbing the ladder of the Writers Association is a long, exhausting, and frustrating process, and success is often not based on fair and professional standards. The Writers Association, like other government institutions in China, is an environment in which power is often abused and professional relations are poisoned by bitter factionalism. The bureaucratic and hierarchical structure is especially problematic for young writers from remote counties who lack connections, like Tian and Tan. By Tian's own account, the Sichuan Writers Association was among the most corrupt in China, in that real literary talent was ignored in favor of promoting well-connected mediocrities.[17]

To add to Tan and Tian's difficulties, beginning in the mid-1980s, reforms to the literary system and reduced government subsidies were making it impossible for professional writers to achieve tenure. Also, with the rapid growth of the popular culture and entertainment industries, the kind of "serious literature" that Tan and Tian wrote—dealing mainly with Sichuan peasants' lives in remote mountain regions—was becoming less and less relevant to ordinary readers, most of whom were urban. The "masses" in the countryside were either illiterate or simply couldn't afford to buy books and journals. With their hopes of becoming full-time professional writers in Chengdu dashed, and facing immediate practical problems such as finding a place to live and supporting themselves financially in an increasingly money-centered society, Tian and Tan had little choice but to find an alternative path to success.

As early as 1984, Tian and Tan had had their first taste of the potential of the popular literature market. They leased a local literary magazine, *Bashan wenxue* (Bashan Literature), from the Cultural Bureau of the local government, and edited a special issue, *Ren yu fa* (People and Law)—which despite the sober title was actually a collection of racy crime stories in tabloid format. They were deeply impressed by the huge market for popular literature and its enormous profit potential. Indeed, this particular special issue received advance orders of twelve million copies from private distributors alone, which would have given each of them hundreds of thousands of yuan in profit. Even though the local government blocked publication of this issue at the last minute, afraid of the "bad influence" it might have on readers, this venture opened Tian and Tan's eyes to a new market and transformed their approach to writing literature. They described its impact as follows:

> The *Bashan Literature* incident was certainly a heavy blow for us, but at the same time it greatly inspired us. It showed us that besides producing pure literature, there are many other things that can be done with writing. It opened our eyes to other people and the world outside. . . . We were dissatisfied with our present situation and felt there must be other ways to reach our goal, and we were just waiting for the opportunity to join literature and society together and to ride the tide of the era.[18]

In the spring of 1987, this opportunity came. Through a literary editor in Chengdu, Tian and Tan were introduced to a book dealer named Xia Guozhong, who asked them to write a novel and as a manuscript fee offered them three times what they would normally have received from a literary journal. Tian accepted the offer first, and quickly produced the outline for a drug-smuggling story set in Hong Kong. Xia liked it and paid him three thousand yuan in cash immediately as an advance, promising another four thousand once the book came out. Tian finished the manuscript within several weeks and immediately delivered it to Beijing, where Xia had already "bought" a book license number from Huaxia Publishing House. Within a couple of months, *Female Couriers* was widely available on the book market, mainly through a private distribution network.

While Tian was still working on *Female Couriers*, Xia asked both Tian and Tan to write more novels for him in the same style. Thus, over the next two years, Tian and Tan completed nine more novels in the series, all paid for in cash by Xia and published and distributed as efficiently as the first one, using book licenses from various state-owned publishing houses. Gradually, the "Xue Mili brand" gained such a reputation for sales that book dealers looking for pulp fiction began trying to break Xia Guozhong's monopoly over the series. The demand became so great that Tian and Tan could no longer meet their deadlines working by themselves, even writing more than ten thousand words a day. So they set up a "Xue Mili Writing Studio" (Xue Mili chuangzuoshi), employing a group of local "literary youth" (*wenxue qingnian*) to collectively write more titles in the series at the rate of a book a month. They adopted a fixed procedure: Tian and Tan would outline the plots, then the others would fill in the details based on some general guidelines. The books would then be edited and published under the name Xue Mili in order to ensure continued strong sales.

By 1988, Xue Mili had become a brand name in domestically produced pulp fiction. The series had become so popular that many bootleg versions began to appear, capitalizing on the name Xue Mili, and even resorting to similar "feminine" titles, such as *Nü daban* (Female Taipan), *Nü zhentan* (Female Detective), and *Nü xiaohua* (Campus Belle). Xue Mili had become the first local (that is, Mainland Chinese) writer to carve out a strong niche in the popular literature market, which had long been dominated by imported best sellers from Hong Kong, Taiwan, and the West. Between 1987 and 1995, nearly one hundred titles—including some fake ones—were published and distributed under the Xue Mili name, including three other trademark series built around the title words *nan* (male), *da* (big), and *ming* (fate). By the early 1990s, Tian and Tan had become millionaires from their writing. Both bought homes in Chengdu, the cultural capital of Sichuan, the city where they had tried for so long to be accepted as professional writers.

Despite their loud disapproval of Tian and Tan's betrayal of the "noble literary endeavor" (wenxue de shensheng) most other Chinese writers were facing a similar dilemma in the late 1980s and early 1990s: "Extreme disillusionment with the socialist bureaucracy and a rapidly increasing role for commercialism in literary publication made the official literary establishment increasingly irrelevant."[19] The economic reforms launched under Deng Xiaoping in 1978 had irrevocably altered many aspects of Chinese society, including the social role and self-identity of writers. They felt abandoned by the government and alienated from ordinary readers; they had great difficulty even getting their works published, let alone making a decent living from their writing; and they were unhappy with their declining social status. Their elitist position—in the political and artistic senses—and their ideals were seriously threatened by the advent of popular literature and by an emerging cultural market that was beginning to replace the system of party and government patronage.[20]

As the 1990s progressed, the accelerated economic reforms initiated after Deng Xiaoping's Southern Tour in early 1992 and the Fourteenth National Party Congress in October 1992 finally penetrated to the culture sphere. The regime's determination to drag culture and art kicking and screaming into the marketplace had become obvious. In his speech to the Fourteenth Party Congress, Jiang Zemin called for the "promotion of organizational reform, and perfection of economic policies related to cultural institutions" (jiji tui-jin wenhua tizhi gaige, wanshan wenhua shiye de youguan jingji zhengce). These organizational reforms, described earlier, tempted and sometimes forced many writers to "dive into the business sea [xia hai]." For the first time in their lives, they had to learn how to survive; however, the threat was not political storms, but rather the economic typhoon that was leading to a "socialist market economy." While broader societal changes progressed around them, more and more writers embraced the market as their only hope. This transformation was not easy for writers, who had to learn not only how to produce literature with mass appeal but also how to promote and sell their work. One of the pioneers in this area was Wang Shuo, and his great success marked a sea change in the behavior of most Chinese writers.

3. Wang Shuo: Writer as Cultural Entrepreneur

Unlike Tian and Tan, whose venture into commercial writing destroyed their literary reputation, Wang Shuo overcame the perpetual controversy surrounding his work and personality, and in doing so blazed a trail that would help transform how writers produced and marketed their works in the 1990s. Starting from the cultural margins in the early 1980s, writing "entertainment literature" with political undertones that mocked the system in his unique and humorous "Beijing hooligan" style, and at one point reviled by elite writers and critics as "zui meisu de zuojia" (the most vulgar writer in China),[21] by the 1990s Wang had moved to the center of the Chinese literary and entertainment scene and become a cultural hero. He was popularly known as an "entrepreneur writer" (xiezuo getihu), not only because of his idiosyncratic style and freewheeling spirit, but also because he introduced a canny business sense both to his writing and to the way in which he promoted it. In many ways, he was a role model for Chinese writers in the 1990s; it was he who showed that it was possible to "marketize" literature for the general audience.

Born in 1958 and growing up in Beijing, the cultural and political capital of China, Wang Shuo spent a good part of his youth wandering, like others of the so-called "lost generation." He progressed from fighting in street gangs as a teenager to a stint in the navy in the mid- to late 1970s; from working in a state pharmaceutical company to smuggling various commodities from the South in the early 1980s. But he claims that most of the time—especially after 1984, when he quit his job to become an entrepreneur (*getihu*) and a writer—he simply "hung out" in the streets and alleys of Beijing, a rapidly changing city full of excitement and contradictions, "lolling about the office, going to films and chasing women."[22]

This close proximity to everyday life and broad contact with real society provided the raw material for his later writings about contemporary street life. It also gave him a shrewd understanding of the needs and desires of ordinary people. In the mid-1980s, most state-supported writers were content to describe the deprivations of peasants or to search for their cultural roots in remote regions; in contrast, Wang's experiences allowed him to develop a unique, urban approach to literature. This involved choosing fresh and relevant subject matter and emphasizing the entertainment function of his writing.

The years 1984 to 1991 were Wang's most prolific. He published more than two dozen stories and novels, ranging from romances such as "Kong zhong xiaojie" (The Flight Stewardess), through detective stories such as "Ren mo yu du" (Nobody Can Touch Me), to coming-of-age novellas like *Dongwu xiongmeng* (Vicious Animals) and social satire—his most successful genre—including "Wan zhu" (Trouble Shooter) and *Qianwan bie ba wo dang ren* (Please Don't Call Me Human). Whatever the genre, all of Wang's writings deal with contemporary urban life and are peopled with young and cocksure urban antiheros who test social and moral boundaries, set up private businesses, and lead unconventional personal lives. Their favorite pastime is mocking the establishment, which includes corrupt bureaucrats, hypocritical intellectuals, or simply boring middle-aged people. In Wang's dialogue-heavy satires, the characters all talk in a fresh, streetwise patois. China's revolutionary past and commercialized present are mercilessly parodied in Beijing street idiom, which is full of irony, cynicism, and clever wordplay.

Wang's fame became impossible to ignore in 1988, when four films came out, all based on his fiction. These included the box office hits *Wan zhu* (directed by Mi Jiashan) and *Da chuanqi* (Samsara, directed by Huang Jianxin). Some media accounts began referring to 1988 as "Wang Shuo year." At a time when the government was withdrawing or reducing its subsidies to literature and publishing, and when most serious writers were having difficulty finding publishers for their work, Wang Shuo was thriving. In fact, he became so popular that even elitist critics could no longer ignore him, as they had done with most other popular writers. They began a heated debate over whether Wang was truly a writer or simply a hooligan, and whether literature should pursue noble standards or pander to the lowest tastes. This debate did not bother Wang. Nor did it touch his readers, for whom the critics were simply irrelevant. If anything, criticisms that Wang Shuo was "vulgar" simply added to the fun of reading him.

There are plenty of reasons why Wang Shuo's writing is so popular—including his sharp business acumen, as we will see below. But in terms of the works themselves, far from being merely "hooligan literature" (*pizi wenxue*)—a label coined by contemptuous critics that barely scratches their surface—most of Wang's novels and stories are complex works that can be appreciated at many levels. As many scholars have noted, beneath their humor and popular touch, they have a much more serious aim that would put many elite literary writers to shame.[23] Through mockery, they constantly challenge and subvert established literary norms and the empty hypocrisies of "Maoist-style language" (*Mao wenti*). Wang adopted and honed Beijing colloquialisms to capture and exploit the contradictory realities and ambivalent social values and attitudes of a transitional society. As for the hobo and hooligan characters that populate his stories, they share many qualities with the antiheroes in well-known Western novels such as *The Catcher in the Rye* (J. D. Salinger), *The Stranger* (Albert Camus), and *On the Road* (Jack Kerouac). That is, his protagonists hold social conventions in extreme contempt and are constantly searching for fresh excitement and real relationships. Wang's works can thus be distinguished from run-of-the-mill popular literature by their depth and complexity.

At the same time, Wang's works have strong appeal for the mass of ordinary readers. They are playful and hugely entertaining, and earthy wisdom spouts from the mouths of the wisecracking "hooligans" who are Wang's stock characters. All of this gives readers a much-needed break from the anguished profundity of most avant-garde Chinese writers. This affinity with the popular stems partly from Wang's unique personality and writing voice, but it is also the result of his strong awareness of readers' needs and his pragmatic view of literature. Wang was among the first serious Chinese writers to publicly acknowledge that literature is a commodity, to treat writing as a private business rather than a public mission, and to see the market potential of literature.

In *Wo shi Wang Shuo* (I am Wang Shuo), Wang attributes his success much more to his business sense than to his literary talent. For instance, when discussing his sentimental romance from 1984, "The Flight Stewardess," which was his first piece to attract popular attention, he wrote, in his usual cynical and self-mocking tone:

Although I wasn't successful when I tried business itself, the experience gave me insight into what businessmen do. I found out what kinds of things could sell well. At that time, I chose to write about a flight stewardess. This was because I thought that this topic, the job of being a flight stewardess, has a mysterious attraction for both readers and editors, and writing about girls has always been a smart thing to do. I was proved right. I didn't even know the editor of the literary journal *Contemporary*, but as soon as I sent that piece out, I was invited to talk with him. If I had written something about peasants, the response would certainly have been quite different.[24]

Elsewhere Wang has declared: "I am very clear about what the masses need, and whatever they want, I'll give them."

This "please the reader" attitude, as Wang terms it, is absolutely necessary for an "entrepreneur writer" who has to make a living solely from writing. He also claims that "professional writers" (i.e., tenured ones with government support) have seldom bothered to consider the demands of readers. For them, the purpose of writing has been either to please their patron, the government, or simply to please themselves. Yet such writers claim to be "serving the people."[25]

Comments like these are somewhat misleading—as I have argued, Wang is a highly gifted writer. That said, it is essential for us to recognize the importance of business acumen to his success. His business sense is apparent in the topics he chooses to write about and in his emphasis on entertaining his readers. It is even more apparent in the approach he took to marketing his works after he became famous. By 1992, he was the most popular and controversial writer in the country, yet he had received very little recompense for his work except for meager manuscript fees from various literary journals, where most of his works first appeared. His few published books had sold quite well, but not to their full potential; their sales were hindered mainly by the underdeveloped and inefficient state-owned publishing and distribution system. Having decided to stop writing fiction for a while, he pondered how "to sell my past writings for a better price."[26]

At the time, many publishers were trying to persuade Wang to bring out a collected edition of his works. But he shrewdly realized the huge market potential of such a project, and he was determined to maximize his own profits. So in June 1992 he published a notice in a Beijing newspaper stating that he was looking for a literary agent. Soon after this, he signed with the Chinese Copyright Agency Company (Zhonghua banquan daili gongsi), one of the first firms in China to deal in intellectual property and cultural products. Through them, he signed an exclusive contract with Huayi Publishing House, a recently established press in Beijing with a reputation for aggressively marketing best sellers. Under this contract, Huayi would bring out a four-volume collection of all of Wang's major works published between 1984 to 1991.

This event was significant for two reasons: first, no publisher in Socialist China had ever published a complete edition of a young and controversial writer like Wang Shuo. The genre of "collected works" (*wenji*, or *quanji*), had long been reserved for older writers as a confirmation of their status—for those who were well established, or dead. But in Wang's case, commercial considerations mattered more to his publisher than political correctness, so the collected edition moved forward.[27] Second, the conditions of Wang's contract included a first print run of twenty thousand with royalties of 10 percent. This was not the first time in China that a publisher had set a high first print run and paid by royalties instead of by manuscript fee, but it was still an innovation—one that would have a strong impact on subsequent publishing practices because of Wang's fame and his reputation as a publishing trendsetter.

The fee system for manuscripts, which had been introduced in China in the late 1950s and restored in 1978 after the Cultural Revolution, was a stubborn holdover from the state-planned economy. Manuscript fees consisted of two parts: manuscript payments and print-run or reprint payments. Both were fixed at extremely low rates throughout the 1980s and early 1990s, with the latter often curtailed completely.[28] For example, in the early 1980s the official range of manuscript payments was 3 to 10 yuan per thousand characters, rising to 15 to 20 yuan by the late 1980s. Not until the early 1990s did some publishing houses and journals begin offering 30 yuan per thousand. As Link correctly observes, it was impossible under the socialist literary system for even an established writer to support a family on manuscript fees; this was even truer in the 1990s, when inflation and overall living costs were rising dramatically. Writers lived mainly off the salaries they earned from their positions in the cultural hierarchy.

By making sure he received substantial royalties from the sales of his collected edition, Wang Shuo became one of the first writers to depend entirely on the market success of his writing. This was certainly more risky than receiving a fixed fee, but the potential rewards were enormous. The four volumes of *Wang Shuo's Collected Works* were a huge best seller throughout the 1990s, with at least a million copies sold, not counting numerous pirated editions. Wang's collection was cheekily referred to as the next "Four Volumes"—a term previously reserved for Mao's *Selected Works*.[29]

The edition's impressive sales were partly the result of a massive promotional campaign, which approached in scale the one that iconized Mao himself.[30] One of the most noteworthy aspects of this campaign was Wang's calculated use of the mass media. As he later wrote: "I realized the power of mass media very early, but I didn't have the money to advertise my books [on television or in newspapers]. So I decided to make myself into a celebrity, and then the mass media would advertise me for free!"[31] Since the huge success in 1991 of *Kewang* (Yearning), the first soap opera produced by the Beijing Center for Televisual Art (BCTA, Beijing dianshi yishu zhongxin), for which Wang Shuo was one of the scriptwriters, television series had become the favorite and most influential form of popular culture in China.

Although Wang himself had quite a critical and elitist attitude toward this kind of popular culture, and although he claimed that his involvement in the television industry was more of an obligation to his friends than a free choice of career, the extremely positive audience response to *Yearning* made him realize the power of television as a vehicle for making himself known to a mass audience: "If I wanted to make a name and promote myself, all I needed to do was go into the business of producing TV serials."[32]

Wang's talent, connections, and reputation as a writer of popular fiction made his success in the television industry almost inevitable. Starting in 1991, he threw himself into the new world of serial production. The most successful of his projects was certainly *Bianjibu de gushi* (Stories from the Editorial Board), which like *Yearning* was a collaboration with the BCTA. As the first situation comedy in China, *Bianjibu de gushi* tapped the distinctive humor that readers had grown to love in Wang's novels. The episodes were set mainly in an office shared by six editorial staff working for a magazine with the ironic name *Guide to Living*. The comedy came from the satirical dialogue and the characters' often disastrous run-ins with magazine readers —situations that amounted to veiled critiques of contemporary Chinese society. Some of the one-liners in the scripts summed up life in China so succinctly that they evolved into catchphrases that were repeated all over the country. The best known of these was "qian bushi wanneng de, meiyou qian shi wanwan bu neng de" (money isn't everything, but without money you can do nothing).

Like *Yearning*, this fifteen-episode sitcom was a huge success—its reruns continued for several years, and a book edition of the script was published, even being distributed in Taiwan. This encouraged Wang to set up his own Sea Horse Creative Studio for Movie and TV Production (Haima yingshi chuangzuoshi). Under his direction, Sea Horse produced more television sitcoms, such as *Haima gewuting* (Sea Horse Dance Hall) and *Ai ni mei shangliang* (Loving You Is Not Negotiable).[33]

These various serials became so popular that all the new entertainment newspapers—which themselves had started to mushroom since the late 1980s —began focusing their attention squarely on television, and Wang's name became a constant fixture in their pages. As early as 1992, with the first broadcast of *Stories from the Editorial Board*, Wang had become one of the most visible media celebrities in China. By his own account, he was interviewed by two or three hundred reporters that year alone. As he had predicted, this "free" publicity had a dramatic effect on sales of his books. By the end of 1992, every title of his had broken the hundred thousand sales barrier.[34]

By 1993, Wang had become a huge celebrity and—in some elite critics' eyes—a figure of controversy as a result of his pioneering efforts to please "the vulgar." Partly to defend his actions and partly to promote himself still further, that year he published *I Am Wang Shuo*, a work of autobiography that would provide a model for many other television celebrities over the next few years. By this time, Wang had demonstrated to all writers that it was possible to thrive in the sea of business. He "show[ed] a way that promised not only survival but also a measure of prosperity, and in 1990s China the intelligentsia . . . increasingly overcame their reluctance and jumped on the Wang Shuo band wagon."[35] A new image for artists leaving the womb of socialism for the marketplace had come into being: the entrepreneur writer whose central aim is to produce and sell best sellers and thereby claim a place in the popular consciousness.[36]

4. Breaking Away: The Implications of Commercialization for Chinese Writers

Xue Mili (Tian and Tan) and Wang Shuo represent two different paths taken by Chinese writers in breaking away from the Writers Association system. The literary crusade against Xue Mili, who liberated Tian and Tan through commercial writing at the turn of the 1990s, exemplified the lingering power of "high literature" and the socialist literary establishment. A few years later, Wang Shuo successfully transformed himself from an outcast into a cultural celebrity, and in doing so announced the coming dominance of market mechanisms in literary production over the rest of that decade. Throughout the 1990s, there was a growing tide toward commercialization, during which Chinese writers gradually became aware that literary works are commodities and tried to establish closer ties with the publishing industry and cultural market, using their literary property as the main currency of exchange. In the process, actual practice often preceded regulatory reform until eventually, a new set of behavioral principles was established for writers, largely based on the profit motive.

Several watershed events occurred in Chinese publishing circles in the early 1990s, especially in 1993; together, they helped extend the innovations of writers like Wang Shuo and make them available to virtually all Chinese writers. The rest of this chapter briefly describes some of the most striking of these events and their effects on the subsequent behavior of writers and the content of their works.

Writers were becoming aware of the value of their literary property, and first demonstrated this by challenging the fixed manuscript fee system. Gradually, they learned how to bargain and receive true market value for their works. In this respect, Wang Shuo was an important influence on other writers: besides skillfully negotiating his own fees, he encouraged young writers, through his Sea Horse Creative Studio and Current Affairs Cultural Consultancy (Shishi wenhua zixun gongsi),[37] to band together to demand their just rewards. The first Chinese Copyright Law (Zhonghua renmin gongheguo zhuzuoquan fa) had been promulgated in 1990; in practice, however, it was often ignored, and few measures to protect copyright and ensure proper payment of writers were enforced, especially in new fields such as television and film production. Also, despite the huge popularity of television series, the big profits made by TV producers and sponsors, and the strong demand for scripts, state-regulated script fees remained extremely low and did not remotely reflect the true commercial value of these works. Wang was the first to propose that market prices be paid for scripts and screenplays based on the demand for and reputation of specific writers. He also called for the splitting of profits among all parties involved in the production according to fixed percentages.[38]

Following Wang, other writers began marketing their works and then selling them to the highest bidder, ignoring the fixed manuscript fees set by state cultural institutions. Many writers even publicly advertised their manuscripts in newspapers and other media. Sometimes this resulted in shockingly high fees being offered. For example, in October 1993, three Beijing writers—Yuan Yiqiang, Xing Zhu, and Gao Lilin—advertised their script for a twenty-episode television series *Hongshun dayuan* (The Hong Shun Courtyard); just a week later, it was snapped up for the astonishing sum of 160,000 yuan.[39]

An event in the fall of 1993 that typified this new trend was the First Shenzhen Auction of Top Manuscripts (Shenzhen shouci youxiu wengao gongkai jingjia). Organized by the newspaper *Shenzhen qingnian bao* (Shenzhen Youth News) and the Guangdong Periodical Development Corporation (Guangdong qikan shiye fazhan gongsi), in collaboration with Hong Kong's Ming Pao Media Corporation, this auction would have a strong impact on how literature was marketed—an impact that would far outweigh its immediate economic return. Most significantly, the auction made it crystal clear that literature could be treated just like any other marketable commodity and sold to the highest bidder. More than seven hundred people applied to have their manuscripts auctioned, and the organizers selected many "hot new" works from famous writers, including *Ying'er*, an autobiographical novel left by the recently deceased poet and murderer Gu Cheng, and *Cong dianying mingxing dao yiwan fujie* (From Film Star to Millionaire), a memoir by the actress turned businesswoman Liu Xiaoqing.

In the months leading up to the auction, the media often reported on various controversies surrounding the preparations for the event—for example, the withdrawal of a group of famous writers from the auction advisory committee as a protest against the exorbitant prices being demanded by "a female writer" for her work.[40] This generated such a frenzy of public curiosity that on auction day, the organizers had to change the venue to escape the surge of reporters. At the auction itself, eleven manuscripts were sold successfully, with total receipts amounting to 2,496,000 yuan. This total did not include some works that were sold before and outside the auction.[41]

The auction did not become an annual event, as the organizers had hoped. Even so, the controversies and media circuses that surrounded it had a strong influence on writers' subsequent behavior. For the first time in several decades, it was almost acceptable for Chinese writers to value their intellectual labor in purely economic terms, and to drastically raise the stakes when negotiating with publishers. As the writer Ye Yonglie put it: "The Shenzhen Manuscript Auction was an act of homage to writers' hard work." Ye's positive evaluation is not surprising, when one considers that he was able to fish 260,000 yuan from the auction for his biographical work *Mao Zedong zhi chu* (The Origins of Mao Zedong). Compare this with the fifty-six yuan he had received for a famous essay he had written that had been reprinted in several million high school textbooks over the decades, but for which he never received a republication fee.[42]

As the 1990s progressed, royalties and large first print runs gradually became commonplace for the works of well-known writers and potential best sellers. Even many serious writers, strongly encouraged by their market-oriented publishers, turned their backs on "pure literature" in an effort to attract a mass readership. In the 1990s, to write something that could sell well—"writing down for the market"—became the norm for Chinese writers. The avant-garde tendencies of the 1980s were fading quickly.

Another watershed event was the publication of *Fei du* (Ruined Capital) by Jia Pingwa in the summer of 1993. Jia, from Shaanxi province, was known as a "peasant writer" (nongmin zuojia) because of his humble family background and the rural themes of his previous works, but also as a stylist (meiwen zuojia) in the sense of cultivating a refined and classical writing style. *Ruined Capital* was the first story by Jia to be set in an urban environment— a place that was named Xijing in the book, but that was obviously a fictional version of Xi'an, the ancient former capital of China where the author then lived. The story centered on Zhuang Zhidie, an established local writer in his middle years, and his circle of friends, including corrupt officials, con artists, scheming maids, and compassionate prostitutes. The style and structure of *Ruined Capital* are vaguely reminiscent of traditional domestic novels such as *Jin ping mei* (Golden Lotus) and *Honglou meng* (Dream of the Red Chamber). However, it depicts a contemporary urban society doomed by moral corruption and spiritual emptiness. The central symptom of decay is Zhuang's decadent and licentious sexual life, which the narrator describes graphically.

Ruined Capital was an immediate hit after it was published by Beijing Publishing House (Beijing chubanshe), first in its literary journal *October* and then in book form. Millions of copies were sold (including various pirated editions) before the government banned it six months later. The book's hot sales were partly a result of the writer's fame—the high reputation that Jia had gained over the past decade. Much more significant, however, was the media hype surrounding the book's publication, which was extreme and which focused almost exclusively on sex and money. In the months before and after the novel was published, speculation raged in the media regarding how much Jia had earned from the book. The sensational figure of one million yuan appeared in many reports even after it was proved inaccurate. Even so, the publisher mined all the speculation to boost sales. The public and various media figures, both highbrow and lowbrow, also fixated on why this highly regarded literary writer had apparently sold out to popular tastes. He had done so quite abruptly, and at the time it was still an unusual act for any writer. Especially ripe for media comment were the abundant graphic sex scenes in the novel and the conspicuous blank squares inside parentheses indicating that "here the author has deleted [X] number of words"—a traditional method of censoring sexually explicit content, here used both to emphasize the sexual nature of the book and to stimulate the reader's imagination.

No matter how carefully Jia Pingwa and others tried to elucidate the novel's hidden and profound intentions—especially its withering critique of contemporary Chinese society—hardly anyone doubted that the book had succeeded commercially mainly because of the publicity surrounding its sexual content, especially since much of that sexual content had obvious parallels with the writer's own life and the lives of his literary and official acquaintances in Xi'an.[43] It is debatable whether *Ruined Capital* truly marked the turning point where "the division between the high and the low in Chinese literature vanished,"[44] but it certainly opened the door wider for serious writers to produce commercially hyped best sellers while justifying their actions by claiming that they were still creating valid artistic works.

This was far from the only time that an orthodox writer had turned to more contemporary urban themes. As Sheldon Lu correctly observes, "the shift from the country to the metropolis, from exploration of deep 'roots' in the rural homeland to fascination with the surfaces and glamour of the city, was symptomatic of a more general cultural aura in the 1990s."[45] In the 1990s, writers came to favor stories about entrepreneurs and the new rich in China's coastal cities, about white-collar women and their modern lifestyles, about love affairs (especially extramarital affairs), and about family relationships in urban centers. These replaced stories about remote rural life and the search for cultural roots—the two themes that had dominated fiction in the 1980s. And from its very beginnings, this new subgenre, urban fiction (*dushi xiaoshuo*), was targeting an urban mass readership, with entertainment as its main purpose. Writers were either pointedly ignoring or only superficially exploring the more disturbing aspects of urban life in contemporary China, such as the huge numbers of unemployed workers since the closing of state factories, and the struggle of migrants from the countryside to survive in a hostile and unfamiliar urban environment.

In this new publishing climate, which revolved around the production and promotion of best sellers, a close business relationship based on contracts and shared financial interests began to develop between writers and publishing houses—a relationship that had not existed under the socialist literary system. For example, in September 1993, the best-selling writer "Zhou Hong"—actually a pen name for two writers who had gained fame for their social and cultural commentary—signed a three-year contract with China Youth Publishing House (Zhongguo qingnian chubanshe).[46] The contract stipulated that over the next three years, "Zhou" would write a certain number of books exclusively for the publishing house, with the topics to be approved by the latter. Payment would be in royalties. In return, the publishing house would be required to "package and promote" the writers' works, and would charge a fee of 3 percent of the total sales to cover promotional costs. Hu Shouwen, the president of the publishing house, claimed that this was an effective new strategy to "promote serious writers and to guide the popular literature market."[47]

Again, cries went up that a writer (in this case Zhou Hong) was "selling out" to a publisher. Yet by now, more and more writers were jumping to develop mutually profitable relationships with publishers and working hard alongside them to promote their works. Writers often cooperated with publishers and bookstores in book promotion and sales events, such as book signings, guest lectures at universities and colleges, and symposia organized to publicize their works. At the same time, many writers were also making efforts to develop business relationships with Taiwanese, Hong Kong, and multinational publishers. This enabled them to earn foreign currency. It also increased their fame exponentially, which rendered more certain the continued success of their subsequent works. Yet another trend developed among writers in the 1990s: inspired by the success of Wang Shuo, more and more of them got involved in the television and film industries. I will discuss this area in detail in my concluding chapter; here, I simply note that writing for television and film was not simply financially rewarding for writers; it also gave them significant media exposure that almost guaranteed healthy sales for their books.

By the beginning of the new millennium, when the Conference of the Sixth National Committee of the Chinese Writers Association opened in Beijing, both analysts and writers agreed that "Chinese millionaire writers have now made their appearance on the cultural stage, and their numbers will gradually increase as the huge market for cultural products continues its steady growth."[48] As this implies, the new market economy and the introduction of business methods to literary production had made it possible for writers to live by their writing; in fact, writing by now could be highly lucrative. Liang Xiaosheng would certainly agree. In *Zhongguo shehui ge jieceng de fenxi* (An Analysis of the Different Social Groups in China), he totaled up all the income and benefits he had received since starting work as a literary editor at Beijing Film Studios in 1979. According to him, the years 1992 to 1997, during which he wrote this book, were by far the most profitable in his entire writing career. He had published three successful novels and two memoirs, for which the royalties ranged between 8 and 10 percent. He had also written three television series based on his novels, for which he collected twenty-five hundred yuan per episode for the forty-five-episode *Nianlun* (Ages), and ten thousand yuan per episode for the other two series. Based on his observations, he claimed that "at least 50% of Chinese writers" now ranked among the middle classes (*zhongchanzhe jieceng*), and that their income was comparable to that of second- and third-rank entertainers, middle-rank artists, small entrepreneurs, Chinese employees in foreign companies, and middle-ranking government officials.[49]

Market mechanisms in literary production have offered many writers financial independence. Just as important, they have brought to prominence for the first time in the socialist era a new breed of writers: those who have broken away from the state cultural establishment, who have rejected state employment, state-supported literary journals and literary critics, and official literary awards. They also resist being controlled by the Writers Association.

As one demonstration of this newfound freedom, consider the results of a questionnaire distributed among various young writers in Nanjing, Shanghai, and Beijing in the spring of 1998.[50] The organizers of this questionnaire were Zhu Wen and Han Dong, two Nanjing writers closely associated with an influential albeit unofficial literary magazine *Tamen* (Them), and leaders of a group of freelance writers in Nanjing. They distributed seventy-three questionnaires; by the end of the survey period, fifty-five writers had responded. The thirteen questions focused on key issues in contemporary Chinese literature, in particular the present role of state literary institutions such as the Mao Dun Literary Award, official literary journals, and the Writers Association.

The survey results were controversial—some critics termed them "collective patricide" (*jiti shifu xingdong*)—and they stimulated much debate in the literary media.[51] From the way the questions were phrased, it was obvious that the organizers were already somewhat hostile toward the establishment. Similarly, the writers' responses were generally contemptuous of many aspects of the literary system, especially the Writers Association.[52] All of this is clear enough from the survey's title: "Duanlie" (Breaking Away). As Han Dong explained: "[We] break away not only in the dimension of time, but also in space: we must break away from the established literary order." Later: "The established literary order refers not only to various aspects of the official literary field represented by the Writers Association, but also to any form of imperious monopoly or authority that tries to manipulate peoples' literary pursuits and aesthetic choices."[53] A writer of the older generation commented that this complete rebellion and bald challenge to the system was "something our generation dares not do, maybe even dares not think about."[54]

These statements can be regarded as the manifesto of a whole new breed of writers who have freed themselves from state control, both financially and spiritually: the freelance writers (*ziyou zuojia*), as they like to style themselves. These writers include those who have quit their state-employed jobs, such as Wang Xiaoni, Lin Bai, Li Feng, Zai Yongming, Zhu Wen, and Han Dong, and those who never bothered to find a job, such as Li Dawei, Wei Hui, and Mian Mian. Most of these writers left their jobs after 1992, when their ability to profit from their cultural products make financial independence possible. Some luckier writers can live just on their income from literary works, which they publish in journals and books; others must support themselves by selling other kinds of writing as well, from newspaper articles and "enterprise literature" (*qiye wenxue*) to television and film scripts and popular fiction. Most also work on a contract basis for various "cultural companies."

Two role models for these contemporary freelance writers are Wang Xiaobo and Yu Hua. Wang was an American-returned writer/scholar who resigned his teaching post at People's University in 1992 to concentrate on writing fiction. Sometimes he also worked with filmmakers and wrote newspaper articles. Wang's writing talents were not widely recognized until 1997, the year he died suddenly of a heart attack; after his death, his humor, his unique facility with language, and his penetrating criticisms of contemporary Chinese culture, made him a cult figure among alternative writers. He had chosen to stay on the margins of society to write truly independent literature—something that inspired other alternative writers to seek independence. Han Dong put it succinctly: "Because of Wang Xiaobo, there exists a different kind of writing."

Wang became a spiritual hero for young independent writers in today's China. Yu Hua represents the enormous success that most of them dream about. Yu Hua was the most prominent writer of the late 1980s. He left his job at a local cultural institute in Jiangsu in 1993 and moved to Beijing to become a full-time writer. Since then he has tempered his preoccupation with experimentation and violence and adopted a simpler and more realistic style. His recent works such as *Huozhe* (To Live) and *Xu Sanguan mai xue ji* (Chronicle of a Blood Merchant) won both the praise of critics and a wide audience, especially after he adapted *To Live* into a film script that became a box office hit under Zhang Yimou's direction. *To Live* sold more than 500,000 copies in China, was translated into several languages, and won a prestigious literary prize in Italy.[55] All of this brought Yu Hua still more fame and financial rewards. Many of his other works have also been published in Hong Kong and Taiwan.

Many Chinese writers hope to do what Yu Hua was able to do—that is, write a serious novel of 150,000 characters and live off the proceeds for four or five years.[56] Put another way, they hope to uphold their rigorous literary standards while still achieving enormous commercial success.

Certainly, the frenzied development of the publishing industry during the 1990s has led to great "diversity and abundance" in literary production compared to previous decades. "There are truly great numbers of people writing in a truly great variety of individual styles,"[57] although admittedly these styles are not necessarily elitist or serious. With the help of enthusiastic publishers—many of them private—Chinese writers are experimenting with new genres and subjects: Ding Tian is writing horror, Li Dawei is writing fantasy, Cui Zi'en is writing about the gay experience, and Mian Mian is writing about the drug-filled lives of urban youth, and these are only a few. Even some former avant-garde writers, like Ge Fei, Bei Cun, and Ma Yuan, have altered their style as well as their attitude toward mass readers. They are now willing to gain readers' appreciation, to work within market mechanisms, and go beyond the narrow boundaries of form-centered modernist writing. Bei Cun, for example, claims that being a novelist is his "enterprise," and being a screenwriter is his "job." In other words, by selling popular works or television and film scripts to support themselves, such writers can afford to write truly autonomous works.[58]

But not every writer can be as lucky or as talented as Yu Hua or Zhu Wen. For most, going freelance has not necessarily brought greater freedom to write as they wish. On the contrary, many freelance writers have found that to maintain their "freedom" from the state, they must sell their written products in great quantities. Yet in order to sell them, they must stick to certain formats or styles that they themselves may not necessarily like. They yearn to write and live freely, but they are in danger of becoming mere producers of narrowly constrained products for the burgeoning cultural market. Indeed, many once serious writers have become so "prolific" that they publish at least one full-length novel every year. This makes it virtually impossible for them to provide any fresh social insights or to experiment with language or forms. They are reduced to churning out literary junk food for an adoring middlebrow readership. Liang Xiaosheng, Zhang Kangkang, and Chi Li are typical of the many overexposed and overprolific writers working in China today.[59]

By the end of the twentieth century, some were declaring that the real enemy of Chinese writers was no longer the politically oppressive "father," the state, but the commercially seductive "friend," the cultural market. Certainly it was this "friend" that enabled Chinese writers to break away from the political confinement they had endured for more than five decades and that offered a "material base" from which they could challenge the established literary order. Yet the risk always remained that they would be too willing to adapt themselves and their writing to suit the market alone, and would end up losing their individual freedom of expression once more.

At the same time, writers today, if they have nothing else, have a much greater choice of publishing venues, including second-channel publishers and television and film industries. Also, they are not constrained by a monopolistic Writers Association with arbitrary entry and selection standards. During the prereform era, Chinese writers had no choice but to become "state cultural workers"; today, they at least have the luxury of deciding how they can best capitalize on their talents. The influence of market reforms on the literary system and literary production has not been entirely benign, but it can still be argued that in China, just the possibility of making a choice already counts as great progress.

CHAPTER 2

Publishing Houses

CREATING A BEST SELLER MACHINE

1. Overview

Since at least the nineteenth century, the publishing industry in the West has been based largely on the profit motive and driven by market forces. In contrast, book publishing in Socialist China was until very recently a centrally planned and controlled arm of the state cultural apparatus. Initial socialist reforms and nationalization of the private-sector publishing industry took place from 1954 to 1957, modeled on the publishing system of the Soviet Union. From then on, all publishing houses were state-owned, closely watched and regulated by a succession of government bodies under the aegis of the State Council. These bodies included the Publishing Bureau (Chuban zong shu) and Publishing Industry Administrative Bureau (Chuban shiye guanli ju) under the Ministry of Culture in the 1950s and 1960s; the State Publishing Industry Administrative Bureau (Guojia chuban shiye guanli ju) directly under State Council control beginning in the mid-1970s; and, from 1987 to the present, the Press and Publications Administration (Xinwen chuban shu), also directly reporting to the State Council.[1]

Like many other state institutes, publishing houses in Socialist China were primarily bureaus for propaganda dissemination, and the government and its various institutes and units were easily their largest customers. The most extreme illustration of this propaganda function came during the Cultural Revolution, when the few publishing houses that stayed in business were virtually forced to specialize in Mao's works. Indeed, after 1967, the Mao Zedong Works Publishing Office (Mao Zedong zhuzuo chuban bangongshi) was established not only to oversee the publication of Mao's works but also to replace the Publishing Bureau under the Ministry of Culture.

To enforce the political function of publishing houses during the socialist era, the state took control of various aspects of the publishing business, from the rationing of paper to the allocation of specific subject matter for publication; from censorship of publications by the Propaganda Department to "guidance" of publishing staff by in-house party committees; from a strict book-licensing system to a complex approval system involving three administrative levels (*san shen zhi*).[2] Within the state publishing system, there was a clearly defined hierarchy among national and provincial publishing houses, with each house assigned its own territory and specialization, from which it could not deviate. For example, there were national divisions of publishers specializing in art and literature (*wenyi chubanshe*), education (*jiaoyu chubanshe*), science and technology (*keji chubanshe*), and "people" (*renmin chubanshe*), with the latter focusing on current affairs and politically oriented titles. Each province adopted the same divisional structure but on a smaller scale, and enjoyed much less prestige.

Furthermore, as soon as the communist government took over the publishing industry, it separated publication from distribution. Apart from periodicals, which were distributed and sold by the post office, distribution and retail were monopolized by the state's Xinhua bookstore system. The Xinhua system originated in the city of Yan'an in the early 1940s and was a typical example of the state-controlled, centrally planned economy. The state-authorized publishing houses had no choice but to sell their products to Xinhua, and these were then distributed to readers through Xinhua branches. As a result, there was no direct contact between publishers and the market—in fact, there was not much of a market in the first place, since prices were fixed according to the central plan rather than based on supply and demand. Understandably, therefore, for several decades Chinese publishers and editors had to be both extremely politically aware and at the same time professionally very conformist and passive. They had no concern about making a profit and no real awareness of market forces and readers' interests. Ultimately, they were just state employees, assigned to their positions by government ministries, overseen by the party, and expected to produce works to order that would benefit the masses.

Under this system, which was devoid of market mechanisms, the idea of producing a commercial best seller would have been anathema to publishers and their overseers. By the mid-1950s, as a consequence of huge "political cleansing" campaigns, the mass production of entertainment fiction and other kinds of politically incorrect publication for profit had been halted.[3] For more than three decades after that, no true cultural market existed in China. Certainly, during the Maoist period many literary works did become popular nationwide, and their writers became cultural icons. For example, during the 1950s and early 1960s, some novels were printed and distributed in the millions, such as *Taiyang zhao zai sanggan he shang* (The Sun Shines on Sanggan River) by Ding Ling, *Qingchun zhi ge* (Song of Youth) by Yang Mo, *Hong yan* (Red Crag) by Luo Guangbin and Yang Yiyan, and *Yanyang tian* (Bright Sunny Day) and *Jinguang dadao* (Golden Road) by Hao Ran. As reflections of revolutionary history or socialist nation building, these titles had an enormous impact on generations of younger readers in Socialist China. However, these works could hardly be termed best sellers in the sense we use the term today, for several reasons.

First, it was a social and political movement rather than market mechanisms that dominated the production and distribution of these books. The authors were assigned to write them as a kind of cultural mission, and they often had to revise them to suit specific party directives from the top leadership.[4] Also, remuneration for writers was based on relatively low manuscript and print copy fees fixed by the state, and print runs were also fixed by the state. This meant that in most cases, even though healthy sales could lead to considerable financial success for some politically correct writers, the fees hardly matched what royalties would have brought. This was especially so during the Cultural Revolution, when even manuscript fees were reduced to almost nothing. Third, the main purpose of these books was to serve as textbooks for "socialist education" during various political campaigns and movements. Hence, most copies were purchased not voluntarily by consumers, but rather by work units, bureaucracies, institutions, schools, and libraries following party directives to "study" particular works. Finally, the publishing houses themselves did not retain the profits from healthy sales of their titles. Any profits from sales were remitted to the state, which then provided a fixed transfer to support the publishers.

The most extreme example of this politically motivated system of literary production and consumption was the success of Mao's *Selected Works* (Mao Zedong xuanji). After first being published on a large scale in the early 1960s, each of the various editions and selections of Mao's works sold in the millions, mainly because every household had to own and ostentatiously display a copy—preferably several copies. Ironically, the sheer variety of new editions of his works allowed Mao to become rich on his manuscript fees, unlike most other writers during the socialist era. But while Mao was alive, no one would have dared to associate his works with commercial best sellers.

In this context, the recent emergence of best sellers is an entirely new phenomenon in Chinese literary production under the socialist system. And the reappearance of best sellers after almost a forty-year gap is tightly linked to the economic reforms that have transformed the publishing industry since the early 1980s.

Several scholars have pointed out that "the government's initial decontrol of the mass media was largely due to economic, not political, reasons," and that "the Chinese opening of the mass media in the early 1980s was aimed at reducing financial losses, not at freeing public discourse. The government slashed subsidies to media organs and allowed the introduction of market forces, including financial autonomy, management decentralization, deregulation, and diversification."[5]

However, economic liberalization allowed an unofficial cultural market to form rapidly at the margins. This peripheral but highly successful new market was dominated by the principle of supply and demand, and it soon began to dictate the direction of subsequent reforms at the center. In this respect, the private or quasi-private (collective) distribution sector became the engine driving the rapid marketization of literary production, and later extended into publishing itself.

In the early 1980s, private individuals began replacing the government as the main purchasers of books, and the "quality" of books became more important, because sales were no longer guaranteed. At the same time, "a rising budget deficit obliged the government to cut funds for publishing houses and tax them at 55% of their profits. Making publishing houses responsible for employees' benefits and bonuses linked profitability with employee welfare."[6] Facing these economic pressures and government cuts, publishing houses urgently began seeking ways to become financially independent through more businesslike management methods. Their hope was to cover their employees' salaries and benefits and still make a profit. As a result, it became imperative for publishing houses to find and produce best sellers instead of politically correct books, simply in order to survive in the increasingly competitive marketplace. It is no surprise, then, that many of them turned to the more efficient and effective private book dealers, initially for help with distribution and sales, and subsequently to establish various profitable, if unorthodox, alliances that would allow them to avoid losses.

Changes in government policies made it possible for publishers (albeit unwittingly) to work with private book dealers in order to improve their financial situation. For instance, in 1984 the government began permitting publishers to establish "cooperative publishing arrangements" (xiezuo chuban).[7] This was originally intended as a measure to allow private dealers to sponsor scholarly books, which publishing houses were reluctant to publish because of their meager sales. In fact, this policy opened the door to deals between publishing houses and private book dealers—deals that had once been under the table. Almost immediately they took advantage of the loophole to publish all kinds of popular reading material, often including "pornographic" and other politically incorrect materials.

The use of state property (including presses and book license numbers) as capital for illegal investments in private publishing ventures has been common practice ever since among state publishing houses, and links between those houses and private book dealers have become ever tighter and more integrated. The heady mix of private entrepreneurs willing to risk everything for enormous commercial returns and state-run publishing houses desperate for extra cash to survive, when added to the sheer scale of the abuses, has rendered government attempts to control such alliances largely ineffective. This is despite numerous campaigns by the government throughout the 1980s and 1990s and harsh penalties against "buying and selling book license numbers and illegal publishing activities [maimai shuhao, feifa chuban]."[8]

Faced with such defiance, the government gradually accepted that further deregulation of the official publishing sector was essential in order to allow it to become a viable industry, although this process has been slow and piecemeal. During the reform period many of the bureaucratic and political restrictions on the content of publications were lifted. For example, as early as 1979 the National Publishing Conference in Changsha was extending more freedom to provincial publishing houses, which until then had been suffering as a result of being restricted to their local areas. They were placed on almost equal footing with national publishing houses with regard to their title selection, and they were permitted to distribute their books throughout the country.[9] Many provincial presses, especially in the South and the East, subsequently became very active; over the next two decades they led the way in publishing reforms and production innovations. My discussion of Chunfeng Art and Literature Publishing House, below, provides a clear example of an innovative provincial press with a national vision.

Then, the government gave state-owned publishing houses a chance to compete with private and second-channel distributors and publishers by removing strict controls on book prices, wholesale discounts, and paper allocation and by encouraging self-marketing. For instance, dual pricing was introduced in the mid-1980s; this allowed publishers to charge market prices for all but a handful of "official" titles, whose prices remained fixed by the government. Furthermore, publishers were permitted to market their own books instead of relying on outside distributors with no financial incentives.[10] These measures transformed official publishing into a potentially profitable business, as shown clearly by the boom in popular literature during the 1980s.

Third, in 1988 the Press and Publications Administration gave the green light to "business management in cultural institutions"; this allowed the introduction of various forms of "responsibility systems" (*zerenzhi*) for publishing personnel.[11] Editorial staff would now be rewarded for producing titles that sold well in the marketplace. Generally speaking, this tying of individual income to sales of books led publishers to take a much more active role in selecting subjects and manuscripts, contracting promising writers, and—no less important—promoting their products in a competitive market. Producing best sellers became the primary goal of editors who hoped to thrive in the new business environment, and organizational reform became the buzzword among publishing house presidents, even those who were reluctant to initiate reforms in practice.

After 1992, when Chinese market reforms accelerated following Deng's Southern Tour, business principles and market mechanisms began to exert even greater control over the Chinese publishing industry. Publishing houses had little choice but to adjust to the new environment. For many, the reforms adopted were reluctant responses to government policy changes. By the early 1990s, publishing houses were still state owned in theory and still had to place "social interests first and economic interests second" (shehui xiaoyi di yi, jingji xiaoyi di er), yet their largest sources of funding were now commercial revenues rather than government transfers. This new economic base inevitably led to the self-liberation of the Chinese publishing industry. Commercial considerations began to take the upper hand; the party line became less and less relevant and at the very least subject to negotiation. During the 1990s, all state-run publishing houses underwent paradigmatic changes; they were being forced to explore various new publishing modes, often termed "Western methods with Chinese characteristics." The market economy also led to the rise of a new breed of editors and publishers, who dared to capitalize on both the state privileges they still enjoyed and the vast opportunities offered by the cultural market.

Even today, these state publishing houses must steer a course between economic success and political correctness, since they can still be closed down if they incur the party's displeasure. Many of them sell profitable popular literature to improve their balance sheets even while continuing to produce "mainstream works" (zhuxuanlü zuopin) in response to government political campaigns. These campaigns, however, now often center on awards such as the National Book Prize (Guojia tushu jiang) and the "Five Ones" Project Prize (Wuge yi gongcheng jiang).[12] Yet as I will show, the general trend since the 1990s has been that publishers, instead of waiting for formal permission from the top, have begun taking the initiative in experimenting with new business models. Their success has often led to further deregulation and policy changes. As with many other areas of economic reform in China today, the government is often reduced to playing a game of catch-up instead of setting the reform agenda in advance.

The "corrosive influence" of market forces on the integrity of Chinese state institutions such as the publishing industry actually reflects a more complex process—one that involves interaction between state policy and reforms from above and market forces welling up from below. Because of this complexity, the best way to illustrate the process of give-and-take between the government and the publishing houses is by way of individual case studies.

In the rest of this chapter, I focus on two state-run publishing houses, one national and the other provincial, and show how each has tried to steer a course between the rock of the market and the hard place of continuing party guidance. Both these publishing houses specialize in literary works; together, they serve as a microcosm of the unprecedented reforms taking place in China's literary publishing industry. The changes and difficulties they have endured in the past decade and the innovations they have attempted, and especially their constant efforts to produce literary best sellers, demonstrate clearly how commercialization has irrevocably altered the literary publication business, which was once one of the most important and tightly controlled cultural institutions in Socialist China.

2. *Writers Publishing House*

An ambiguous saying made the rounds among publishers and book editors in Beijing during the late 1990s: "Zhang Shengyou [president of Writers Publishing House] is like a fish stirring the clear waters of the publishing industry." This characterization was probably not originally intended as a compliment. Even so, up-and-coming writers were only too happy to sign a contract with Writers Publishing House (WPH), despite its president's "water-muddying" tendencies. This apparent contradiction can be resolved only by examining the changes that have taken place at WPH in recent years —in particular, by explaining its amazing ability to produce one literary best seller after another over the past decade. Its success lies both in its challenge to the former socialist publishing model outlined earlier and in its thorough implementation of a new, market-oriented model that allows writers, editors, and WPH itself to maximize income and profits.

The offices of WPH are on the fifth floor of the famous Federation of Literary and Art Circles Building (Wenlian dalou) in southeastern Beijing, a building that also houses other once-important cultural institutions such as the editorial boards of *Renmin wenxue* (People's Literature) and *Xiaoshuo xuankan* (Fiction Digest) and, of course, the China Federation of Literary and Art Circles (Quanguo wenlian). Partly because of its stark contrast with the shiny new luxury hotels and commercial office buildings along this section of Beijing's second ring road, the gray, 1950s-style building looks quite despondent, even though the fancy cars parked outside the entrance indicate that it remains a "powerhouse" in its own cultural terms.

The corridors on the fifth floor are dark and crowded. All six editorial sections of WPH, and the president's and vice presidents' offices and a conference room, are crammed onto this one floor. The area seems even more crowded because of the piles of books overflowing from the various offices and the many posters and newspaper clippings pasted on the walls—all signs of a prosperous business. Apparently, four or five editors share each office, although most of the time not all of them are present. Envelopes and manuscripts are heaped up on the desks, and newly published books are stacked on the floors, under the desks, and anywhere there is space. The garish posters and well-printed glossy books contrast strangely with the crowded offices and dark corridors. It's as if the publishing house is a bird that has strayed inside and become trapped, yet one day will break the confinement of this dark cage and fly away to a brighter and more spacious home.

On a wall along the corridor leading to the offices of Bai Bing, WPH's vice president in charge of external affairs and public relations, a big bulletin board is covered with photocopies of recent news reports and book reviews. When I visited in the spring of 2000, the house was promoting *Zhisheng Dongfang Shuo* (The Wise Sage Dongfang Shuo) by Long Yin. The copy for its half-page advertisement:

It has set five records for Chinese Fiction: it was the first book published in the new millennium, at 0 o'clock on Jan. 1, 2000; it was the first Chinese work whose global copyright was purchased by an American company "Getaway" before it was even published; it was the first work of Internet fiction to attract over a hundred thousand viewers; it is the first literati-errant novel [*wenxia xiaoshuo*] which will compete with Jin Yong's famous knight-errant novels [*wuxia xiaoshuo*]; and it will be adapted into a TV serial to challenge the ratings of "Liu the Hunchback Minister" [Zaixiang Liu Luotuo, one of the most popular Chinese TV series of the late 1990s].[13]

The three-volume book was impressively packaged. A golden book belt stamped with promotional phrases tied the three thick volumes into one set, and each volume had its title emblazoned in gold, silver, and shining red. Inside each set was a collector's card printed in gold and red, with a declaration on the back by the Beijing Public Notary's Office (gongzhengchu) confirming that WPH had in fact published this book at exactly 0 o'clock on January 1, 2000.

This is only one example of the packaging and promotional work for which WPH has become famous. Apparently this particular promotion was very successful. Even at a steep price of 48 yuan for the three-volume set, the first print run of this book was 10,000. Within four months it had been reprinted three times to satisfy demand. The number of copies printed so far has reached 170,000,[14] even though during the period immediately following the book's release, many media reports exposed the campaign's false claims—including the nonexistent plans for a television version—and criticized its pallid imitation of knight-errant fiction and its complete lack of historical accuracy.

Clearly, WPH has found a highly effective way to appeal to the huge Chinese reading market. Indeed, *The Wise Sage Dongfang Shuo* was a relatively minor best seller by the standards of the house, which in the latter half of the 1990s earned a reputation for being one of China's premier makers of best sellers. Among its most successful titles: the novel *Lailai wangwang* (Coming and Going, 300,000 copies) by the popular woman writer Chi Li; the personal essay collections of Yu Qiuyu, including *Shuangleng changhe* (Frost on the River, 520,000) and *Qiannian yi tan* (Sigh of a Thousand Years, 360,000); and memoirs by entertainment stars such as CCTV's most famous anchor and host Zhao Zhongxiang (*Suiyue qingyuan* [Passion for Life]), CCTV entertainment host Ni Ping (*Rizi* [Days]), and television and film star Zhao Wei (*Xiaoyanzi: Nüsheng Zhao Wei* [Little Swallow: A Girl Named Zhao Wei]), all of which have sold more than 200,000 copies, some even reaching 900,000 copies—and very quickly. In 1999, WPH easily led the best seller lists, with eight titles among the thirty-nine books that appeared on the monthly top-ten lists. In 2000, it had eight titles among the forty-three books on the monthly lists, and thirty-two of its titles had first print runs of more than forty thousand.[15]

It would be inaccurate to say that WPH did not produce any best sellers before 1996. For example, in the late 1980s, the translated novels of the Czech writer Milan Kundera brought the publishing house both fame and profit, and in 1994, the poet-murderer Gu Cheng's autobiographical *Ying'er* was also a national best seller. However, these titles sold well because of the novelty and high quality of the works themselves (in the case of Kundera), or because of the sheer dramatic force of the real-life events they described (especially in the case of Gu Cheng). In this earlier period, WPH's ability to produce best sellers remained sporadic and unpredictable. Only after 1996, when Zhang Shengyou took over its reins, was WPH transformed into a consistent producer of best sellers. This is clear from an examination of Zhang's management reforms and their dramatic effect on WPH's sales figures.

WPH was originally a branch of People's Literature Publishing House, the most famous and privileged literary press in China, which had been established in 1949 as the preeminent literature and art publisher in Communist China. In 1984, WPH was spun off from People's Literature, becoming an independent publishing house of national scope affiliated with the Writers Association, with a mandate to promote and publish works by contemporary writers. Between 1984 and the mid-1990s, WPH mainly published anthologies for the Writers Association, with an emphasis on young writers. For example, the series Twentieth-Century Literary Stars (Ershi shiji wenxue zhi xing), which lasted for more than a decade, was completely subsidized by the Writers Association. In effect, WPH was an in-house publisher of the Writers Association, specializing in "pure" literature, and thus was a typical official cultural institution.

Which meant it was in a poor position when economic reforms began affecting the publishing industry—especially during the late 1980s, when sales of "pure" literature suffered a sharp decline and government funding was simultaneously cut. Like many other state-run publishing houses during this earlier reform period, WPH occasionally cooperated with private book dealers in publishing popular fiction titles to compensate for its financial losses. However, this was a temporary and shady practice, and the directors of the publishing house would probably have been ashamed to admit it in public. Overall, therefore, WPH remained an elitist and unprofitable institution into the mid-1990s.

Zhang Shengyou, previously an editor and writer, became editor in chief and vice president of WPH at the end of 1995 and immediately set about transforming the house into a producer of best sellers. In the process, he introduced many modern marketing and business methods, thus setting a standard for successful commercialization that other state-run publishers have since scrambled to emulate.

After graduating from the journalism program at Fudan University in Shanghai in the early 1980s, Zhang was among a group of ambitious "sent-down urban educated youth" who were young enough to board the train to the future, but who were also equipped with abundant social experience as a result of their hardships during the Cultural Revolution. While working as a reporter and features writer for *Guangming ribao* (Guangming Daily), he witnessed the economic reforms spreading through Chinese society and their impact on cultural institutions. He became convinced that running a publishing house would give him the chance to prove his theory that reformed cultural institutions could become viable business ventures. In his first speech to the WPH staff after he took over, he made his vision perfectly clear: "We will do whatever it takes to make money, no matter whether it's big money or small money!"[16] This blatant profit-seeking approach, although he later refined it, would underpin his reform efforts over the next five years.

Zhang started by overhauling the inefficient and sluggish management system that was a holdover from the state-planned economy. The editorial offices had been divided into six divisions—fiction, poetry, prose, popular literature, foreign literature, and literary criticism—with each exclusively responsible for its single field of expertise. This structure, although logical under a nonprofit socialist system, inevitably led to unfair results under a market-oriented system, since some divisions had clear advantages over others in terms of producing salable books. For example, the fiction division would certainly have the chance to produce more best sellers than the poetry and literary criticism divisions. Zhang replaced this structure with six nonspecialized editorial offices designated only by number—Office One, Office Two, and so on. He then permitted them to publish titles in any of the six categories.

Zhang also introduced reforms at the next level of administration, establishing three divisions to coordinate and supervise the work of the entire pub-lishing house: first, the Final Deliberative Group (Tushu zhongshen xiaozu), which checked the political and artistic merit of books; second, the Quality Control Group (Tushu zhiliang xiaozu), which oversaw editing, proofread-ing, and printing standards; and third, the Market Assessment Group (Shi-chang lunzheng xiaozu). This last group was especially innovative for a state-owned publisher, and indicates the importance that WPH now attached to proving the potential market for its products.

Regarding personnel, Zhang made great efforts to implement a responsi-bility system, replacing automatic tenure with contracts based on perform-ance. To encourage more efficient performance, the managers (or leaders, *lingdao*) in each division were not directly appointed from the top; instead they had to go through a competitive selection process. Likewise, to ensure employee satisfaction, the members of each editorial division were chosen based on a two-way selection process: individual staff editors could choose which office and colleagues they worked for and with; at the same time, the leaders of each division had the final say regarding whom they accepted as their underlings. Zhang also gave much more autonomy to individual edi-tors, all the way from subject selection and manuscript acquisition to cover designs and final promotion.

Most of these reforms were highly innovative in the context of Chinese cultural institutions, especially institutions of national scope. They have also been extremely successful. As Zhang put it, his "executive editor responsi-bility system" (*zhe bian zhi*) has greatly "liberated the productive forces" within WPH and has resulted in a remarkably motivated and hard-working editorial staff.

Without a doubt, the most effective method Zhang has developed to mo-bilize his editors is a bonus system that associates each editor's rewards and penalties directly with his or her work. The bonus system is a carefully cal-culated method for increasing company profits while motivating staff. In China, such systems are much more common in the private sector than in the Byzantine cultural institutions. Each book WPH publishes is evaluated under three headings, called "cards"—a costs card, a sales card, and a profits card. Bonuses are based on sales and profits after costs are deducted. An edi-tor who produces a title that makes a profit of up to 100,000 yuan will re-ceive a commission of 6 percent; for a profit of 100,000 to 300,000 yuan, 8 percent; for a profit of more than 300,000 thousand yuan, 10 percent. If a book earns a profit of more than 500,000 yuan, the editor will be given the chance to travel abroad, with all costs covered by the publishing house. For designers (or art editors, *meishu bianji*), bonuses are fixed at 1.5 percent of the book's profits.[17] Under this responsibility system, editors will obviously concentrate all their energies either on producing a huge best seller that can make them rich, or on discovering several marketable writers and producing a string of saleable books in order to maintain a substantial regular income.

The opportunity for financial success has had a strong impact on the morale and work habits of the editors at WPH. This is reflected in the house's higher pretax profits. In 1995, WPH made a pretax profit of just 2,590,000 yuan; by 1997, its profits had broken the 20,000,000 yuan mark; in 2000, its profits reached 25,000,000 yuan. This means that in 2000, based on the total number of approximately one hundred editorial staff at WPH, on average each staff member made a profit for the publishing house of nearly 100,000 yuan. On average, their individual incomes rose from a respectable 8,000 yuan in 1996 to the extremely high 60,000 yuan in 2000.[18]

These figures help explain the determination and workaholic habits of one WPH editor, Wang Shuli, who is responsible for two best-selling books by the famous contemporary essayist Yu Qiuyu: *Frost on the River* and *Sigh of a Thousand Years*.

Yu Qiuyu, professor and former president of the Shanghai Academy of Drama (Shanghai xiju xueyuan), became a household name after the publication of his prose works *Wenhua ku lü* (Cultural Journey of Pain, 1992) and *Shan ju biji* (Notes of a Mountain Hermit, 1998). These two books are based on his observations and reflections on his many trips to cultural sites and historical ruins, in China and abroad, and on his own reading and life experiences. They are written in a culturally uplifting tone and have strong emotional resonance for ordinary readers.

Since the mid-1990s, Yu's works had been extremely popular. Publishers were keen to bring them out, and many pirated editions had appeared. In 1998, while scouting for manuscripts in Shanghai and conducting market surveys in southern China, Wang Shuli learned from booksellers that Yu Qiuyu's books were selling remarkably well. She made extraordinary efforts to contact the writer and gain his trust. It happened that Yu was extremely frustrated by the many pirated editions of his books, and he was looking for another publisher that had sufficient resources—especially in the areas of marketing and distribution—to preempt pirated versions of his next work. Soon after meeting Wang, Yu agreed to sign a contract with WPH for his forthcoming *Shuangtian huayu* (Discourses on Frosty Days). Wang's editorial proposal for this book was quickly approved, and she received the full support of the publishing house.

Wang then took drastic measures to prevent pirated editions from coming out at the same time as or even earlier than the WPH edition. This effort would greatly enhance the book's profitability. She herself went to the airport to pick up Yu when he delivered the manuscript to Beijing. And during editing and production, Wang typed the text herself and forbade anyone else from looking at the manuscript. Finally, after the book was sent to the printer, she watched it throughout the entire process. As soon as the copies were printed, she had them all immediately sealed in the warehouse. Even with such careful security, WPH had to change the book's title in mid-process from *Discourses on Frosty Days* to *Frost on the Long River*. A reporter had revealed the original name in a newspaper article, and this could have given a head start to potential pirates. The first print run was 250,000, and Wang made sure that plenty of copies appeared in the bookstores of five major cities all on the same day, again to prevent unofficial editions from being sold before the authentic ones arrived.

Of course, these precautionary measures would have been wasted had potential readers not known that the book was coming out. Wang therefore also organized an extensive marketing campaign. One week before the book came onto the market, she held a press conference and sent excerpts of the book to numerous review magazines and newspaper book columns. She also arranged for Yu Qiuyu to give speeches in various colleges and to sign his books at several major bookstores. Overseeing the book's production and promotion was like leading an extended battle, according to Wang, who claimed that "for seventeen days in a row, I hardly went home or had a regular sleep."[19]

Wang Shuli's hard work consolidated her position at WPH—she had once been just a lowly clerk in the editor in chief's office. It also cemented her working relationship with Yu Qiuyu. As a result, in 2000 Yu arranged for her to edit another essay collection based on his transmillennium trip to the Middle East, *Sigh of a Thousand Years*. This book brought Wang another award for top performance as well as a fat bonus. Besides earning an astounding 200,000 yuan annually in 1999 and 2000, she also won herself a trip to Europe arranged and paid for by the publishing house. When I interviewed her in the summer of 2001, she declared that her sense of achievement went far beyond the money; she was just a high school graduate, and her success showed her that she was just as good as all the college graduates around her. But she had paid a price for her success. Although only in her mid-forties, in the past several years her health had seriously deteriorated, and she had lost almost all her hair.

Besides reforming its personnel and organizational structures, WPH also adjusted its title selection criteria. Previously, it had focused almost exclusively on serious literature by contemporary writers, showcasing the achievements of the Chinese Writers Association. It has since embraced the concept of "literature broadly defined" (*da wenxue*), and under this convenient rubric is enthusiastically seeking out all kinds of manuscripts on a wide variety of topics. Indeed, the publishing house has been willing to consider almost any genre that is even remotely connected with "literature" as long as it can more or less guarantee healthy sales. Thus, besides publishing works of fiction and prose by contemporary writers—especially popular authors such as Chi Li, Wang Anyi, Han Shaogong, Mo Yan, and Yu Qiuyu—which fall squarely within WPH's earlier publishing mandate, the house has also made strong inroads into nonfiction, often setting new trends and stretching the boundaries of "serious" publishing.

Among the most popular new genres promoted by WPH has been so-called autobiographical writing by entertainment celebrities. In fact, the publishing house's top best seller during the 1990s was *Days*, a memoir by the television star Ni Ping, published in 1997. A former stage actress, Ni has hosted various entertainment programs for Chinese Central TV over the past decade, most notably the annual Chinese Spring Festival Gala (chunjie lianhuan wanhui), which attracts an audience of some 500 million. She is well known for her "natural and approachable" smile, and early on won viewers' hearts as a sympathetic and loveable "sister," "lover," or "daughter," depending on the viewers' own particular fantasies. In her book, Ni does write about her career success, but she focuses mainly on her daily life and her feelings toward family, friends, and colleagues, always presenting a respectable and approachable public image. Helped by Ni Ping's wholesome image and extremely high name recognition, this mediocre and sentimental work quickly sold nearly a million copies in less than half a year.[20]

Another category that WPH has successfully targeted is works related to youth culture and high school education, which appeal to younger readers and their parents. Because of the fierce competition surrounding college entrance exams and the dominance of only children among high school students in 1990s China—a result of China's one-child policy—books that offer advice for success to this readership group and their anxious and ambitious parents are guaranteed healthy sales. In 1999, to capitalize on this, WPH bought the rights from the literary journal *Mengya* (First Growth) to publish the prizewinning pieces from the national New Concept Composition Contest (Xin gainian zuowen dasai), an annual event organized by *First Growth* and cosponsored by several top universities. The main selling point of this book was that those awarded prizes in the contest would be recommended to top universities without having to go through the extremely competitive entrance exams; hence, prospective entrants to the contest could learn from the model compositions and possibly find an alternative route to entering university. Not surprisingly, this book was an immense success. Its first volume sold more than 560,000, its second, 300,000. It has been published annually since then.[21]

Another recent best seller published by WPH, and one that combines biography and education, is *Hafo nühai Liu Yiting* (Harvard Girl Liu Yiting), a true account of a Chinese girl who managed to become a Harvard undergraduate, written from the point of view of her parents. This 2001 hit gives a detailed description of how Liu's family trained her to be a star student, and how she ultimately got to study in the United States. It also offers many practical tips for parents and students, including even the questions and answers that Liu gave in her Harvard entrance exam. Its appendix contains various sample official application forms for American colleges. In less than a year, the book sold more than 860,000.[22]

Besides publishing these nonfiction works, WPH sought to exploit the market of younger readers by promoting "teenage writing," where problems with the current school system and the "growing pains" of teenagers are examined in raw works written by teenagers themselves. The best seller *San chong men* (Triple Door) by Han Han, a Shanghai high school dropout, established this trend. Han imitated the satirical and cynical tone of the famous writer Qian Zhongshu in depicting the materialistic lives of today's high school students. Although not original in aesthetic or literary terms, the book does reveal many of the ridiculous and even absurd aspects of the current Chinese education system as well as the growing pains of a whole generation of only children from an insider's point of view.

Also helpful for the book's success was Han's unusual personal experience. Despite winning first prize in the inaugural New Concept Composition Contest, this Shanghai teen subsequently failed six courses before suddenly dropping out of high school, declaring that he was fed up with the education system and would follow an alternative path to success. His shocking choice became a strong selling point for the book and was hyped skillfully by the publishing house through television interviews, newspaper articles, and a book-signing promotional tour. The media's heated coverage greatly helped sales, which jumped to more than 740,000, with more than ten reprints in a single year (1999–2000).[23] This huge success led to a tidal wave of books by teen writers in 2000 and 2001, including those by Han Han, Yu Xiu, Yang Zhe, Gu Zi, and Jin Jin. This bald attempt to profit as much as possible from these mainly immature teen writers has generated much controversy among parents, students, educational workers, and publishers over the past year.[24]

WPH's success at publishing best sellers relies heavily on innovative and clever packaging, marketing, and promotion. Until quite recently, most books published in China were produced in plain, undistinguished editions without illustrations; the cover designs had very little to attract the reader. In general, printing, binding, and paper quality were all very poor. Of course, all of these defects were the result of the nonprofit, state-sponsored publishing system, specifically, the extremely low book prices set by the government. During the 1990s, reforms in the publishing industry led to dramatic improvements in all of the above—especially in cover design and the overall look of books. In this respect, Chinese publishers have clearly learned a lot from Taiwanese and Western publishing methods.

WPH has been at the forefront of these improvements. It has deliberately increased the appeal of its books by creating eye-catching cover designs and texts with unique formats. One example is Chen Danyan's two collections of personal essays, *Shanghai de fenghuaxueyue* (Colors and Sounds of Shanghai, 1998) and *Shanghai de jinzhiyuye* (Daughter of Shanghai, 1999). In these collections, Chen Danyan, a woman writer famous for her "Shanghai style" of lyrical and subtle language, describes Shanghai's people and their daily lives and culture in the pre-1949 period. WPH turned her books into works of fine art. First, it inserted many old black-and-white photographs of Shanghai from the 1920s to 1940s, not just to complement the books' nostalgic tone but also to fully exploit the craze for old photos (*lao zhaopian re*) that had swept through Chinese publishing in the late 1990s. Also, the page margins and cover designs were in Victorian style, with floral patterns and soft but faded colors; for most Chinese, this style embodied exquisite European taste. By catching the wave of "nostalgia chic" at the fin de siècle, Chen's books sold well among new, middle-class urban professionals and college students and proved WPH's ability to make the most of a book's visual potential.

The design of *Shiyan xiju dang'an* (Files of Fringe Theatre)—a collection of plays directed and in most cases written by the avant-garde artist Meng Jinghui—reflected another kind of chic: radical, innovative, genre disrupting, all characteristic of the experimental theater that Meng so enthusiastically promotes. This book's cover imitated the look of the personnel files kept by work units (*dang'an*)—files that had once been a disturbing part of every Chinese person's life: brown manila paper, bold black characters, even a dated red wax seal imitating the official seal on all such files. Also, the book's text was arranged as files: stage pictures, invitations, advertisements, posters, signed tickets and brochures, musical scores, and even the notes and letters exchanged among the artists were all bundled together with the script, to make the reader "feel like" he or she was holding an actual historical record of the development of experimental theatre in 1990s China. The resulting slightly subversive aura had a clear appeal for the new urban yuppie class.

Along with design, marketing and promotion used to be the weakest departments in state-run publishing houses, not least because of the artificial separation of publishing and distribution under the state-planned economy. In this respect as well, WPH has led the reform trend. The very act of setting up a Market Assessment Group in 1996 showed the publisher's new marketing awareness. For every book, the editor must now write a proposal that indicates its market potential; only after satisfactorily answering all questions raised by the group's members and convincing them that the book will be salable is the editor given the green light for the project.

Similarly, WPH realized early on that to reap the rewards of potential best sellers, strong efforts to develop a more efficient distribution network would have to be made. So it established the rule that the profit from each book would be divided among the executive editor, the arts editor, and the distributor. This immediately linked the interests of editors with those of distributors and encouraged constant feedback between the two formerly separated groups. Throughout the entire production process, from the first stages of market assessment to the final stages of advertising and promotion, both sides would now work together to find the best way to make a book appealing and profitable.

The chance to make large bonuses motivated distributors to improve their efficiency and also to seek out better and broader distribution channels to compensate for the weaknesses of the Xinhua bookstore system. To the same end, WPH set up its own wholesale center, which developed more flexible business relations with private and semiprivate brand-name bookstores. As a result, in 1997 the publisher's book sales through unofficial private channels were 60 percent of the total; in 1998, 40 percent; and in 2000, 50 percent. The number of distribution companies contracted to WPH also increased, from just over two hundred in 1996 to more than eight hundred in 2000. The house also established an after-sales assessment system, with sixteen distributors tracking market reaction to its latest titles.[25] Through methods like these, WPH created a much more efficient and flexible distribution network that has certainly been a major contributing factor to its success.

The benefits of an improved marketing and distribution system can be demonstrated with the Chinese translation of *The Horse Whisperer* (Ma yu zhe), by the American author Nicholas Evans. This was an unlikely best seller in China—most urban Chinese readers should have had difficulty identifying with the down-home lifestyle and folk philosophy of the main characters. Even the copyright agent thought the book would sell at most fifty to seventy thousand. But it turned out to be one of the top best sellers of 1998, with more than 230,000 copies sold. Much of the demand was certainly the result of WPH's "carpet-bombing" promotional campaign.

Bai Bing, the vice president of WPH and the book's executive editor, himself wrote numerous promotional articles for the book, declaring that the house would "present" its readers with a stupendous "love story" that had taken the European market by storm, a story similar in style to *The Bridges of Madison County*. This inaccurate characterization of *The Horse Whisperer* would probably have offended the author, but it was certainly an effective strategy for hooking Chinese readers, since *Bridges* was one of the most popular works of foreign fiction published in China during the 1990s. Simultaneously, Bai leaked the news to the Chinese media that Hollywood had just spent three million dollars for the film rights to *The Horse Whisperer*, and coincidentally, that the publication of the Chinese translation had been delayed owing to fierce competition from several publishers for the Chinese copyright. These kinds of hyped reports raised readers' expectations even higher.

Once the book actually came out, WPH launched its promotional campaign. First, it set out to persuade readers that the book was not merely for European and American audiences but would also appeal to Chinese tastes and values, such as the Chinese idea of natural harmony. Next, the marketing team emphasized the high cultural values and literary merit of the book by inviting experts and critics to a symposium and then having their speeches published in the media. Finally, the team collected market information "proving" that the book was short of stock due to high demand—doubtless partly because the publishing house purposely limited its supply in areas outside Beijing in order to achieve the effect of "the fewer, the better" (*wu yi xi wei gui*).

To deal with distribution and retailing, in which the main problem was competition from pirated editions, WPH adopted a clever two-stage strategy. First it saturated the Beijing book market with tens of thousands of copies, which it made available simultaneously through both main and secondary distribution channels. At the same time, it made sure that all the main Beijing media outlets hyped the book, but that provincial media outlets were shielded from the adulation as much as possible. As a result, provincial book dealers doubted the book's sales potential and hesitated to invest in pirating their own versions. Thus, the publishing house was able to fully exploit the Beijing market before moving on to other major cities.[26]

3. An Boshun and the Cloth Tiger Series

In Chinese literary publishing circles during the late 1990s, a name often mentioned in the same breath as Zhang Shengyou of WPH was An Boshun, editor in chief of Chunfeng Art and Literature Publishing House (Chunfeng wenyi chubanshe), based in Liaoning province. Like Zhang Shengyou, An has been a pioneer in new modes of book publishing and distribution based on profit margins. Unlike Zhang, however, his success and reputation are based squarely on a single product line—the Cloth Tiger series (Bu laohu congshu)—and on his highly focused efforts to promote the subgenre of romantic fiction under the Cloth Tiger label. But what really has distinguished An Boshun from his editorial peers is his insight that the business techniques for creating recognizable brand names—"labels" that guarantee a high degree of quality and style—can be successfully adapted to the production and promotion of literary works.

By examining the development and operations of this literary branding process through the rise of the Cloth Tiger series, we will see in clear relief how a progressive provincial publisher/editor has successfully adapted to the new market environment—with occasional setbacks—and how, in the process, he has helped alter the entire manner in which literature is written and consumed in China today.

The Cloth Tiger series was launched in 1993. That year, An Boshun, then a rank-and-file literary editor, signed contracts with ten famous writers, including Wang Meng, Tie Ning, and Jia Pingwa, paying each a manuscript fee of one hundred yuan per thousand characters (a record amount at the time) to write a popular novel. An styled this series as "Popular Novels by Famous Writers." He later gave the series the name Cloth Tiger, registering the name as a trademark along with its distinctive logo—a folk-style cloth doll in the shape of a tiger. Because of their consistently readable stories, their well-packaged albeit middlebrow appearance, and An's creative marketing and promotion strategies, the dozen Cloth Tiger novels published over the next three years sold extremely well. The first print run for most novels in the series was 100,000, in some cases even 200,000. By 1996, Cloth Tiger had become a recognizable and successful brand name in the literary market.

In 1997, An Boshun launched another three-year campaign, capitalizing on the Cloth Tiger brand to solicit what he called "Golden Cloth Tiger" manuscripts, for which he offered to pay a one million yuan fee. This campaign helped Cloth Tiger recruit several promising new writers and works; it also refocused the Cloth Tiger brand to produce romances—a genre for which An Boshun had discerned a huge demand among Chinese readers.[27]

By the spring of 2000, when Chunfeng was ordered to suspend its business after publishing the controversial *Shanghai baobei* (Shanghai Babe), the name Cloth Tiger represented not just a single literary series, but an enormous cultural enterprise publishing a variety of romance-related works, including a line of romantic novels for younger readers (the "Red Moon" series) and Chinese translations of Harlequin romances.[28] The company that An Boshun established, Cloth Tiger Cultural Enterprises Limited (Bulaohu wenhua shiye youxian gongsi), had also built up a national distribution network and opened a Beijing editorial office. After the *Shanghai Babe* incident, An Boshun was forced to resign his position as editor in chief; even so, the "legend" of Cloth Tiger carries on.[29]

An Boshun's branding of the Cloth Tiger label was one of the most successful examples of introducing business practices and market awareness into Chinese publishing. I will examine the main aspects of this branding process in more detail, beginning with the advertisement for the above-mentioned Golden Cloth Tiger Manuscript Contest.

The advertisement first appeared in the November 12, 1997, issue of *Zhonghua dushu bao* (China Reading Weekly), an authoritative newspaper in the publishing industry. It took up a full page in the advertisements section. The main part consists of a "call for manuscripts" (*zhenggao qishi*), which announces that from November 1997 to November 1999, the editorial board of the Cloth Tiger Series will hold a contest for "Golden Cloth Tiger Romance" manuscripts. The ad provides guidelines and criteria for the submissions. The novel "will fully embody the artistic spirit of Classical Chinese Romanticism" and "emulate the transcendence of life and suffering demonstrated by Liang-Zhu's 'Butterfly Lovers.'"[30] The setting "should describe urban life of the 1990s," and "the plot should be realistic, but its inner spirit should transcend everyday reality." The ad notes that "the form of the novel should be modeled after the techniques and methods of classic novels." In particular, it advises potential contestants that "the conflicts of the story should not be based on the perverted psyche of destitute literati"; in other words, no elitist avant-garde novels will be accepted. Once a work is selected by a special jury of experts, consisting of five famous critics and scholars, and approved by the customary three administrative levels, Chunfeng Art and Literature Publishing House will sign a contract with the author and purchase the exclusive publishing rights for one million yuan.

The layout of this advertisement is just as notable as its content. At the top, there are several lofty-sounding slogans about Cloth Tiger being a new business model for literary publishing. Below the announcement, there is a list of in-house products for sale, including reprints of the original Cloth Tiger series and two new lines of Cloth Tiger spin-offs. Obviously, An Boshun is using this "call for manuscripts" as an opportunity to advertise Cloth Tiger's products as well as to increase its name recognition. He trumpets the success of Cloth Tiger in purely financial terms: "According to the Liaoning Provincial Center for Estimating Invisible Capital and the State-Owned Capital Management Bureau, in 1996, the invisible capital of [the Cloth Tiger] brand was 100,020,000 yuan, and it had a total readership of 34 million." An credits this outstanding success to the publisher's efficient business operations and market awareness: "Yesterday's Cloth Tiger has created today's glory; tomorrow's Cloth Tiger will work with book distributors to create a wonderful future using a highly effective intellectual management system, a large-scale enterprise operation and a scientifically regulated market service."

The deliberate extravagance of this advertisement—especially the sky-high award of one million yuan—immediately caught the attention of both the media and the masses. The ad was "reported" (that is, as a free ad) by more than 240 newspapers and magazines over the next few months. At the same time, the editorial board was besieged by telephone inquiries and flooded with manuscripts, which almost overwhelmed the three-person office set up to administer the contest. Over the next two years, more than 730 manuscripts were received, including more than sixty by professional writers.[31]

The success of this ad was not accidental; rather, it was was the culmination of a lengthy and meticulous branding process for the Cloth Tiger series initiated as far back as 1993. I will now look more closely at five principles and techniques of commercial publishing revealed in the advertisement, and show how each was deliberately developed by An Boshun as part of his broad strategy to elevate Cloth Tiger romances to the status of a famous and marketable brand.

As we mentioned, the first noticeable feature of this advertisement is the strict editorial guidelines channeling writers into producing a particular kind of literature: romantic novels about contemporary urban society. The ad provides clear and detailed instructions regarding the kind of story and setting required and the language, style, and aesthetic values of the ideal entry. Such formulaic literature did not originate with this call for manuscripts; it had all along been a central feature of titles produced under the Cloth Tiger label, the result of An Boshun's careful investigation of current market demands.

Even before he started Cloth Tiger, An Boshun was convinced there was a shortage of original romances aimed at Mainland Chinese readers. He had edited a series of romantic novels by contemporary women writers in 1992 to "resist the unhealthy influence of imported Romances by Taiwanese and Hong Kong writers, and other foreign fiction."[32] Although Cloth Tiger wasn't originally defined as a romance novel series, most of the initial titles were formed from the primary romance ingredients of love and passion. By 1997, many titles in the series had been tested by the market; the most successful turned out to be those by women writers dealing with the confusing world of love and marriage. The most successful of these was Zhang Kang-kang's *Qing ai hualang* (Gallery of Passion and Love); its first print run was more than 210,000, and its success was reflected in the number of pirated editions that sprang up around it. An Boshun was greatly inspired by this notable success, and so in his 1997 advertisement, he further tied the Cloth Tiger series to the romantic novel category, deliberately seeking to guide his contracted writers into that genre. He declared in an interview: "When everyone is disillusioned by the lack of real love, this romantic Utopia, though it is just a fantasy, can give readers a noble feeling that they cannot find in real life. . . . This is the selling point of Cloth Tiger."[33]

Besides recruiting writers through this advertisement, An Boshun planned to organize a workshop for writing romance novels, to train young women to produce a steady stream of them.[34] According to An, the cooperative agreement he signed with Harlequin Books in January 2000 to introduce their romances to China was designed mainly to further familiarize Chinese readers with the genre of romantic fiction, thus increasing the market potential for his own Chinese romances. Ultimately, he hoped to use this alliance to introduce and sell Chinese romances on the international market.[35]

From the start, besides defining the particular subgenre and its characteristics, An Boshun actively involved himself in producing the titles, working directly with the writers. When he first signed up ten writers to produce the original Cloth Tiger series in 1993, he made it clear in the contract that, first, the novel should be easy reading; second, it should be about contemporary urban society, with an emphasis on the "world of feelings" (*qinggan shijie*); and third, it should be "idealistic" (*lixiangzhuyi*)—that is, uplifting and sentimental like a daydream. Before signing the final contract, he would listen to the writer's description of the story and give his own concrete opinions and suggestions for revisions, making sure the writer understood his guidelines. Only then would he agree to publish the book. In return for all this, he guaranteed a first print run of fifty thousand.[36]

This formalization of a specific literary category for writers is closely tied to a second aspect of commercial publishing adopted by Cloth Tiger—identifying and analyzing potential readers / consumers in an increasingly heterogeneous society. As the Golden Cloth Tiger advertisement states, "the intended readers are urban educated."[37] Indeed, the Cloth Tiger series was solidly based from the start on An's analysis of this new urban literary market—an analysis that involved intense market research in the form of commissioned surveys and data provided by his own distribution network. He concluded that in urban China of the 1990s—especially in developed areas, coastal cities, and special economic zones—mainstream society included large numbers of well-educated public and private employees working in various companies and institutions. This group he defined as "professional intellectuals" (*ligong zhishi fenzi*) in the "white-collar class" (*bailing jieceng*).[38] He realized that this newly emerging urban middle class had both purchasing power and intellectual curiosity; thus, he made them his target customers for literary books.

An did not stop at delineating the objective features of this new market segment; he also engaged in some makeshift psychological analysis of potential readers' expectations. He predicted that as an upwardly mobile class benefiting from the reforms, these potential readers would generally support the present social system; also, they would hold a positive view of life, while longing for a society with moral and social stability. Culturally, however, they would be conservative, with a high regard for classic writers as well as for tradition. Thus, for this reading group, literature should not function as social criticism; rather, it should "meet their spiritual need for self-cultivation and emotional nourishment, and enhance their sense of well-being and taste."[39]

This careful market research and identification of a potential readership is again inseparably related to the third aspect of Cloth Tiger's business plan: the adoption of a production and marketing strategy whose aim is to appeal to the middlebrow market. An Boshun consistently defined Cloth Tiger's titles as "popular literature by famous writers" in order to differentiate them both from pulp fiction—better known in China as "market-stall literature" (*ditan wenxue*)—with its crude language, sensational stories, and poor production values, and from overly intellectual and "pessimistic" elite literature, which he declared was "based on the perverted psyche of destitute literati." Thus, the principal aim of the Cloth Tiger series was a hybrid one, to "please both the refined and the popular audience" (ya su gong shang).

To that end, these novels usually focused on true-to-life stories dealing with popular topics such as personal life, family relations, and everyday situations. They avoided probing deeply into serious social issues. They were well written and carefully structured but did not draw attention to their style. And they were proofread thoroughly, printed to high standards, and packaged elegantly—all to appeal to the professional readers.

To give a more concrete illustration of this middlebrow approach, let us examine the content and style of Zhang Kangkang's runaway best seller *Gallery of Passion and Love*. The story centers on the love affairs between a Beijing artist and his three lovers, two of whom are a mother and her daughter. Zhou You is a talented and charismatic Bohemian artist in constant search of the ultimate marriage of love, beauty, and art. While wandering through Hangzhou, a beautiful town famous for its long cultural history and beauties romantically related with scholars, he falls in love with a "classical beauty," Qin Shuihong, an art history professor. At the same time, Qin's teenage daughter, Ni, falls completely under Zhou's thrall. All of this inspires Zhou, on his return to Beijing, to produce several sensational works based on his dual love for the mother and daughter, which he sends to Hangzhou. Bombarded by Zhou's love letters on canvas, Qin lets her suppressed desire for love and passion burst through. She leaves her daughter and husband—the kind-hearted but dull surgeon Wu, the heir to an illustrious family—to go to Beijing and pursue her own dreams.

The two lovers share their passion for love and art in their own little Eden. Zhou's talents are fully stimulated by the perfect female body of his lover Qin, and Qin finally becomes aware of her own beauty through her lover's brush. But the harmony between them only accentuates the terrible consequences to others of their passion. Wu's family, once widely admired in the town as a model of domesticity, is shattered after Qin leaves. Wu remarries but cannot find happiness again, and his new wife is soon murdered during a break-in that targets the family's collection of art and antiques. Shocked by the changes to the family, and tortured by her unrequited love for Zhou, the daughter Ni loses her mind. Meanwhile, back in Beijing, the love nest of Zhou and Qin is threatened. Zhou's former girlfriend Li, an affectionate and energetic businesswoman, returns from Shenzhen a dollar millionaire and is determined to reclaim her lover. But she cannot compete with Qin's talent and beauty, and especially with Qin's true love for Zhou, and instead becomes their best friend. With the help of Li—who is now his agent—Zhou's works sell very well. Qin and Zhou are able to build their dream home not only with love but also with money. Ni and Wu also gradually recover, and Ni's youthful beauty is bound to bloom under the gaze of a local entrepreneur who had been an admirer of her mother for years.

The novel is a stimulating fantasy that combines spicy ingredients with the twists and turns of a popular story. At the same time, it offers a "refined and tasteful" account of the life of urban elites and is elegantly written by an accomplished and renowned writer. It concerns itself with profound issues such as the conflict between different kinds of love and the relationship between love, beauty, and art; but it is also crowded with enviable if unconvincing characters—gorgeous women, passionate artists, cultivated professionals, and successful entrepreneurs. In sum, it is market-stall literature for middle-class professionals—presumably the goal of An Boshun's "middle-brow approach."

A fourth aspect of the Cloth Tiger approach—and perhaps the most innovative in the Chinese publishing context—was An Boshun's deliberate attempt to create a recognizable brand name. This strategy had been employed successfully by Western labels such as Harlequin for many years. Golden Cloth Tiger's "call for manuscripts" was clearly a branding event in itself, designed as much to remind people of all the values Cloth Tiger represented and to give the brand further media exposure as to solicit new novels. According to the ad, these values included the following: "creating eternity, writing nobility, and giving a dream back to the masses!"[40] An Boshun promised that the manuscripts he accepted as a result of his call would exemplify the highest achievements of Cloth Tiger, that their brand-name quality will be recognized by a jury of respected experts, and finally, that the winning books would be sealed with a golden logo on the cover.

This branding practice was always central to the success of the Cloth Tiger series. An always promoted the brand by pointing to the high profile of its writers, by ensuring good production quality, and by emphasizing strong stories and elegant writing. He was one of the first Chinese publishers to register a literary series name and logo as a trademark, and he was careful to create uniform packaging for the series, complete with a standard logo and similar cover designs. Later, with the reprints, he further upgraded the quality of the series by introducing clothbound editions that were much smoother and more elegant than the originals.

In itself, the conception of a "series" was a meaningful marketing gesture, since in Chinese publishing circles, *congshu* (series) are normally associated with the classics and with authoritative editions. Clearly, An's aim was to encourage readers to associate the Cloth Tiger brand with quality fiction, so that later on they would continue to purchase books under that label, no matter who the writers were, knowing that they would be guaranteed a similar reading experience.

This strategy reveals one of An's key insights: his target readers were young, educated professionals who were generally keen to purchase all sorts of brand-name products. It also clearly demonstrates that he saw literature as a salable commodity. As he had stated, best sellers could be produced as a uniform series following the "principle of duplication" (*kaobei yuanze*): with consistent content, with a brand-name guarantee of quality, and consequently, with predictable sales figures, even if sometimes this required "repression of the writer's creative individuality."[41]

The final noteworthy aspect of the Cloth Tiger approach related to the use of commercial gimmicks and media hype. As already noted, the real purpose of the extravagant Golden Cloth Tiger ad was to make a media splash, and as a result of being printed in more than 240 newspapers, it achieved this goal beyond the publisher's wildest dreams. Over the years, An Boshun repeatedly came up with similarly extravagant strategies to hype his Cloth Tiger series as the "number one" product in the competitive world of literary publishing. These included his original idea of contracting ten famous writers simultaneously by offering them unprecedented fees, and his decision to register the Cloth Tiger trademark—something seldom done in book publishing before his time.

Another publicity method that An used repeatedly was "soft advertising"—in other words, using literary criticism and book reviews for advertising purposes. This has since become common practice in Chinese publishing. For example, Cloth Tiger "sponsored" a regular column, "Shidai wenxue" (Contemporary Literature) in *China Reading Weekly*; in return, that newspaper often reported on new books from Cloth Tiger, book signings by its writers, and other Cloth Tiger news. Some of these articles amounted to blatant promotional copy.[42]

Also, there were many forums and articles in other journals that seemed at first glance to discuss the Cloth Tiger phenomenon objectively; at second glance, their uniformly positive tone suggested that An Boshun had actually worked closely with the writers and editors to make sure they would speak well of his product. A typical example of this is the section "Forum on

Brand Names" (Pinpai luntan) that suddenly began appearing in the journal *Nanfang wentan* (Southern Cultural Criticism). Its first installment was dedicated entirely to Cloth Tiger, with An Boshun's own article leading the chorus of praise. Likewise, Chunfeng itself arranged regular "symposia" to publicize individual titles. For example, in April 1997, An Boshun hosted a symposium in Beijing to discuss the first novels of two young female writers: *Kewang jiqing* (Thirst for Passion) by Pi Pi and *Yingsuhua* (Poppy Flower) by Wen Xi, and to promote them as a fresh new generation of romance writers who could carry the torch for Zhang Kangkang.[43]

The outcome of the Golden Cloth Tiger manuscript contest made it clear that it was largely just another publicity gimmick. At the end of 1999, after the original two-year deadline for manuscripts had passed, the editorial board announced that the evaluation committee was disappointed with the quality of the nearly seven hundred entries. It had found only one work, Pi Pi's *Biru nüren* (Such as Women) that even came close to meeting the criteria. So An Boshun announced that he would extend the contest deadline for one more year. Many critics expressed cynicism, suggesting that An had never intended to pay the million-yuan prize to anyone and that from the start the contest had been a massive fraud. Then in April 2000 the editorial committee suddenly declared that it had at last found a worthy Golden Cloth Tiger, Tie Ning's *Da yunü* (Bathing Woman). A symposium on *Bathing Woman* was then held in Beijing, with all of the attending critics and reporters receiving special collector's editions of the book.[44] However, Tie Ning later turned down the prize, since she felt her work was not "confined to the narrow category of a Romantic Novel."[45]

All of these twists and turns, with their attendant media hype and controversy, resulted in very healthy book sales for both Tie Ning and Pi Pi—something that An Boshun had conveniently predicted by authorizing first print runs of 200,000 for each. Generally, all of these commercial gimmicks attracted a great deal of media attention and greatly increased the name recognition of the sort that a provincial publishing house such as Chunfeng desperately needed in order to survive in the competitive book market.

The branding techniques of the Cloth Tiger series and the extensive organizational reforms at WPH demonstrate clearly that in China today, literary publishing is undergoing a thorough transformation. From a state cultural institution, publishing is evolving into a profit-oriented industry in which individual publishers can exert great power in defining writing styles and producing best sellers. As a result of the new concept of literature as commodity, publishers are now keen to explore the best ways to identify their customers, to deliver the most marketable and desirable products to them, and to do all of this efficiently. The effect of this new market-oriented publishing model extends beyond the publishing business itself. Publishers like An Boshun are tempting highly esteemed writers to alter their preconceptions about literature and are training a new generation of writers to produce works that satisfy commercial demand. As we saw in Chapter 1, the new publishing model has changed the "business" of writing literature.

As with any system in transition, many problems remain in the Chinese publishing world. Not the least of these is continued state ownership, with all the inefficiencies and occasional state interference this implies. The case studies presented in this chapter exemplify the pacesetters among Chinese cultural institutions on the cusp of wholesale paradigmatic change. Many publishing houses have begun to imitate the new business methods and reforms that brought so much success to WPH and Chunfeng; but many others are still held back by editorial staff who lack initiative but cannot be removed, who are burdened by their responsibility to pay and house their employees, and who lack any of the modern management and business skills that might allow them to adapt to the market. As state-owned institutions, they must also take care not to produce content that will offend the Communist Party leadership or cause "bad social influence," no matter how marketable and profitable such books may be. This is because the government still has the power to deny them their precious book licenses and still often cracks down on politically incorrect publishers.

Even experienced editors occasionally fall afoul of the censors. This happened to An Boshun in the summer of 2000; his publishing business was suspended for eight months and his Beijing editorial office was closed down after he brought out the sexually explicit and "immoral" *Shanghai Babe*. Walking on similarly thin ice, Zhang Shengyou has developed a "balancing strategy" approach to publishing reform. He has been careful to publicly state that WPH is more than a "best seller machine" and that 90 percent of its titles are still "mainstream works" (*zhu xuanlu zuopin*) and "serious literature" (*chun wenxue jingpin*). And the 10 percent of his books that are "high-quality best sellers" (*youxiu changxiaoshu*) in effect subsidize the sales of other kinds of books.[46]

Despite the above problems, and even though publishing houses and government leaders do not always interpret the latest market reform policies in the same way, the spillover effect from economic reforms in Chinese society has led to a remarkable degree of self-liberation among publishers. As the following chapter will show, the fierce competition from the private and quasi-private sectors infiltrating the publishing business—the "second channel"—and the reduction of government funding have gradually forced the centralized and inflexible state-controlled houses to open up and adopt more aggressive business management styles simply in order to survive. This in turn has prompted complaints by state publishers about the present regulatory and ownership system—about the "nonmarket factors" (*fei shichang xingwei*) that hinder their marketization and profitability.

Zhang Shengyou eloquently expressed the point:

> There are a number of causes of the present chaotic situation in the book market. . . . One is the government, another is second channel publishing. . . . Yet the root of all these causes is the system. Publishing must be changed to run like a proper business, and publishing houses must become truly competitive in the market economy, operating autonomously, financially independent, self-regulating and able to develop and expand freely. In due course, the approval system [*shenpi zhi*] should be abolished and replaced with a business registration system [*dengji zhi*]. Only then will the publishing industry be truly "industrialized" [*chanyehua*] and integrated into the market economy.[47]

Clearly, unleashed market forces have contributed to the "acceleration of institutional decay" and exerted a corrosive influence on the integrity of the centralized and inflexible state-controlled economy. And although "the primary goal of economic reform was improving the efficiency of the state-owned enterprises without changing their ownership,"[48] the effect of this marketization and enterprise management reform is likely to be much greater and more far-reaching than the Chinese government could have expected. It may ultimately undermine one of the basic foundations of socialism—ideological control—and cause party influence over the cultural sphere to completely give way to market forces.

CHAPTER 3

"Second Channel"

ACCORDING TO SHEN CHANGWEN, veteran publisher of the Joint Publishing Company (Sanlian shudian) and former editor in chief of *Dushu* (Reading) monthly in Beijing, by the end of the 1990s, there were five to ten thousand private book dealers (*shushang*) in China—at least ten times the number of official publishing houses. Shen calls these book dealers, most of whom often engage in unlicensed publishing activities, "shadow" publishing houses (*yingzi chubanshe*).[1] Shen's assessment is confirmed by Nicolas Driver, although the latter's figures are more conservative. According to him, some five thousand private publishers operate by unofficially obtaining ISBNs (what I refer to as book license numbers) from six hundred state-owned publishers, and most of these unofficial publishers focus on literature, culture, and the arts.[2]

The gray area of publishing that Shen and Driver describe is also known in China as the "second channel" (*er qudao*)[3]—a term that includes both unofficial publishing and private book distribution. The second channel was an almost inevitable consequence of economic reforms in the cultural field, and emerged to supplement the often inefficient, uncoordinated, and slow-to-reform "main channel" (*zhu qudao*) of state publishers and the Xinhua bookstore system. In one sense, therefore, the second channel represents the most commercialized and liberated area of book publishing and distribution.

The conflicting regulations regarding the second channel and the obstacles it constantly faces to becoming an officially recognized business sector reveal a growing chasm between conservative government directives and actual practice in a market economy. On the one hand, publishing in China is still officially a state-owned and state-run cultural enterprise. The government exerts control over existing publishing houses through various administrative and regulatory bodies, and attacks as "illicit publication" (*feifa chuban*) all other forms of unofficial publishing. This means that private-sector book distribution—especially if it involves unofficial production of books—remains a high-risk venture and that private book dealers are vulnerable to various government campaigns, with few legal safeguards to protect their property and rights.

Yet on the other hand, market forces and the chance to make a large profit have inexorably led to significant self-liberation within the state publishing industry, as well as to de facto cooperation with unofficial book dealers and publishers, some of which has even been triggered by changes in government policies. As a result, during the past two decades, private-sector book publishing has continued to develop rapidly and expand its reach. From its unsavory beginnings among shady dealers hawking trashy market-stall literature and pirated best sellers in the 1980s to its present semirespectable state, in the hands of a new breed of unofficial publishers calling themselves special editors, studios, cultural corporations, and book producers, the second channel has consistently tested the boundaries of economic reform. It continues to survive and even thrive because of its amazing success at producing best sellers, because it plays a necessary role as a financial support for unprofitable state publishing houses, and because of its ability to exploit loopholes in the regulatory system.

To gain a full understanding of the changes taking place in the field of literary production and distribution in China, it is essential to examine closely the growth of the unofficial book publishing and distribution business and its increasing penetration of the literary book market. My research shows that contrary to the often negative depiction of "illicit publication" in government documents and official sources, the second channel has played an important and generally positive role in the Chinese book and cultural production market over the past two decades. The second channel has brought out many culturally challenging books, some of very high quality, that would otherwise have remained unpublished; it has also published general entertainment books and works of fiction that have enriched the book market. Furthermore, it has filled the huge gap left by the main-channel publishers, which have failed to satisfy the huge public demand for books.

The rise of the book dealers, their growing influence over all stages of publishing during the 1990s, and their transformation into semilegal businesses, are the most fascinating aspects of the chaotic and innovative world of second-channel publishing in China. I will begin this chapter with a brief history of second-channel book dealers, the perils they have faced, and their recent evolution into *de facto* publishers. Then I will present two case studies on the new breed of second-channel publishers and book retailers in China today, focusing especially on the Alpha Book (Zhengyuan tushu) group and the Xi Shu Bookstore chain. These case studies will demonstrate just how closely intertwined the official and unofficial publishers and distributors have now become, to the point where it is almost impossible to tell whether a book was produced in the main or second channel. In the concluding section, I will argue that the growth of the second channel in Chinese publishing reveals the most intriguing and contradictory reality of the present dual-track system from a cultural perspective. Many serious problems have emerged in the world of second-channel publishing, mainly because of the lack of a proper legal framework or clear rules of ownership for such businesses; as a result, the reputation of this publishing sector remains precarious, as does its very existence. However, as with private enterprises in most other business sectors in China, it is likely that market forces will eventually make the present approval system irrelevant, and that restrictions on both publishing houses and book numbers will disappear, replaced by an open registration system for publishing houses. This in turn will allow the demand for popular books to be satisfied by the most efficient book publishers, whether state owned or not, acting through a true free market.

1. Chinese Book Dealers: Fact and Fiction

Second-channel book dealers and publishers have contributed greatly to the prosperity of the Chinese book market since the early 1980s, yet until recently the government adopted discriminatory policies against their retail outlets, known as private or quasi-private bookstores (*minying shudian*), and equated all unofficial publishing with illicit activities such as spreading pornography and subverting the moral and social order. It is no surprise, then, that the term "second channel" is often used in a pejorative sense, and that many articles and speeches about the second channel continue to emphasize its negative effects on the publishing industry—how its dealers have become rich by selling filth, and how they violate laws and regulations.[4]

This negative official attitude means that few objective studies on second-channel publishing and distribution are available. It is extremely difficult to locate official materials and information about this field, especially private-sector book publishing. Even direct interviews with book dealers can be difficult to get, since those who are willing to talk do not always provide reliable information about how they do business: they are too afraid of being charged with illicit activities. But, as traditional wisdom teaches us, "fiction often reveals what cannot be told in the official histories." There are plenty of fictional works describing in great detail the world of Chinese book dealers, from their beginnings two decades ago right up to the late 1990s.[5] So to set the scene for the facts I provide below, I will first introduce some key episodes from a fictional work, *Zhongguo shushang* (Chinese Book Dealer), by Yang Zhijun, which depicts the rise of unofficial or second-channel publishers in China. This novel graphically illuminates both the huge rewards and the serious perils awaiting those who dare to publish books outside regular official channels.

The novel opens with a ghost taking a taxi to a bookstore, telling everyone he meets: "Give me back my money! I was going to use it to buy a book license!" As it turns out, this is the ghost of the manager of a private bookstore called Heaven and Earth Books (Tiandi shudian) in the fictional city of Haguo, who was executed during a government campaign against illegal publishing in the late 1980s. It seems obsessed with its failure to obtain book licenses. Elsewhere it cries: "Why do they all have book licenses, but I can't get hold of even one?" ("They" here refers to state publishers and some lucky and cunning book dealers.) This ghost reappears several times in the book, and is obviously intended to provide a disturbing contrast with the dazzling success of the hero, the owner of Heaven and Earth Books and foster brother of the ghost when it was alive.[6]

The ghost having established the novel's refrain, the story now focuses on a panoramic history of underground book publishing in reform-era China. It follows the hero, Zhou Yikuai, as he progresses through the three main stages in the growth of second-channel publishing.

The first stage depicts his childhood and early career. An orphan, he has barely enough schooling to appreciate children's cartoon books, which he rents to other children to earn his first money. While working as a clerk in the local Xinhua bookstore in the late 1970s, he finds that many books in demand are not on the store shelves, even though they are available in storage. He decides to satisfy this demand by setting up his own private bookstore, first simply obtaining books at wholesale prices from Xinhua. Through his continued access to the Xinhua bookstore, he manages to obtain advance information about books, along with the addresses of publishing houses, and begins to order books from the publishers directly, cutting out the Xinhua purchasing office and reducing his costs. By keeping good credit and often paying immediately in cash transfers, he establishes good business relationships with publishers; before long, he has gained control over book distribution to all the private bookstores in his region. He also hires people to set up street bookstalls, and they too all buy their books from him. Ultimately, he establishes a distribution network throughout northwest China; from this, he expands both inland and out to the East Coast.

In the second stage, Zhou moves into unofficial publishing. Having by this point done plenty of business with publishing houses, he realizes that publishing could offer him much larger profit margins than distribution. A friend,

Liu, who once worked for a state publishing house, invites him to become a business partner and explains how the system works. The costs include the following: manuscript fees, which are extremely low at that time (zero, for pirated foreign titles); a book license fee of several thousand yuan, necessary to "buy" permission from the publishing house to print and distribute a book; cover design costs of several hundred yuan; printing costs, including typesetting, labor, and paper fees; and, finally, packaging and shipping. He then quickly calculates the profits they could make on a book priced at five yuan: "If you print 80,000 copies, your gross income is 400,000 yuan, and the costs wouldn't exceed 150,000. Even if you give the wholesalers a 15% discount, or 60,000 yuan, your profit will still be a whopping 190,000 yuan.[7]

Zhou is easily persuaded by this logic. With Liu's access to book license numbers and local printing houses, coupled with Zhou's efficient distribution network and a clever selection of popular titles, within just three months they make astronomical profits—almost a million yuan. Zhou is now collecting money from two sources simultaneously: bookselling and publishing.

Having tasted this success, Zhou immediately sets up a company in Beijing, Otter Cultural Enterprises (Hanta wenhua fazhan gongsi),[8] to fully exploit the potential of the publishing business. He pirates the works of famous Hong Kong and Taiwanese writers, such as the romantic novelist Qiong Yao and the martial arts novelist Jin Yong. His company also establishes "business" alliances with dozens of financially struggling state publishing houses by offering them "administrative fees" (*guanli fei*) in order to obtain their book license numbers. Publishers are happy to oblige in order to offload some of their surplus license numbers and make some profit themselves. The desperate-for-work printing factories also require little persuasion to do just as Zhou asks.

Despite fierce competition from other second-channel publishers and distributors, Otter quickly develops into one of the top book dealers in the country, largely owing to its excellent distribution network and Zhou's ruthless methods—for example, stealing others' titles and "preempting" their publication. Otter evolves into an independent and highly efficient publishing house, one that carries out all the tasks that were once the sole province of official publishers, such as acquiring manuscripts, editing them, designing, printing, and shipping books, selling subscriptions, and of course collecting money from booksellers.

At its peak, Otter has ninety-seven book projects going at the same time: thirty-six waiting for distribution, twenty-two in print and being sent to bookstores, fifteen awaiting book licenses, and twenty-four in the process of being written. Setting an ironic tone, the narrator sums up the secret of his success:

In fact, even with such a grand and complex operation, there are only three things that the head office need to look after: the first is checking the title selection, to make sure that no title produced contains anti-government content. Zhou Yikuai thought this was even more important than making money, because Otter doesn't oppose the Party or the government. It is just a cultural enterprise, cultural, that's all.[9]

In the novel's third section, Zhou continues to expand his business, investing in printing plants and paper factories to gain control over yet another stage of book production. But his main effort now is to forge alliances with other book dealers and unofficial publishers, in order to lobby the government for policy changes that would allow them to come out of the shadows and be recognized as legitimate businesses. At the (fictional) Second Channel Workers Association Conference, Zhou gives a rousing speech in which he sums up the achievements and continued problems of unofficial publishing in China—in particular, the fact that their colleagues are still often pursued and arrested simply for "providing a much needed service to the masses." He also expresses his vision for the future, his ambition to draw together all the major second-channel publishers and build an International Book Plaza (guoji tushu dasha) in Beijing where they would be able to pool their resources and divide their profits. And he dreams of holding a Book Dealers' Representative Conference in the Great Hall of the People—something that would truly demonstrate their acceptance by the Chinese government and their emergence as respectable and orthodox business entrepreneurs.

Chinese Book Dealer provides remarkably vivid and detailed insight into the rise of second-channel book distribution and publishing in China. Its hero, Zhou Yikuai, does become an extremely successful businessman, yet the book does not downplay the problems and dangers confronting second-channel dealers. This is clear in the recurring figure of the bitter ghost, and in the constant battles Zhou must fight to maintain his book distribution network in the face of incursions by clever, unscrupulous, and sometimes violent competitors not too dissimilar from himself. There is also ambiguity in the book's ending, when the narrator notes that Zhou has recently disappeared. Some say that he has been executed for illicit publishing, just like his foster brother; others, that he has been elected to the Chinese National People's Congress and been made responsible for the publishing industry!

Yang Zhijun's novel, which was itself produced by a second-channel publisher, provides a brief history of unofficial distribution and publishing in China over the past two decades; the hero, Zhou Yikuai, is presented as an archetypical private-sector publisher. The offbeat ending and the author's obvious ambivalence toward his main characters make it clear that on the one hand, the second channel is a positive force, one that is opening up new territory in the culture / business wilderness; on the other hand, until the Chinese government recognizes second-channel publishing as a valid enterprise, it will remain a dangerous business that attracts a strong criminal element. The ambiguous identity of the second channel is inherent in its very nature and always has been.

Turning to the facts, it is true, as the novel points out, that the second channel gained its original toehold in the distribution sector. For decades, Xinhua bookstores and state-owned publishing houses enjoyed a strict monopoly over the publishing and distribution of books. All books produced by publishing houses were sent directly to Xinhua, which then sold them at its retail outlets, the only bookstores in China. This system allowed the government easy control over the publishing industry, but led to serious inefficiencies in distribution owing to a lack of competition and market incentives. It also increasingly became a burden on the state's finances.

As early as 1980, in order to solve the problems of urban unemployment and to deal quickly with the so-called "book famine" (*shu huang*)—a huge demand for reading matter of any kind following the deprivations of the Cultural Revolution—the government permitted the development of the "urban nonagricultural private-sector economy." This included allowing private book retail and distribution in the form of street stalls, newsstands, private bookstores, and later, wholesale operations.[10] As we saw in *Chinese Book Dealer*, this private sector grew rapidly during the 1980s and gradually invaded the territory of the Xinhua distribution system, especially once private individuals overtook state institutions as the main customers in the book market: "In 1979, state-owned Xinhua bookstores controlled 95% of the book retail market; by 1988, private and collective stores gained control of nearly two thirds of that market. The government-controlled postal system's monopoly on the distribution of newspapers and magazines fell to 42% by 1988 as private newsstands gained market dominance."[11] Like the fictional character Zhou Yikuai, these early booksellers were generally poorly educated urban unemployed, who sold books purely for profit, just as they might sell fruit, clothes, or any other commodity. But after 1988, the government further reformed book distribution. At that point, many higher-quality private and collective bookstores appeared, such as Beijing's All Sages Bookstore (Wan sheng shuyuan) and Women's Bookstore (Nüzi shudian), to satisfy the demands of more diverse customers.

Increased consumer spending power during the 1980s led to strong growth in the demand for leisure books and popular literature, part of a burgeoning new entertainment industry. Private booksellers were familiar with the market and able to satisfy its demands better than state publishers, and they quickly moved into book production, which was more lucrative than what they were doing. The main obstacle for them was that for ideological reasons, the government controlled publishing through a book license number system; thus, it was illegal to produce, print, or sell books without those numbers. For a while, private book dealers could only gaze at this tempting and highly marketable fruit beyond their reach.

However, beginning in the mid-1980s, the government began introducing deregulatory policies to encourage state-owned publishing houses to manage themselves more like businesses—to reduce their debts and become financially independent. For example, in 1985 the publishing houses were urged to introduce a responsibility management system, whereby salaries and bonuses would be linked to employees' performance, and to become financially independent from the government. Around the same time, outside funding was severely curtailed, and policies encouraging dual pricing (i.e., removing price controls from all but a few select titles) and self-marketing by publishers (unnecessary in the past, under the Xinhua system) were introduced. These changes caused publishing houses, which were concerned about their very survival, to experiment with various new business practices and alliances, some of which were technically illegal.

One deregulatory change that was absolutely critical for the growth of the second channel was the policy introduced in 1984 permitting "cooperative publishing arrangements."[12] Originally this policy was intended to give publishing houses an incentive to produce scholarly books, which normally lost money. It allowed publishers to sell book license numbers for scholarly books to authors or other individuals willing to pay the costs and bear the risks of producing such titles. In practice, however, publishing houses defined "scholarly books" extremely loosely, if at all; they were delighted that this policy entitled them to offload their surplus license numbers for a profit.[13] Private book dealers were quick to see this opportunity to buy book numbers and lease literary journal numbers; the policy amounted to a green light for them to print and distribute books legally in the names of orthodox state publishers. This is why Zhou Yikuai, the fictional book dealer described earlier, was able to break into publishing with the help of his editor friend Liu.

The result of this deregulation was the great blooming of popular literature that we discussed in Chapter 1 in the context of the Xue Mili phenomenon. Although all of these popular books were published in the name of state-owned publishing houses, in the vast majority of cases their actual publishers—those who chose the titles and did the required work—were private book dealers. Because of the huge demand for popular literature and light reading and the low cost of these crudely made and badly printed books, most of the first generation of Chinese book dealers/publishers grew rich overnight. The enormous commercial returns in this trade soon enticed a variety of entrepreneurs into private publishing. Some were in-house editors, much like Liu in *Chinese Book Dealer*, or people with good connections in the cultural world; others were merely daring businessmen like Zhou himself, armed only with "scissors and paste" (*jiandao jia jianghu*). Unofficial publishing grew so rapidly that "some bought the publishing permits of government-run publishing houses and newspapers. . . . Others set up underground publishing houses or masqueraded their unlicensed publishing outfits as government-owned operations."[14]

Not surprisingly, in this atmosphere of wheeling and dealing, many pornographic and politically suspect titles were also published in the name of state publishing houses. This led to repeated government campaigns against illegal publication in the late 1980s and throughout the 1990s. In 1990, all publishing houses were subjected to reregistration, and a national regulatory body called the Anti-Pornography and Illegal Publications Office (Sao huang da fei bangongshi) was established to sniff out offenders. The crackdown on a major illegal publishing group in 1991 demonstrated how serious the problem had become. This publishing network had distribution arms in 27 provinces involving 257 publishing houses, printing facilities, and bookstores; it had produced 1.3 million copies of 230 different titles of what were deemed "highly subversive antisocialist materials, and pornographic and superstitious works."[15]

Since 1991, almost every year there have been directives from the Press and Publications Administration prohibiting the selling, assigning, or leasing of book license numbers to private publishers, and occasional crackdowns have shut down or suspended some publishing houses. But the huge, quick profits and relatively small costs compared with other products—especially since the deregulation of book prices—have made publishing a gold mine for efficient entrepreneurs, however risky it is. And the sheer numbers of offenders have made the government's enforcement efforts virtually useless. Indeed, selling licenses has become a regular practice for most state publishing houses, and as long as no really controversial books are produced through this system to attract the censors, it seems that all sides—the government, publishing houses, and private book dealers—are happy to let the practice continue, as will become clear below.

During the 1990s, private publishers continued to penetrate more and more aspects of the industry. The most notable changes in private-sector publishing in the 1990s compared with the 1980s were as follows.

First, the private publishers and state publishing houses became more tightly integrated and intertwined, so that it was often difficult to tell who was involved at each stage of producing the books. Some private publishers, after buying the license numbers, became responsible for the entire publishing process; others only contracted to complete certain stages, especially planning and production (*cehua*), cover design (*meishu bianji*), and promotion (*yingxiao*).[16] In still other cases, book producers worked closely with bona fide state publishers to produce and market high-quality series that would have languished unsold under the previous system.

One such literary agent/book producer is Xing An. Having worked as an editor at the journal *Beijing wenxue* (Beijing Literature) for almost two decades, he was acquainted with many local up-and-coming writers. At the same time, he had developed contacts at other literary journals and at publishing houses. Like many editors, he began freelancing while still at *Beijing Literature*. He established Xing An Studio in 1998, made it his mission to discover and promote young writers who had fallen through the cracks of the state publishing houses and the book dealers, who focused strongly on best sellers. He subcontracted with Hundred Flowers Art and Literature Publishing House (Baihua wenyi chubanshe) in Tianjin to edit a literary series, Intellectual Women (Zhishi nüxing congshu), and published prose collections by four Beijing female writers. The books in this series shared a well-chosen theme—urban intellectual women's experience—and stood out for their unique and lively design, with pictures scattered throughout. Although not runaway best sellers, the titles sold around twenty thousand each, which made them a success in the "serious" literature market.

In 2000, having quit his job at *Beijing Literature* to focus full-time on his studio,[17] Xing An began producing a new series, Readable Novels (Haokan xiaoshuo), a joint project with China Youth Publishing House, for which he conducted some of the project planning and executive editorial work. Backed by the high reputation and financial strength of China Youth, he had plenty of resources to develop his new project: a genre fiction (*leixing xiaoshuo*) series that would include horror, fantasy, and science fiction. Although commonplace in Western publishing, genre fiction was still relatively new in China, and Xing An wanted to exploit its market appeal. He discovered and successfully published several new authors through this series.[18]

A second way in which private or second-channel publishers of the 1990s differed from those of the earlier reform period was that they were generally better educated; many had extensive professional training. In fact, most of the successful second-channel publishers during the 1990s were editors or former editors of state publishing houses. Many continued in their regular jobs while beginning to moonlight as private agents and book producers running independent studios (*gongzuoshi*). They struck deals with their own and other publishing houses, and in the process gradually expanded their business activities.

For example, in 1996 and 1997 the Liu Fang Studio (Liufang gongzuo shi) produced two novels for Writers Publishing House (WPH): *Zhao bu zhao bei* (Getting Lost) and *Shui bi shui sha* (Who Is the Dumbest of All?), both by Zhao Qiang. The studio's director, Liu Fang, was also a literary editor at WPH, and he not only carried out the usual editorial work on the manuscripts, but also took charge of the entire production process. Furthermore, he promoted the books through various media; this involved full-page advertisements in newspapers and a prime-time television commercial on Beijing TV. With this project, it was impossible to establish where Liu Fang's work as editor for WPH ended and where his work as Liu Fang Studio's director began.[19]

During the late 1990s, many such studios developed, often named after their directors. Typically, a studio began by working closely with one particular publishing house where the director was an editor, and then gradually developed ties with other state publishers until it became an independent business entity. These studios had a variety of functions: helping large state publishers discover new talent, acting as writers' agents, planning new publishing projects, doing promotion and marketing under contract, and working their connections with second-channel publishers to smoothly integrate the different stages of the publishing process. Many of these studios expanded into cultural corporations (*wenhua gongsi*), with major private investment. Some even purchased paper mills, printing presses, warehouses, and distribution networks, which allowed them to participate in every stage of the publication process.[20]

According to *Zhongguo tushu shangbao* (Chinese Book Business Review) (July 24, 1998), by 1998 there were more than one hundred such studios or cultural corporations. Most of them had been established by former editors or by people with strong links to the publishing industry. Since then, they have been the predominant form of "book dealer." They are very different from their often shady and ignorant predecessors, who opened up the second-channel distribution market back in the 1980s. Some sources estimate that more than one-quarter of the books published in China today are produced by this sector, and this figure is likely to continue growing. In the next section, I will examine Alpha Books, one of the most impressive examples of this new version of the second channel, which certainly represents the publishing wave of the future.

A third difference between second-channel distribution and publishing of the 1990s and that of the previous decade is that, partly owing to increased market competition and the entry of more educated and professional players, the second channel began producing much better books in terms of both content and production quality. Today, many top-quality books with high production values and challenging themes are being produced and successfully marketed outside the state system. There is no doubt that private or independent publishing guided by market forces now represents the liveliest action in Chinese publishing today. This sort of publishing has quietly begun to take over the book market; it is setting publishing trends and demonstrating the true potential of a free-market book-production system.

An example of a challenging literary work championed by the second channel is Yu Hua's *To Live*. As noted in Chapter 1, Yu Hua became famous in the late 1980s for writing about the cruelty of Chinese society and the struggle for survival of the Chinese people and for his narrative and stylistic experiments. He continued to evolve as a serious writer, and *To Live* was one of the finest literary works produced in the 1990s. It was turned into an award-winning film by Zhang Yimou in 1995 and was translated into several foreign languages, winning the prestigious Carvo Prize in Italy. In China, sales of the novel were poor at first, largely owing to feeble promotion by its state publisher, Changjiang Art and Literature Publishing House (Changjiang wenyi chubanshe). Between 1993 and 1998, the novel sold fewer than ten thousand.[21]

In 1998, Ding Xiaohe, an independent book agent and former "literary youth," decided that Yu Hua's novel deserved a better fate. He contracted with Nanhai Publishing Company (Nanhai chuban gongsi), a newly established provincial publishing house with offices in Beijing, Shanghai, and other cities, to repackage some contemporary literary works, starting with Yu Hua's *To Live*. First he hired the well-known Kang Xiaoyu Studio to design the book's cover and format. The result was an unusual pocket size with a distinctive modernist cover design that proved to be a great attraction. To grab the attention of browsers, the front and back were covered with catchphrases and with gushing reviews from overseas. When promoting the book, Ding capitalized on the commercial success of the film version, especially on Ge You's best actor award at Cannes and the film's subsequent ban in China. Finally, he made sure there would be enough copies of the novel to satisfy the subsequent demand, and that the book would be distributed through both main and second-channel networks.[22]

In one year, Nanhai's edition of *To Live* sold more than 200,000 copies, and the publishing house had to reprint it every month to satisfy the demand. Yu Hua's other novels, such as *Zai xiyu zhong huhan* (Crying in the Fine Rain) and *Chronicle of a Blood Merchant*, have since received similar repackaging, along with a number of other underappreciated works by serious writers such as Wang Anyi. The result has been a string of best sellers for Nanhai Publishing Company.

Repackaging, or in local terms "edition upgrading" (*banben shengji*), has become a common approach to collaboration between second-channel producers and struggling state publishing houses, which are still hobbled by bureaucratic, financial, and political restrictions. Many private players, including Ding Xiaohe, have established regular working relationships with one or more state publishing houses and are helping them produce readable and salable books. As a result, since 1999 many new editions of challenging literary and academic works that had once been undermarketed have made the best seller lists. Elegant cover designs, attractive illustrations, and immaculate proofreading and printing have all contributed to the feel of these books as "quality products" (*jing pin*). This has established a new trend in literature and art publishing, one that appeals especially to newly affluent urban Chinese.[23]

Private book dealers have "hollowed out" the most inefficient state-run publishing houses, leaving them with little to do besides "manage book licenses." Other state publishers have succeeded in transforming themselves, but only by borrowing methods from and increasingly joining forces with entrepreneurs. The attitude of state-run publishing houses toward independent book agents and producers has changed. Back in the 1980s, the editors and administrators of publishing houses were contemptuous of book dealers, who dealt in bags of cash and cut shady deals for license numbers. Even though publishers were happy to take their money, there was a great deal of prejudice and resentment against these entrepreneurs, whom publishers viewed—with some justification—as a bunch of "uneducated opportunists." By the late 1990s, the situation had been transformed. Publishing houses were eager to do business with the independent producers, not least because by this time they belonged to similar social and cultural circles. And their expertise ran the gamut, from distribution, marketing, editing, and cover design, to recruiting new writers and discovering potential best sellers.

No doubt these independent book producers and literary agents were motivated by profit, which they either split with the publishing houses or kept for themselves. But many of them truly did want to promote new and interesting literature, applying market mechanisms to turn works of high art into best sellers. In fact, with few exceptions, most literary works that have come out under the imprint of art and literature publishing houses since the late 1990s have actually been produced by freelance book agents like Xing An and Ding Xiaohe. These people function as editors, critics, academics, and entrepreneurs, and they have a deep knowledge of both literature and the book market. These independent publishers have without a doubt changed the whole structure and attitude of the publishing industry, and they will continue to do so.

In this section, I have focused on the contrasts between second-channel publishing and book distribution in the 1980s and 1990s. To give a taste of the probable future development of the second channel in China, in the following section I will examine in detail two of the most aggressive players in the private publishing and book retail market, Alpha Books and Xi Shu Bookstore. Their success and the sheer scale of their operations will add weight to my argument that the second channel has led—in fact, virtually forced—all the major deregulatory trends in Chinese publishing over the past decade or so. It is highly likely that as a result, before long the government will take even more steps to liberalize the publishing industry to keep up with the most recent second-channel innovations. This liberalization will allow second-channel publishers to compete with state-run publishing houses on more equal terms, with their legal rights fully protected, in contrast to the current situation, in which they are still technically illegal. It will also force state publishers to accelerate reform of their outdated business practices, and reduce their burden on the national economy.

2. Alpha Books

Alpha Book Co. Ltd. (Beijing Zhengyuan tushu gongsi, hereafter Alpha Books) was registered as a book sales and distribution company in August 1999. Prior to this, the company had been engaged in book publishing for more than a year under the name Alpha Books Studio (Zhengyuan tushu gongzuoshi). Before becoming an independent business entity, it had been (since April 1998) a division of the National Forest Book Center (Beijing Guolinfeng tushu zhongxin), one of the most influential private bookstores in Beijing. Both National Forest Book Center and Alpha Books were (and still are) owned by the Guofeng Investment Corporation (Guofeng touzi gongsi), a joint-stock company (*gufenzhi gongsi*) based in Beijing and founded by several graduates of Peking University, whose business interests also included advertising agencies, restaurants, a travel agency, and cultural enterprises such as a television and film production company. The Guofeng Investment Company established a good working relationship with the government of Haidian district, which extended it land use and other administrative permits. The local government even established a cultural corporation, Haidian District Cultural Development Ltd. (Haidian qu wenhua fazhan gongsi), with Guofeng as its partner. Complex links between private bookstores, second-channel publishers, larger business corporations, and local governments have been typical of the book market environment since the mid-1990s, and partly explain the second channel's successful growth despite the official restrictions on such activities.[24]

Alpha Books was the brainchild of a group of idealistic Chinese, many of whom had obtained degrees from American universities. Among them were Ouyang Xu, Xu Xun, Liu Junning, and Shi Tao, the general manager in 1999 and 2000. Their decision to set up a book-publishing venture could not have come at a better time. The year 1998 was the hundredth anniversary of Peking University, and among the first books Alpha produced was *Beida chuantong yu jindai Zhongguo—ziyou zhuyi de xiansheng* (The Tradition of Peking University and Modern China: Prophet of Liberalism), edited by Liu Junning, who was then a researcher at the Chinese Academy of Social Sciences. This book argued that freedom and democracy were the precious legacies of Peking University and that all progressive liberal intellectuals should embrace these values as the cornerstones of modernization. The book circulated widely among social science scholars and college students and was included as one of the top ten books of 1998 by many reviewers, including the reviewer for *Xin zhoukan* (New Weekly), a trendy new magazine for urban yuppies. A second title produced by Alpha Books that year, a collection of the speeches given by President Bill Clinton during his 1998 visit to China, also sold extremely well and attracted still more readers to the new imprint. These two books established Alpha Books as a savvy producer of high-quality and intellectually challenging titles, of the sort overlooked by ordinary publishers, both state owned and second channel.

Since then, Alpha Books has focused strongly on bringing out scholarly books that address contemporary social problems of the sort that have engaged modern Chinese intellectuals for more than a century—books "to make readers think and possibly change their lives." These have included translations of Western writings on modern law and legal culture, freedom and democracy, and political systems. All of these titles reflect Alpha Books's basic aim, which is "to thoroughly investigate the true sources of major issues and problems" (zheng ben qing yuan).[25]

Alpha Books has also had considerable success producing general cultural titles, some of which have been best sellers. Several have appeared in the Alternative series (Linglei congshu), edited by Shi Tao, who has described this series' lofty purpose as "to improve the general quality of popular culture" with "class and taste." This series consists mainly of translations from foreign works in cultural studies. One book in particular, *Gediao: Shehui dengji yu shenghuo pinwei* (Class: A Guide Through the American Status System), a translation of a book written in the late 1970s by American cultural critic Paul Fussell describing the social classes in American society and their identity, tastes, and status, made Alpha Books a household name among general readers. Within two years (1999–2000), the book had been reprinted several times and sold nearly 300,000.[26] It also created two new terms in Chinese: "class" (*gediao*) and "alternative" (*linglei*). Introduced, translated, and edited by Shi Tao in 1998, *Class* was snapped up by Chinese readers, especially urban yuppies, who seemed to overlook its ironic tone. The book allowed them to satisfy their strong curiosity about American society and lifestyles; it also served as a kind of behavioral guidebook for those who had accumulated wealth and who now wanted to raise their cultural awareness to match their new social status. For example, the CEO of a large private company in Shanghai purchased a hundred copies for his middle-level managers to help them improve their dress habits, their behavior, and their conversation. The success of *Class* launched a trend among Chinese publishers toward books with similar themes: "style," "taste," "dress codes," and the like.[27]

Alpha Books has also been active in the field of literature, where it has concentrated on promoting "alternative" writing of the kind neglected by conventional publishers. An example is its "No" Fiction series ("No" xiaoshuo congshu). The concept for "No" Fiction was developed by Zhang Fu, who had earned a Ph.D. from Peking University before serving as a guest editor for Alpha Books. Zhang declared that "No" Fiction "should be individualized, true, and sensual; it should open up a fresh spiritual space for the new generation, revealing their existential state and inner experience."[28] "No" Fiction would stand up against the literary ideas and practices of elite literature, which required far too much attention and education, but also against the light and fluffy pulp fiction and romances imported from Hong Kong and Taiwan.

A concrete example will help illustrate Zhang's rather vague concept: the works of a young Beijing writer, Shi Kang. Shi was born in 1968 and witnessed both the idealism of the 1980s and the spiritual crisis and moral vacuum of the 1990s, a time when China was rapidly transforming itself from a bankrupt socialist state into a dog-eat-dog society more materialist than the West. The titles of Shi Kang's three novels, published sequentially under the "No" imprint between 1999 and 2001, reflect the growing intensity of his feelings about this transformation: *Huanghuangyouyou* (Swaying and Staggering), *Zhiliposui* (Fragmented), and *Yitahutu* (Completely Messed Up). All three books are semiautobiographical. They record the private life, writings, and reflections of an angry and confused young "I" from high school to his early thirties. For example, in *Fragmented*, the "I" is a thirty-something writer/dropout, a marginal figure who observes the world spinning around him at the speed of business but somehow always feels left out. The narrative is itself fragmentary: the story is told through monologues, observed scenes, reflections, and memories, in a colloquial yet reflective style. The narrator expresses the anxiety and confusion that afflict modern Chinese youth. Within his cynical monologues one senses nostalgia for the romance that had been vanquished and ridiculed during the 1990s.

Writers like Shi Kang, with their negative views of contemporary Chinese society, would have found it difficult to reach an audience without the support of private publishers like Alpha Books. Before being taken up by Alpha, Shi's first novel *Swaying and Staggering* was turned down by several publishers. Shi's friend Yang Kui, a veteran editor at the relatively progressive Writers Publishing House, finally got it published there in 1996 after deleting and rewriting some paragraphs to make it less "pessimistic" and "alternative," but it sold only a couple of thousand copies. WPH felt that it "lacked potential" and was undeserving of a full promotion campaign.[29]

Then in 1999, Alpha Books began to champion Shi Kang's novels as "alternative"—as a new kind of writing that resisted the easy sentimentality of mainstream best sellers. At that point, they took off in the market and Shi suddenly gained respect as a literary pioneer. All three of his novels have sold so well that they have since been reprinted by Yunnan People's Publishing House (Yunnan renmin chubanshe). Even more significantly, the marketing vision of Alpha Books in defining and promoting this new genre of "alternative literature" has started a new trend among Beijing's young writers. Recent successful alternative works include Chen Tong's prose collections *Meiyou ren zhidao ni shi yi tiao gou* (Nobody Knows You Are a Dog) and *Meiyou ren zhidao ni dasuan huai duojiu* (Nobody Knows How Long You Plan to Be Bad); also, Yin Lichuan's *Zai shufu yixie* (A Bit More Comfortable); Zhang Chi's *Beijing bingren* (Beijing Patient); and Gouzi's *Yige pijiu zhuyi zhe de zibai* (Monologue of a Beer Worshipper). Some of these titles were produced by Alpha Books, others by Bookoo Books (Boku shuye), which Shi Tao joined after he left Alpha in early 2001.

In an interview conducted in May 2001, when asked how difficult it was to publish books when one's registered business is actually distribution, Xin Jiping, the general manager of Alpha Books, replied: "In fact both the Propaganda Department and the State Administration of Press and Publications know exactly what Alpha Books is doing, but they prefer to keep one eye closed as long as we don't cause 'political' trouble." This is partly because the huge number of second-channel businesses makes it impossible for the government to monitor and control any but the worst offenders. According to Xin, there are more than five thousand independent publishers like Alpha Books, which refer to themselves by a variety of names: studios, cultural companies, creative salons, or simply bookstores. The government seems to realize that such companies can play a useful role by filling gaps in the market that state publishers cannot. Hence, although they all register under other names and trades, they rarely need to hide the fact that their businesses take part in the entire book-publishing process, from manuscript acquisition to final printing. The only anomaly is that the imprint on the book cover is not theirs. Clearly, these book agents and "shadow publishers" constitute a gray area—one that keeps expanding as it attracts more and more private investment and that is developing a momentum of its own.

As companies like Alpha Books have shown, these profit-seeking private publishers have done much to shape the world of Chinese publishing. Throughout the 1990s, they brought out many politically and stylistically provocative books—titles that otherwise might never have seen the light of day, let alone made a profit for their authors and producers. The logic behind their approach is refreshingly simple and pragmatic. Shi Tao explained in an interview with an American newspaper: "We do a lot of critical books because people want to read them, and we want to make money."[30] At their best, therefore, second-channel publishers have attained what is surely the ideal for all respectable publishing houses: to consistently bring out thought-provoking, high-quality, well-produced titles that will satisfy readers and make good money.

Obviously, this benefits controversial writers, such as Mo Luo, a young cultural critic and dissident intellectual whose daring and challenging essay collection *Chiruzhe shouji: yige minjian sixiangzhe de shengming tiyan* (Notes from the Humiliated: A Folk Philosopher's Life Experience) was published by another private book agent, He Xiongfei. Mo Luo declared: "The fact that I am now able to publish my books is entirely thanks to the emerging marketplace. In the current consumer environment you can't survive by publishing books that are dull and boring. So the liveliness of the publishing world has opened things up, and there is a much wider space for speaking out."[31]

3. Xi Shu and the Rise to Respectability of Private Bookstores

It is not only second-channel publishing that has experienced a sea change since the early 1990s. Bookselling has also seen enormous change, in both distribution and retailing. As with publishers, this has resulted in greater official acceptance of the second channel and much better service for the book-buying public. In this section I outline the main developments in book retailing over the past decade; then I introduce the Xi Shu Bookstore, the first private book retailer in China to set up a national chain in competition with the Xinhua system.

In Chapter 39 of *Chinese Book Dealer*, the hero Zhou Yikuai summons China's leading booksellers to Beijing to discuss their plans and to collect funds for the construction of an "International Book Plaza." The author presents this meeting as a parody of a National People's Congress meeting or Party Conference; it includes windy speeches from the industry's leaders, a conference agenda, and even the singing of the national anthem. The only difference is that the delegates are all private entrepreneurs engaged in illegal publishing—something that in real life is supposedly anathema to the government.

Just as in real life, throughout the book, despite all the efforts of the government to control it over the past decade or so, the unofficial book trade (*minying shuye*) has become increasingly flexible in business methods and better at providing quality. This has helped improve the structure and business awareness of the Chinese publishing industry. The fictional character Zhou claims in his speech that Chinese booksellers have led a "second Cultural Revolution," and have been at the forefront of all the many publishing trends established since the early 1980s: "We have trained and supported a whole new group of Chinese writers, improved the taste of ordinary readers, decreased or eliminated the distance between serious and popular literature, and exerted a subtle influence on the reading habits of the whole nation." He concludes with a confident prediction: "In a couple of years, the first National Congress of Book Dealers will convene in the Great Hall of the People, right in the heart of the nation's capital Beijing!"[32]

When *Chinese Book Dealer* was published in 1996, this vision of political respectability for unofficial book dealers must have seemed like political satire—especially after the Chinese government tightened its control the following year by closing down several famous second-channel retail operations, including Yellow Mud Street (Huangni jie) in Changsha and Hufangqiao and Baiwanzhuang alleys in Beijing. At that stage, it seemed more likely that many book dealers would end up in prison or even executed for illicit publishing activities. But sometimes truth can be more surprising than fiction. When the Beijing Book Fair (Beijing tushu jiaoyi hui) convened in January 2001, more than fifteen hundred private bookstores were invited to attend, and their representatives donated one million yuan for the Hope Project Charity (Xiwang gongcheng), a government foundation that builds schools in poverty-stricken regions. Not only that, but the donation was accepted at the Great Hall of the People, with several high government officials present.[33] The newspaper *Xinwen chuban bao* (Chinese Press and Publishing Journal), mouthpiece of the Press and Publications Administration, reported the donation on January 10, 2001, under the headline "Second Channel Makes Its Voice Clearly Heard" (Erqudao dasheng yaohe maishu lou). This was a major step forward, considering that the Xi'an Book Fair, held five years earlier, had been the first occasion when private book dealers were even allowed to attend alongside the state-run main-channel bookstores.

One major reason why the government now accepts private bookstores and book dealers is the great improvement in their overall quality over the past two decades. Shady-looking street bookstalls and private bookstores like those of the 1980s still exist in China and are still the main point of sales of pirated books. But in the 1990s, high-quality bookstores run by well-educated book lovers began to emerge, and these are committed to making bookselling a respectable and viable business venture. Three such stores are located in Zhongguancun, in Beijing's Haidian district, which is known as China's Silicon Valley and is surrounded by the campuses of Peking and Tsinghua universities.

Forestsong (Feng ru song) is a million-yuan investment by Peking University professor of philosophy Wang Wei and his partners, who established this bookstore in early 1996. This store focuses on the arts, literature, and social sciences and has a regular stock of around twenty thousand titles. Forestsong has a café corner where university students can sit and read. It publishes a weekly New Books list and a members' newsletter.

Not far away, outside the South Gate of Tsinghua University, is All Sages Bookstore (Wan sheng shuyuan), which was founded in 1993 by a small group of history graduates from Peking University. Unlike the relatively spacious Forestsong, All Sages started out as a small, narrow shop with shelves up to the ceiling. It sold mostly academic books, especially premodern Chinese literature, history, and philosophy, generally carrying only one or two copies of each title. This made All Sages popular among college students, professors, and researchers. In the fall of 2001, All Sages moved to larger premises in the same district, an indication of its success. It now has room to display a generous selection of art books and imported English scholarly books and fiction. Yet it still retains the same jumbled book lover's charm.

Quite close to these two stores, within the newly renovated Haidian Book Town (Haidian tushu cheng), is National Forest Book Center, which opened in 1997. This store represents another mode of investment—the large, private cultural company. As noted earlier, Guofeng Investment Corporation owns both National Forest Book Center and Alpha Books, along with many other business interests. The initial investment for the Book Center was seven million yuan. Its normal book stock is twenty to thirty thousand titles, mostly in humanities and social sciences, although the store also carries computer texts and English books. The center is very well organized and devotes an entire section to titles produced by its affiliate, Alpha Books. It also puts a great deal of effort into marketing and advertising. For example, there is a regular review column in *Chinese Reading Weekly* that promotes selected titles from National Forest.

All of these private bookstores offer relatively efficient and friendly service, with discounts for club members, and provide a comfortable, music-filled environment that includes Western-style cafés, which are popular with local college students and teachers—their main customers—and with book dealers and local artists. These stores often organize talks, readings, and book signings by well-known writers. When one adds to this pleasant atmosphere their carefully selected titles—many of which are not available elsewhere—it is clear that such bookstores have become unique cultural spaces, havens from the hectic and dusty transitional urban society outside. The calligraphic banner hanging at the entrance of Forestsong sums up this feeling: People Living Lyrically (Ren shiyi de qiju). This is a major contrast from most of the Xinhua bookstores, whose clerks are often ignorant, whose book selection is limited almost solely to educational and administrative tomes, dictionaries, and language textbooks, and whose decor is dowdy and unwelcoming.[34]

The great improvements in private bookstores have transformed people's preconceptions about the second channel. In the 1990s, these private bookstores became the de facto mainstream or first channel for book retail in many subject areas, especially in the arts, humanities, and social sciences. To show how this trend is likely to evolve, I will introduce the main innovations of perhaps the most ambitious—and certainly the most imaginative—private bookseller of the 1990s, Xi Shu.

Xi Shu is a legendary figure in China—a cultural entrepreneur perfectly suited for the new market of the 1990s, during which culture became just another commodity. He first gained fame as a calligraphy teacher, after developing a quick and easy method for writing Chinese characters stylishly with a ballpoint pen. This method had strong appeal for Chinese consumers, most of whom still consider fine handwriting a sign of good breeding. As a result, *Xishu yingbi shufa sucheng* (Xi Shu's Short Cut to Great Pen Calligraphy), published in 1992, became a national best seller. Xi Shu capitalized on this by opening a nationwide chain of calligraphy schools and distance learning centers named after himself. He cemented his brand-name appeal by coining the schools' advertising slogan: "Want to write well? Come to Xi Shu!" (*Yao lian zi, zhao Xi Shu*), a phrase that appeared often in the national media throughout the early 1990s.

In 1994, Xi Shu invested his profits from the calligraphy schools in another business venture: instructional videos. He boasted of having hired "the best high school teachers in China" to record this series of videos, which were aimed at teaching children various subjects, from mathematics and science to the English language. Once again, this venture had broad market appeal, owing to the importance Chinese parents place on giving their children the best education possible. The expense and variable quality of "in the flesh" home tutors discouraged many parents from hiring them; the reasonable prices that Xi Shu charged and the guaranteed quality of his tutors made his videos an excellent alternative. Hence, this new venture became another runaway success.

Xi Shu's achievements have been based on two crucial gifts. First, he knows how to capitalize on Chinese consumers' pragmatism and materialism and within that framework makes his cultural products as appealing and marketable as possible. Second, he acts without delay as soon as he sees a new business opportunity, and he knows when to change direction before imitators saturate the market. Besides all this, he has a monumental vision that drives him to launch all his ventures on a national scale and to make a big promotional splash in the media.

In 1996, Xi Shu decided to apply his successful approach to yet another business, chain bookstores. In August of that year, in Beijing, to much fanfare, he opened the first branch of Xi Shu Bookstore. He had hired the famous interior designer Zhang Yonghe to decorate the store in unique fashion—for instance, the bookshelves had cartwheels attached to them, alluding to a well-known Chinese saying: "To be a scholar you need five cartloads of books" (xue fu wu che). He had also invited Fei Xiaotong, China's most famous sociologist, to write the characters on the bookstore's sign, so as to lend the store intellectual weight. For the first day of business, Xi Shu invited many well-known writers, critics, and scholars, and of course the media, to visit the bookstore, and he made the most of his fame by giving out signed copies of books.

Soon afterwards, Xi Shu opened further branches in Shanghai, Wuhan, Nanjing, Guangzhou, and even San Francisco, all with the same kind of media exposure and with endorsements from famous celebrities. Steadily he realized his aim of establishing the first national franchise bookstore in China specializing in the arts, humanities, and social sciences.

Xi Shu also carved out his own business niche, which he described as "selling titles that you can't find in the Xinhua bookstores; titles with very small print runs that publishing houses worry about selling; and titles that only appeal to a handful of professionals but are difficult to locate." He established close relationships with publishing houses from the beginning. For example, in 1997, he invited the presidents and editors in chief of many houses in Beijing and Shanghai to a huge Chinese New Year party. For their part, these publishers were happy to do business with a private bookstore run by such a famous figure who was willing to sell all their odds and ends. As a result, more than sixty houses agreed to write dedications to Xi Shu Bookstore in a publicity piece that appeared in *China Reading Weekly*. Through this network of relationships, Xi Shu was able to beat other competitors in locating hard-to-find books, especially older titles and specialist academic books unavailable in most bookstores.[35]

Also in 1997, Xi Shu was inspired by the methods of the multinational publisher Bertelsmann to adopt a bookselling method relatively new to China: the book club. Chinese book clubs had existed since the early 1990s, but most were simply mailing services that offered no information about the products they sold. Xi Shu's Good Book Club (Haoshu julebu) introduced several innovations, mostly based on the sales methods of foreign publishers and retailers. The most impressive of these was his bimonthly *Hao shu* (Good Book Newsletter), in which experts from different fields offered guidance on new titles. For the rapidly developing Chinese book market in which more than 100,000 titles were being published each year, this newsletter provided well-written book reviews by professionals that enabled potential readers/customers to make informed decisions about their purchases, and perhaps even to improve their appreciation of books. The newsletter also provided content summaries, page counts, and detailed sales information, including discount and members' prices. The *Good Book Newsletter* is still by far the best consumer guide to new books available in China—a useful combination of literary review and catalogue.

In the new millennium, Chinese entrepreneurs are being attracted to e-commerce and its potential—this, despite the large numbers of Western dot-com failures. Internet bookstores mushroomed in the spring of 2000, all claiming that they would become the Chinese Amazon.com. As usual, Xi Shu was among the first to exploit the new trend, starting up Xi Shu E-Commerce Ltd. (Xi Shu dianzi shangwu youxian gongsi), again with plenty of media exposure. Unlike many other online bookstores, however, Xi Shu had already developed a national network of bookstores with excellent ties to publishers to support his operation. For him, therefore, e-commerce was simply another platform, like the book club, for selling his books and expanding his retail channels. His bookstores around the country had access to a centralized computer database that included all book titles and prices; these stores could now function as warehouses and distribution centers for his e-bookstore and book club. He even employed his own delivery personnel in order to ensure efficient service.[36]

It is too early to judge how successful Xi Shu's venture into e-commerce will be. However, by the summer of 2000 he had built up a multidimensional book retail kingdom, with eleven chain stores and more than 112 special partner bookstores (*texu jingying jiameng dian*) across China, as well as a membership of more than seventy thousand in the Good Book Club and its online equivalent, Jingqi.com.[37]

Most of Xi Shu's business techniques have long been familiar in the West. For Chinese retail, especially cultural retail, they have been innovative. Xi Shu has not always been the first to employ such methods in China, but his company has commonly been perceived as the trendsetter. This is for several reasons. First, he has fully exploited the commercial potential of celebrities and the media to spread the fame of his business throughout China. Second, he has developed a brand name that is truly national in scope, so that customers know they will receive equally good service and an excellent choice of titles no matter which of his branches they frequent. Other Chinese bookstores may have friendlier and more knowledgeable staff and a more interesting selection of books, but so far they have failed to compete with the sheer scale of Xi Shu's operations. It is therefore likely that Xi Shu's approach will set the standard that other bookstores—including the Xinhua system itself—will have to meet if they hope to survive.

4. Perils of Second-Channel Publishing

I have argued that second-channel book publishing and distribution has on the whole been a positive force in the once rigid and inefficient Chinese book market. It has allowed many interesting and alternative books overlooked by state-run publishing houses to see the light of day and even become best sellers. Just as important, its introduction of market mechanisms and competition into the publishing and book distribution industry has encouraged much-needed organizational reforms at state-run publishing houses. In a rapidly developing society such as contemporary China, there is inevitably a gulf between the government's administrative directives and actual practices within economic institutions. In the business arena, more often than not it is practice that precedes policy, with unapproved but economically successful business methods ultimately leading to corresponding policy changes down the line. In terms of the Chinese publishing industry, it is the second channel that has pioneered most of the innovations and systemic reforms that have helped make publishing a viable industry. So it is quite possible that fairly soon the urgent need to reform state-run publishing will lead to further government deregulation that will allow second-channel companies to become publishers in name, not just in fact.

But for the time being, second-channel publishing—as opposed to distribution—is still officially prohibited. The contradictory and unstable business environment arising from the present dual-track system and the incomplete reforms in the publishing industry have led to many problems that threaten the survival of unofficial publishing.

The most serious problem has been the government's repeated attempts to crack down on "illicit publishing." All second-channel publishing is technically illegal, which means that all who engage in it are in a very insecure position. Government crackdowns generally fail to remove many of the worst pirates and pornographers. They also tend to be quite indiscriminate, in the sense that they fail to take into account the astonishing variety of second-channel publishers—all are accused of "illicit publication." Those who are charged with it may be fined heavily or even imprisoned, and may see their property confiscated.

Moreover, the state, although it has softened its hard-line approach to ideological control, often still uses campaigns against "illicit publishing" as an excuse to ban politically controversial books and to pursue those who bring them out. This was the case with He Xiongfei and his Wilderness Tribe Studio (Caoyuan buluo chuangzuoshi). Through his personal connections with intellectuals, especially his friendship with Qian Liqun, a Peking University professor famous for encouraging many young talents, He Xiongfei had access to some of the most challenging and inspiring writers of the 1990s, including Yu Jie, Mo Luo, Kong Qingdong, and Zhang Jianwei. The result was his Dark Horse books (Heima xilie),[38] a series of essay collections addressing contemporary social and intellectual issues from a liberal and radical perspective.

Yu Jie, the first Dark Horse author, was then a young graduate student at Peking University. His essays discussed the importance of dissent, the moral awareness of intellectuals, and the widening gulf between rich and poor in

China, among other pressing issues. Although widely circulated among college students in handwritten copies, Yu's essays were considered far too risky
for state-run houses to publish. He Xiongfei's Dark Horse edition of Yu Jie's
essays came out in early 1998 under the title *Huo yu Bing: yige beida guai jie
de chouti wenxue* (Fire and Ice: Writing Locked Away in the Drawer by a
Peking University Prodigy). On the back cover were listed several of the
most daring essay titles, including "Blood from the Massacre," "The Trai-
tors," "Fascists: Lingering Ghosts," and "The Real Face of Our Leaders."[39]
Surprisingly, this book became one of the most successful and talked about
titles of that year. He followed up with several other politically challenging
works by Yu Jie and other similar-minded young writers, such as Mo Luo.

He's books were all published through state publishing houses, although
he handled virtually all of the production and editorial work himself. These
houses cooperated, either for the money or because many of their editors
supported He's project. He Xiongfei became a legend in Chinese publishing
circles for his heroic idealism, and he gained a wide following. He even led
his "Dark Horses" on tours around the country, during which they gave
speeches, especially on university campuses.

But in the spring and summer of 2000, the government launched a crackdown on the publishing industry during which dozens of houses were given
warnings or temporarily suspended.[40] As a result, He Xiongfei lost the cooperation of the state publishers. His Dark Horse stable, having produced
nine books, was forced to close its doors.

During political campaigns and crackdowns on the publishing industry,
private publishers are the most vulnerable group. State publishing houses
have also been punished by fines and suspensions, and individual editors have
been sacked; however, the state houses do not depend on sales of confiscated
books for their livelihood and can soon resume publishing. It is a different
story for second-channel publishers, who may face financial ruin after a single government campaign, no matter how high the quality of their titles.

The second problem facing second-channel publishers, again because of
their murky status, is that they have few property rights. This is not just a
problem when the government confiscates their books. The fact is that their
very success over the past two decades has led to much greater competition.
Many would-be publishers have entered the industry, and as a result, the supply of second-channel books now often exceeds the demand. So instead of
paying cash like they used to, booksellers are now in a position to take books
on consignment. In other words, they need not pay the publisher until those
books are sold. When a bookseller then refuses to pay its debt, the second-
channel publisher cannot expect much support from the courts, because it is
engaged in an "illegal" business.[41]

A third problem is the general instability and vulnerability of the second-channel book industry, which has resulted in a high turnover of qualified personnel and the constant disappearance and reappearance of companies under new names and guises at new locations. For example, the personnel at Alpha Books—especially the editorial staff—have turned over rapidly over the past three years. In late 2000, one of Alpha's founders, Shi Tao, left the company to head a competing second-channel company called Bookoo Books (Boku shuye) that combined book production with Internet publishing. Then in 2001, Miao Hong, the project manager who replaced Shi Tao, also left after less than one year in that position. Similarly, He Xiongfei has often had to change his direction in order to gain the cooperation of state publishing houses. In particular, he has often had to turn down politically challenging projects.

Of course, frequent changes like these are also the result of the freedom and flexibility that private business makes possible, and are not necessarily a bad thing. Even so, the unstable and unprotected business environment undoubtedly discourages consistent quality in the industry, and makes it very difficult for second-channel firms to establish themselves long enough to really compete with state-run houses, especially when they are handicapped by restrictions on book license numbers. It also means that few second-channel publishers are likely to aim for the high end of the market in the manner of Alpha Books and He Xiongfei. Instead, they are more likely to seek quick profits by selling pirated titles, and then disappear before the authorities catch them.

The above problems threaten the second channel's survival. In addition, the underground and illicit nature of second-channel publishing seems to foster one particular "social evil"—namely, piracy. Indeed, the most reliable way to learn which current titles are selling best in China is not to read the best seller lists in newspapers or book review columns, since they all differ so much that you don't know which to believe. Instead, visit the discount booksellers that advertise themselves as "five-yuan bookstores" (wu yuan shudian), or the temporary bookstalls set up on the streets after nightfall, or even the Weekend Book Fair (zhoumo shushi) at Peking University. There you will find the answer immediately, in the form of pirated editions of all the recent best sellers.

Despite numerous government campaigns against illegal publication and piracy since the late 1980s, the problem has gotten worse. Various forms of piracy have developed, two of the most common being pirated printings (dao yin) and pirated editions (dao ban). Pirated printings are simply photocopies of books that have already been published; of course, they are sold at much lower prices. This form of piracy can be highly profitable due to the low investment required. Except for copying and paper costs, the perpetrators need not pay anything—not manuscript fees or royalties, not editorial costs, not the book license "administration fee," and certainly not taxes. Of course, this method is also the easiest to detect because of the low quality of the printing, so it is very risky. The other main method, producing pirated editions, involves editing an unauthorized new version of a popular book, or producing a "fake" and attributing it to a popular writer. The writer's or publisher's name is used without permission, and the book is published without a license number or with a fake license number. For example, there have been many unauthorized editions of Yu Qiuyu's popular essay collections, ranging from pirated printings to pirated editions. On one occasion, Yu pointed out a bookstore display containing sixteen different titles or editions of his works; fifteen of them were pirated, and many of them had come out even before the authorized editions.[42]

A visit to the Weekend Book Fair on the campus of China's illustrious Peking University helps explain the continued appeal of pirated books to Chinese consumers. Every Saturday and Sunday, the open space beside the graduate students' dormitory becomes a marketplace where local private bookstores and discount bookstores (*tejia shudian*) set up stalls to sell their goods. Many of the stalls are operated by the private bookstores in nearby Haidian Book Town. Besides textbooks, reference books, and various English-language, MBA, and law school test papers, all of the latest literary and general best sellers are available, with every stall selling virtually the same titles, most of them pirated. Two kinds of titles are especially susceptible to pirating: runaway best sellers like the works of Zhang Kangkang, Chi Li, and Yu Qiuyu, and the most recently banned novels. In 1999, the latter included Li Peifu's *Yang de men* (Sheep Gate) and Wang Yaowen's novel *Guohua* (Chinese Painting), the two best-known examples of a recent popular subgenre, "official circles" fiction (*guanchang xiaoshuo*).[43] In 2001, various titles by banned *Shanghai Babe* author Wei Hui were readily available, including many hastily edited pirated collections. In fact, nowadays a government ban is often the best possible advertisement for a book—a kind of nationwide jolt of publicity that immediately gets people flocking to the private bookstalls. Collected works of popular writers are also often pirated, partly because they are among the top best sellers from regular publishers, but also because they offer the best value for money. In the late 1990s, the multivolume collected works of Zhang Ailing, Wang Shuo, and Jin Yong were all available at private bookstalls for about one-quarter of their fifty- to sixty-yuan cover prices. In other words, one could buy a writer's complete novels for the price of a single volume at a regular bookstore.

Although the booksellers obviously do not admit that most of their stock is pirated, any title that is sold below 50 percent of its cover price is certainly not an authentic edition. Likewise, one can normally tell genuine from pirated editions by examining them closely. With the latter, the cover art and the printing are not as sharp; the text usually contains many wrong characters and typographical errors; and the books are often produced in a much denser and smaller font to save paper costs. Yet despite these defects, there are still plenty of customers, many of them students who are short of money but can't resist the temptation of books.

The fact that pirated books continue to be sold like this on the campus of China's top university and throughout the city in private bookstores, despite repeated government campaigns, reveals several things. First, there is a huge market for pirated books largely because prices of the originals have increased so sharply. On average, regular book prices are 17 times higher than in 1979, whereas peoples' average incomes are only 7.9 times 1979 levels.[44] As a result, most Chinese readers simply cannot afford to buy many legally published books, and they are inevitably drawn to the bookstalls, where prices are more closely geared to their income levels. This problem is especially acute for students subsisting on their low monthly stipends, which explains the size and popularity of the fair at Peking University.

Second, when officially published books do become best sellers, in many cases the inefficient state publishers and Xinhua bookstores simply cannot keep up with the demand. Pirate book producers and distributors are quick to step in and fill the gap. Consumers generally prefer to obtain a pirated best seller immediately (especially at a discount) instead of waiting around for the main channel to get its act together.

Third, selling pirated books is highly profitable because the booksellers select only those titles for which the market has already been proven, such as best sellers and banned books. Also, they need not carry large stocks of titles that cannot be sold, which is what the regular bookstores must do. As a result, after a government crackdown, plenty of new pirates soon appear, willing to take the risk for the sake of the high profits.

Fourth, although the government does often attack illicit publishing, and has closed down some of the more notorious pirate book markets—such as Yellow Mud Street in Changsha and Baiwanzhuang Alley in Beijing—it clearly lacks the political will to stamp out piracy at its roots. The Peking University Book Fair has actually grown over the past three years, and now comprises several dozen stalls spread over a wide-open space on the campus, and is a weekly fixture, with its hawkers apparently holding official permits to sell their wares. Only when especially controversial or politically sensitive titles appear on the market does the government take action, and even then its crackdowns are of limited scope. It obviously lacks the resources to concern itself with the vast majority of literary, entertainment, and educational titles that do not cause social harm or political disturbance.

In advanced Western countries, it is not so much governments that attack book pirates. That task falls predominantly to piracy's main victims, the writers and publishers, who lose profits when their titles are pirated. Large Western publishers in particular are quick to go to court against producers and even sellers of pirated editions. The risk of prosecution deters most commercial book dealers from engaging in piracy—although of course plenty of copyright violation still occurs on a smaller scale, in the form of book photocopying for personal use and the "sharing" of texts over the Internet.

So far, the prosecution of pirates has been much less common in China, for several reasons. First, owing to local protectionism in the Chinese political and court system, local governments, police, and courts may be unwilling to enforce judgments against major book-pirating factories in their regions, since this will damage the local economy. And even if enforced, judgments often underestimate the amount of damages, so that often the award received by the plaintiff is less than the costs of bringing the lawsuit. Second, most state-run publishers are still not attuned to the realities of a market economy—in particular, the need to maximize profits. As long as they can sell a fixed quota of their books, they rarely concern themselves with the many alternative editions of the same titles appearing in the bookstalls, especially when to take action would involve so much effort and risk and when little legal assistance is at hand. Also, state-run publishers are still partly subsidized; these subsidies, when added to their income from selling book license numbers, are usually enough to pay their salaries. In contrast, those few publishers who have truly introduced market reforms and tied their staff salaries to book sales—Writers Publishing House, for instance— have been extremely vocal and active in seeking to protect their copyrights and to prevent piracy of their titles.

As for the writers themselves, some have tried to stand up against pirates, but with limited success. For instance, in 1998 Yu Qiuyu published "Yu Qiuyu jiaoshou jing gao quanguo duzhe" (an announcement by Professor Yu Qiuyu to his readers nationwide), in which he protested the rampant piracy of his books. This was completely ineffective, and a year later, another pirated book, *Qianxi riji* (Diary of the Millennium) came out even before its authorized WPH edition, *Sigh of a Thousand Years*. Yu could only express his frustration by announcing that he planned to stop writing altogether.[45] Like other efforts by publishers and government enforcement agencies, Yu's attempt to defeat the pirates was just another drop of water that evaporated in the summer sun.

Most if not all of the above problems with second-channel publishing and distribution result from the inherent contradiction of the present dual-track system, and could be solved by abolishing the current license number system and replacing it with an open registration system for publishers, properly regulated and protected by the law. Under such a system, any company that fulfilled the basic requirements for establishing an enterprise according to Chinese law would be permitted to do business as a publisher and bring out as many books as it felt able to, based entirely on market demand. Setting up such a registration system would also remove the unfair advantage extended to state-owned publishing houses, and force those houses to reform their business structures in order to survive. This is certainly the hope and expectation of all the unofficial publishers whom I have interviewed during the past year.[46] Recently they have been encouraged by the government's deregulation of film production, another actively commercialized cultural industry. Now, any individual or corporation with sufficient funding can apply to make a film, and approval doesn't depend on the applicant having a studio license number.[47]

The development of the second channel over the past two decades exemplifies the ongoing and tenacious struggle between the state and the market in a reforming, dual-track Chinese society.

The market mechanisms first introduced by the state led to many policy changes in the cultural field and opened up an unexpected space for the second channel. Stimulated by market forces, the second channel sprouted like wild grass despite various administrative and ideological obstacles. This rapid development of the second channel and its deep penetration into China's book publishing and distribution sectors have caused the state to loosen its rigid ideological control in various ways. The iron fist of the censorship system now seems almost powerless to block publication of "politically incorrect" best sellers of the kind the second channel has been bringing out over the past decade.[48] At the same time, many new business methods initiated by second-channel publishers and distributors have since been adopted by state publishers, which are desperate to survive in an increasingly competitive cultural market. This has led to further official deregulation to catch up with the preemptive changes in the industry. Certainly, further changes are required before China has a truly market-based publishing system free from government interference, but the cracks in the old system are becoming more and more noticeable. In this respect, the second channel has served as a catalyst for reform, quietly but steadily undermining the foundations of the socialist publishing system.

CHAPTER 4

The Economics of Privacy

PUBLISHING WOMEN'S WRITING

The year of 1995 should forever be remembered by Mainland Chinese women. . . . That year, the UN's Fourth
World Conference on Women and the NGO forum, a
significant event in the history of the world women's
movement, was solemnly held in Beijing. . . . Chinese
women, together with their sisters from all over the world,
enjoyed an unprecedented carnival. . . . Chinese women's
writing also experienced a spell of unparalleled ecstasy. In
1995, there was a sudden blooming of Chinese women's
studies, and the publication of all kinds of writing and research by Chinese women. Various international symposia
on women's subjects and on individual woman writers
were held in quick succession; numerous literary journals
published special issues on women writers; and a plethora
of academic research on women's writing competed for
attention. Countless series and anthologies of women
writers grandly emerged onto the market, surrounded
by a mass of other reading materials for women.[1]

IN THE ABOVE PASSAGE, Xu Kun, who witnessed the events of 1995, is re-
membering the significance of that year for Chinese women and women's
literature. Xu, a researcher of women's writing at the Chinese Academy of
Social Sciences in Beijing, is a rising "feminist" writer in her own right. In
1995, *Nüwa*, her first collection of novellas and short stories, was published as
part of the Red Poppy (Hong yingsu) series by Hebei Education Press
(Hebei jiaoyu chubanshe). As I will describe below, the appearance of this
series exclusively devoted to women writers was one of the most acclaimed
publishing events of that frenzied year. Based on her participation in and observation of these events, Xu wrote a vibrant personal essay, "Cong ci yue lai
yue mingliang" (Brighter and Brighter from Now On) to record her feminist reflections on the exploding interest in women and women's writing.

She remembers 1995 as a year of political opportunism and showmanship, of excitement and betrayal, of paradoxes and irony: "This year was like a bull market for feminism. Our gender became the hot stock of the moment, and was hyped and overvalued by a swarm of discriminating male brokers."[2] Xu Kun's use of a market metaphor is not accidental. Based on her close involvement in publishing and promoting the Red Poppy series and her careful observation of the UN Women's Conference and the Chinese response to it, in her essay she questions the sudden enthusiasm for women's studies in general, and women's literature in particular, among publishing houses and the mass media. She argues that the increasing commercialization and mass consumerism of Chinese society did much to initiate and sustain this collective hype of gender and sexuality. Although certainly the profile of women's writing was raised dramatically, at the same time various vested interests guided women into specific fields of exploration and tried to make them more marketable and commercially viable.

A detailed analysis of the eventful year 1995 is a suitable starting point for this chapter, as it clearly demonstrates the influence of the marketplace on women's writing under the dual-track economic system of 1990s China. Indeed, as I will show in my discussion of several key publishing events of that year, although women were empowered by the burgeoning cultural market to make their voices heard to an unprecedented extent, they were also pigeonholed by that same market in order to satisfy the demands of consumers. After this survey of 1995, I will shift focus to a representative genre that emerged and flourished after the mid-1990s—women's "privacy literature" (*yinsi wenxue*). I will show how publishers have used the concept of privacy literature to exploit and capitalize on women writers' sexuality and private lives, and how, at the same time and in turn, women writers have more recently exploited their own sexuality to gain notoriety and huge financial rewards. I will consider two case studies in particular: Lin Bai's *Ye ge ren de zhanzheng* (A War with Oneself), published in the mid-1990s, and Wei Hui's *Shanghai baobei* (Shanghai Babe), published in the late 1990s. Through these examples, I will investigate the complicated dynamic that has developed between women's writing and the cultural market, and the various social and economic forces—especially as they relate to the recently deregulated commercial publishing industry—that guided and shaped the writing and publishing of women's literature in the 1990s.

1. *1995*

Twenty-two of the most active contemporary women writers in the Chinese literary field today have recently proposed what they call "the largest-scale series on women writers in

Chinese publishing history," entitled Red Poppy Series. In choosing the name Poppy, the main ingredient for producing opium, this series has stimulated interest and controversy. The publisher claims that "the poppy combines the healing qualities of a beautiful flower with the dangers of temptation." And one writer declared: "Due to prejudice, we have not been able to mention the name of this outstandingly beautiful, vigorous, and unique flower, the poppy." . . . But some readers have expressed the feeling that naming the series Red Poppy means these books will be both poisonous and extremely beautiful; or alternatively, that women themselves are both beautiful and poisonous. The series will be published by Hebei Education Press.[3]

This report from a provincial evening newspaper gives a vivid sense of the mixture of hype and mystery that women's writing inspired in the publishing industry and the media during 1995. Judging from its comments, the publisher of the Red Poppy series, Hebei Education Press, clearly wanted to exploit stereotypical feminine qualities—beauty, treachery, seduction—in planning and promoting the series. A closer examination of the events surrounding the launch of this series shows that the above comments were simply part of a much broader marketing strategy in which the writers, *as women*, were employed—more or less willingly—to play a central role.

At least as early as the summer of 1994, many state publishing houses and private book dealers sensed that the upcoming UN World Women's Conference would be an unprecedented business opportunity—specifically, a means to revive sales of literary and art books, which were declining in the early 1990s. The government, in typical fashion, treated this event as a rare chance to showcase for the outside world its achievements in women's liberation and gender equality. Thus, it gave the green light to countless cultural projects relating to women, even providing generous funding for some of them. Many art and literature publishing houses took advantage of the easy money to plan their own contributions; most of them, predictably, would publish one or more series by women writers.

As an educational publishing house that could accumulate capital by producing textbooks and other materials for the Chinese school monopoly, Hebei Education Press had a distinct financial advantage over arts and literature publishing houses after economic reforms spread to cultural institutions in the 1980s. This meant it had plenty of resources to make a big impression when the craze for publishing and selling women's literature began in the mid-1990s. Xu Kun observed:

In the summer of 1994, a number of publishing houses started planning their women's series, intending to take advantage of the upcoming UN conference in Beijing. If one includes private book dealers in the total, there must have been around a hundred thousand people hoping to profit by "selling women." The difference between Hebei Education Press and the others was the sheer scale of their operations. While others sold their goods furtively, one piece at a time, Hebei decided to sell theirs on a grand scale and with the utmost fanfare. They invited one of the most famous male writers in China to take charge of the project, and they managed to catch all the major women writers in their net.[4]

Wang Meng, highly respected author and former minister of culture—the "famous male writer" to whom Xu Kun refers here—agreed to become editor in chief of the series. The publisher sent invitations to fifteen young and middle-aged women writers, signed by Wang personally, asking them to attend a workshop at the well-known northern seaside resort of Beidaihe. There, they would work on a publishing project in which each of them would select and edit a collection of their own works. By the time of publication the following year, the list of writers had been lengthened to twenty-two. At the workshop, the participants chose the sensational name Red Poppy for the series, and all the writers signed publishing contracts with Hebei under which they agreed to accept a 10 percent royalty. This was quite an eye-opener, since at the time most publishers still paid a fixed and rather low manuscript fee for literary books. Despite its heavy investment, Hebei was confident that it would make high profits. It immediately shifted its promotional campaign into high gear, touting the series in the national media as "the largest-scale women's writing project in Chinese publishing history" before any of the titles had been printed.

Media hyping was apparent again once the Red Poppy series finally appeared. The day the books were placed on sale in Beijing, a special symposium was held to discuss the series. In its August 19, 1995, edition, *Xinwen chuban bao* (Press and Publishing Journal), the official newspaper of the Press and Publications Administration, carried a full-page colour advertisement for the series, which included photographs of all twenty-two writers. Wang Meng's preface to the series was published in the elite book review journal *Dushu* (Reading). In that piece he adopted a teasing tone, claiming that Chinese literature was now dominated by women writers and that women writers ought to establish their own separate writers' association to avoid diverting all the attention and glory from their male colleagues.[5] The trade magazine *Chuban guangjiao* (Publication Panorama) printed a special promotional piece from the editor of Hebei about three recently published series of women's literature. Besides the Red Poppy series for contemporary Chinese women writers, there was also a Golden Spider Series (Jin zhizhu) for novels by Overseas Chinese women writers, and a Blue Stockings series (Lan wazi) for twentieth-century world women's literature, with each volume focusing on one country or region.[6]

Throughout all this media hype and marketing frenzy, the women writers were more than willing to help promote their books. On August 18, 1995, more than twenty of the series authors attended the Beijing premiere and symposium, and their presence attracted news photographers. Over the next three days, at various branches of the Xinhua bookstore in Beijing, these writers signed books and helped sell them to curious customers. On August 22, most of them went on to Shijiazhuang, the capital of Hebei province, to meet readers and again sign books. There they received an even warmer welcome, since for two weeks the local television station and newspapers had been reporting on this series and on the writers themselves, treating them like cultural superstars. The writers all converged on the biggest Xinhua bookstore in downtown Shijiazhuang and in one hour signed more than three thousand books. Some of the more popular titles, such as the collections by Chi Li, Zhang Kangkang, and Tie Ning, sold out immediately, and all of them sold out their initial print runs of fifteen thousand within half a year. Each writer received fifteen thousand yuan as a first royalty payment, and reprints were quick to appear.

Encouraged by the enthusiastic response from readers—especially by their curiosity about the personal lives of these young, talented, and in some cases beautiful "red poppies"—Hebei decided that the eight pages of photos it had included at the front of each volume were not nearly enough. It quickly decided to capitalize on the interest it had generated by producing a new series focusing on the women themselves. This time it asked the woman writer Tie Ning, president of the Hebei Writers Association and vice president of the Chinese Writers Association, to take charge of the project. The series, Photo Albums of Women Writers (Nü zuojia ying ji), consisted mainly of personal and studio photographs of eight young writers, including Tie Ning, Chi Zhijian, Chen Ran, and Chi Li. Each volume included one hundred photos of the writer, recording her growth from childhood to the present, with brief explanatory paragraphs alongside the photos. These titles were published in 1997 and were lavishly produced; they were obviously meant to be "quality products" (*jingpin*), the equivalent of coffeetable books. Although the print runs were quite small, around five thousand each, they were priced very expensively to ensure high profit margins.

The public display of women writers at the symposium and book-signing ceremonies—especially the curious stares of readers and the furious clicking of news photographers—struck Xu Kun as rather incongruous. She claimed that these events made her suddenly realize the dilemma facing feminist writers such as herself:

We all yearn for success, but we cannot attain it on our own by directly combating the patriarchal culture. So instead we participate in this collective show, creating a spectacle in order to "sell" ourselves. They [the male-dominated publishers, editors

and mass media] can sell us at a higher price than if we tried to sell ourselves. . . .
Our lost and forgotten gender and sexual identity are now suddenly remembered
with the approach of the UN World Women's Conference. Captivated by the huge
potential profits, they deliberately emphasize our femaleness, and we feel that we
cannot escape from our sex. . . . We certainly need not worry that the tickets won't
sell and our performance will have no audience. But who are the viewers and the director? And who the performers? Who will watch our naked parade and see us per-
form our earnest striptease?[7]

　　This sort of collective hyping and marketing of women's literature by men
and their female collaborators would not end in 1995; for the remainder of
the 1990s women's books would be one of the hottest fields in publishing.
The number of women writers was not necessarily greater than during the
1980s; the difference now was that their gender and their "unique female experience"—supposedly so different from that of their male counterparts—
was being exaggerated and celebrated to a much greater degree, to the point
of hysteria. From "little women's prose" (*xiao nüren sanwen*)[8] to semiautobiographical "privacy literature" (*yinsi wenxue*) and "alternative writing" (*linglei
xiezuo*) by post-1970s "babe writers" (*meinü zuojia*), women's experience and
sexuality, gender consciousness, and writing became a prominent focus of
public discourse during the 1990s. Yet in many ways, "this struggle to gain the
right of free speech was unfortunately confined to the existing terms of the
discourse of power."[9] Indeed, the craze for women's literature during the
1990s vividly demonstrates what Dai Jinhua, Chinese feminist scholar and
critic, called "the exploitation, utilization, and rewriting of women's literature
and identity by the consumerist culture."[10]

　　Since the early 1990s, series or collections (*congshu*) had become fashionable among publishers. By producing sets of quality books on a grand scale,
they could reap higher profits and enhance their reputations and at the same
time "carve out a territory" (*pao ma quan di*) in an increasingly competitive
industry. Yet early on, few such series focused on women writers. Beginning
in late 1994, however, a slew of women writers' series began appearing on
the market. One of the most distinctive of these was the Red Chili Pepper
series (Hong lajiao congshu) from Sichuan People's Publishing House
(Sichuan renmin chubanshe), a five-volume prose collection edited by Chen
Juntao, a male literary critic at the Chinese Academy of Social Sciences. This
collection included five contemporary women writers, notably Fang Fang
and Zhang Kangkang. There was also the Trendy and Talented Female Writers series (Fengtou zhengjian nuzi congshu) from Huayi Publishing House
in Beijing, produced by Wang Shuo and Chen Xiaoming, who used their
extensive literary networks to serve as intermediaries between the house and
the writers. This series comprised seven collections of fictional works by
young and middle-aged women writers, including Wang Anyi and Lin Bai.

Finally, there was the Them series (Tamen congshu) from Yunnan People's Publishing House, a long-term project that gathered both fiction and non-fiction works by contemporary women writers. This project, launched in 1995, had reached its fourth series by 2001.

With all these competing new series aimed at virtually the same market, it became difficult for publishers to draw attention to their products. Those which had the resources, like Hebei with its Red Poppy series, could afford to attract the most talented writers, pay them well to pose for publicity pictures, and saturate the media with promotional copy, as we saw earlier.

Other publishers took less costly but more sensational approaches, spicing up their titles and cover designs to appeal to readers' baser instincts. One such example is the Contemporary Women's Literature series (Dangdai nüxing wenxue shuxi), published by Chunfeng Art and Literature Publishing House. This project was planned as early as 1992, and like most other series of this kind, its editor in chief was a male scholar—Lan Lizhi, a professor at Beijing Normal University. The original goal of this series was to bring out ten volumes of serious works in various genres by recognized women writers such as Wang Anyi, Tie Ning, Dai Qing, and Shu Ting. According to Lan's preface, the series would "give a comprehensive and complete review of contemporary women's writing and theory."[11] It would offer four volumes of fiction and one each of personal essay, prose, poetry, reportage, feminist writing from Hong Kong and Taiwan, women's writing since the May Fourth Movement, and feminist literary criticism. The editing of this ambitious and academically rigorous series was completed by mid-1993; however, it did not come out until the summer of 1995.

By then, the publisher had drastically altered the titles and cover designs of the volumes. They were now shockingly vulgar, little different from the pulp fiction and popular magazines sold at private bookstalls. This was quite incongruous, considering that their content had not changed at all. The sensationalism of the changes is clear when we compare some of the new titles with the originals: *Memory and Feeling*, the original title of the personal essay volume, had become *Trapped Women: Women's Confessional Literature*; and *Privacy Revealed*, one of the fiction volumes, became *Imprisoned: Women's Sexual Literature*. Other title changes: the wicked-sounding *Dream Demoness: Feminist Literature* instead of the innocuous original, *Endless Sadness*; and *Variations: Women's Heretical Literature* instead of the rather sober *One Kind of Memory and Emotion*.

Clearly, the new titles were meant to grab the attention of casual browsers. This effect was heightened by equally crude and colorful cover designs. For example, the cover for *Imprisoned* showed a naked woman painted in traditional style on the front cover, and on the back a Star Trek–like Westernized cyborg. Next to the seductive yet threatening cyborg were these phrases:

"[This series] is dedicated to the Fourth UN World Conference on Women" and "Produced by the Chinese Women's Talent Association." The publisher obviously wanted to package women's writing so as to maximize its market appeal—to attract more ordinary readers and not just serious scholars and urban intellectual women, who had been the original market. The publisher seemed unconcerned about the obvious incongruity between the packaging and the content, and did not even bother to notify the editor about the changes.[12]

The newly commercialized publishers were certainly exploiting women's appeal and recent events such as the 1995 UN World Women's Conference, and in some cases they "effectively packaged and led serious literature, especially women's literature, in the direction of commercial writing."[13] Yet it is too simple to say that women were merely victims of this process. In fact, some women writers were happy to exploit their sexuality for their own ends.

In the following sections of this chapter, I will demonstrate this point in detail by focusing on the cultural phenomenon of "privacy literature" (*yinsi wenxue*). According to Xu Kun, the term privacy literature was coined in 1994 by the journalist Han Xiaohui to refer to a group of recent autobiographical novels by Chinese women writers that focused on women's private lives, especially their sexual experiences.[14] Han and other critics subsequently published many articles debating the merits of this form of writing, and the heated debate helped spread the concept much more widely. Early works of privacy literature included Lin Bai's *Yige ren de zhanzheng* (A War with Oneself, 1994), Hainan's *Wo de qingrenmen* (My Lovers, 1994), and Chen Ran's *Siren shenghuo* (Private Life, 1996). More recently, younger women writers such as Wei Hui (*Shanghai Babe*, 1999) and Mian Mian (*Candy*, 1999) have also been placed—or have placed themselves—in the privacy literature category, despite the strong contrasts between their works and those of earlier writers.

Privacy literature has caused a storm of controversy over the past eight years. Feminists have defended its descriptions of "gendered experience" (*xingbie jingyan*); moral apologists have accused it of being little different from soft pornography. Much of the controversy has revolved around the misleading impressions given of these women writers' works, first spread by publishers and the media and, more recently, encouraged and exploited by the writers themselves. I will focus on two representative works of privacy literature: Lin Bai's *A War with Oneself* and Wei Hui's *Shanghai Babe*. I will show that the development of privacy literature and the media's heated response to it demonstrate how various social forces—especially in newly emerging commercial publishing—have engaged in the collective hyping of gender and sexuality, and also how women writers have sometimes been complicit in the process of commodifying Chinese women's writing.

2. 'A War with Oneself'

A War with Oneself is not the kind of book that one expects to become a best seller. With its first-person, self-reflexive narrator, this novel is highly experimental at the narrative level. It follows a psychological order based on memory or consciousness to develop its account of growing from girlhood to womanhood. In terms of language, the novel is strongly lyrical, with occasional touches of symbolism.

Yet after coming out in 1994, *A War with Oneself* caused a sensation that still hasn't ended, and became one of the most talked about and controversial books of the 1990s. Five editions of it have already been published in China, as well as various pirated and Overseas Chinese versions. This is the book that inspired the new genre of privacy literature by women. Lin Bai has since written three more novels, all of them taking a similar autobiographical approach. Together, these works provide a picture of an entire literary generation.[15] Yet when we examine more closely this novel's feverish reception, we soon encounter serious discrepancies between its content and its increasingly distorted image among the reading public.

The novel centers on a woman named Duomi and describes her literary ambition, her sexual desires and frustrations, and her personal journey from a remote provincial town to Beijing, the Chinese capital. Having grown up in the hinterlands in a single-parent family, with her mother—a public health nurse—often absent on trips to rural areas, Duomi is a sensitive and lonely girl. She discovers early on that she can console herself through masturbation—an insight that will influence her later experiences both in writing and in relationships. She also develops a fascination for beautiful women. She starts writing in her late teens; like many, she hopes her writing will empower her to escape the deprivations of her backward social environment. At first, her literary talent is a blessing; she manages to publish several poems and lyrical prose pieces. Later, however, the blessing becomes a curse; when she is nineteen, she is punished for plagiarism. As a result of that humiliation, during her college years she cuts herself off from the outside world and gives up writing. Only after traveling across China after her graduation does she recover her enthusiasm for life and writing. On one of these trips, the inexperienced Duomi loses her virginity to a married man, and finds the sexual experience rather disappointing.

Later, she gets a job at the provincial library, where she can spend her days writing and reading poems, and where a lesbian admirer becomes her close companion. As a reward for her literary achievements, she is soon transferred to the provincial film studio. There, she falls hopelessly in love with a male director, but he is afraid of long-term commitments. As a result, she is compelled to have an abortion. Emotionally scarred by this experience, she es-

capes to Beijing, where she marries a much older man in exchange for a secure place to live.

A War with Oneself is a Chinese woman's bildungsroman. To those familiar with modern Chinese writing, it exemplifies the trend toward personal
writing (*geren xiezuo*) in fiction by writers of both sexes, a trend that began
in the late 1980s. These works often adopt a first-person narrator; also, they
turn away from social and historical concerns to emphasize personal and domestic life, and do so to such an extent that even descriptions of collective
historical experiences are often conveyed through the lenses of personal
memory and flawed narrators. The narratives thus tend to be highly subjective and psychological. This "inward turn" in Chinese fiction reflects a collective consciousness that is attempting to reconstruct the self as an individual in a postrevolutionary era.[16] Lin Bai has differed somewhat from most of
her contemporaries in writing from a determinedly female perspective, but
in other respects, her works clearly belong to the "personal writing" trend.

Two other aspects of this novel made it marketable for publishers—much
more so than other works in this genre. First, there is an intriguingly close
relationship between the writer's personal life and the fictional world she offers. *A War with Oneself* was published as a "novel," yet throughout it the author seems to be blurring the boundaries between reality and fiction. For
example, there are frequent juxtapositions of fictional figures with real people; and we find that the main character's life story overlaps to a great extent
with the personal realities of the writer Lin Bai. Examples: her poetry writing and literary friends, her personal journey from her provincial hometown
to Beijing, her real family, her love affairs, marriage, and separation, her life
as a single mother, and her recent experience of being laid off.[17] At the narrative level as well, the novel clearly adopts an autobiographical approach.
Lin Bai employs a first-person heroine whose reflective, subjective perspective often confirms the author's own intense involvement. As a result, the
writer is very ambiguous regarding whether she is writing a novel at all, or
simply offering readers a lyrical description of her actual experiences.

Second, the book breaks several taboos in contemporary Chinese writing.
In particular, from a clearly feminine perspective, it explores issues relating to
female sexual desire and physical experience—narcissism, masturbation,
abortion, rape, adultery, and lesbian affairs. These experiences are offered up
in poetic language, and often indirectly through metaphors and imagery.
Notwithstanding its techniques, this novel was virtually unprecedented in
that it dealt with women's desires and bodily experiences openly and unabashedly, and did so in a semiautobiographical manner.

However, we should note that sexual desire and experience are not the
constant focus or main content of *A War with Oneself.* A careful reading of
Lin's novel shows that sexual experience is only one part of the complete ac-

count Lin offers of a woman's experience growing into adulthood; further-more, her account is honest and thorough. There are no explicit descriptions of sex, nor do the heroine's sexual experiences overwhelm the story—less than one-third of the book deals with sexual experiences. Furthermore, the narrator's other experiences, especially those relating to her literary ambi-tions and writing life, are dealt with in extended detail. But when the novel was being promoted and controversy began to rise around it, publishers and critics paid little attention to the book's overall artistic structure and focused almost exclusively on its sexual aspects.

To demonstrate the book's thematic concerns and narrative style, and also the reasons for its notoriety, I will analyze the following controversial passage:

A war with oneself means slapping yourself in the face, blocking yourself with a wall, destroying yourself like a withered flower. A war with oneself means a woman mar-rying herself.

This woman often closes her doors and windows, and stands in front of a mirror. Her clothes on the chair are full of dynamism, as if there is an invisible vitality hid-den within them. Looking at herself in the mirror, she is both filled with self-love and a lurking feeling of self-loathing. Any woman who is married to herself will cer-tainly possess two contradictory natures. Just like a two-headed monster.

Her bed cover is like a large lily placed there casually. And the soft cotton is ca-ressing her burning skin, just like an indescribably large male organ stroking her body, up and down. She feels that she is swimming in water, her hand moving up and down on her wave-like body. And the spring-water in the deepest recesses of her body comes surging out unceasingly. She is soaked by transparent liquid. She struggles with all her strength, her lips half open, emitting desperate moans. Her hand, searching, hesitating, stubbornly advances. Finally it reaches that wet and messy place. Her index finger feels for the damp and soft opening of that chaotic centre. She screams as if she has made contact with an electric current. She devours herself. She feels that she has turned into water, and her hand into a fish.[18]

These three paragraphs—smoothly followed by a childhood memory of her first discovery of masturbation—appeared as the epigraph for the first chapter when the novel was first published, and quickly became the main reason for the controversy surrounding the book. Obviously, the main prob-lem for critics was the sensual description of the protagonist's masturbation. Yet it would be reckless as well as too simplistic to conclude that this book is "illicit pornography" on the basis of this single, brief and metaphor-laden de-scription of the protagonist's sexual desire. In fact, when we place this passage in the context of the novel as a whole, we can hardly avoid the opposite con-clusion: that this passage is absolutely necessary to the novel's artistic aims.

As we discover throughout the book, Duomi's relationships with others, especially with men, are bleak and disappointing. Her first physical en-counter with a man involves a failed rape; her first love affair is with a cheating married man, and her loving devotion for him ends in abortion; finally, she exchanges her youth for a marriage of convenience that will provide her with a resident's permit for Beijing. Masturbation thus becomes the only way for her to reach physical ecstasy and gain some sexual satisfaction. The passage encapsulates this young woman's fate and her need for self-love, as well as the novel's dominant mood of narcissism. Also, the language here is poetic, refined, and symbolic, emphasizing the psychological experience of sexual pleasure, which is described with great intensity and originality. It should hardly be treated as merely a graphic physical account intended to arouse the reader's baser instincts. Seen in this light, the passage is crucial to the work's main theme, and its position at the very beginning of the novel is readily justifiable.

Unfortunately, although *A War with Oneself* is a well-crafted work with serious artistic aims, during its promotion, publication, and circulation phases the book was misidentified, and as a result, the vast majority of readers and critics came to see it as a piece of "soft pornography" (*zhun huangse*). We will now consider this process of social circulation in more detail.

A War with Oneself was first published in the 1994(3) issue of *Hua cheng* (Flower City), an influential literary journal well known for bringing out controversial and experimental works.[19] This first version attracted little notice, but soon afterwards a book edition put out by Gansu People's Publishing House (Gansu renmin chubanshe) appeared and was widely distributed through various channels, including bookstalls and private bookstores. According to Lin Bai, this heavily commercialized edition caused her to suffer "many personal attacks, vicious insults and misunderstandings."[20] In this book edition, the publisher deliberately created the sensation of a "sexual novel" by tailoring the text to satisfy commercial aims, and in doing so sacrificed the artistic integrity of the original work.

The first thing one notices about the Gansu edition is its cover. It is an "artistically executed" photograph of a steamy lovemaking session, which is discernible even though the very dark tones. Next, one probably notices that the paragraph describing the protagonist's masturbation has been moved from the beginning of the first chapter to a separate page following the title page, where it serves as epigraph for the entire book. This strengthens the impression that the novel that follows will be almost exclusively about sex. Furthermore, the novel now has a longer title and an extra chapter. The title is now *Zhiye: yi ge ren de zhanzheng* (Body Fluid: A War with Oneself).

According to Lin, this extra title and the added chapter belonged to a novella, *Zhiye* (Body Fluid), which she completed shortly after *A War with Oneself*. This later work is a story about two women trapped in illicit affairs with men they don't love. They attempt to improve their lives by making use of their sexual relationships. *Body Fluid* is Lin's most explicit and powerful study of female sexual desire and the use and abuse of the female body. But in content and style, it has very little connection to *A War with Oneself*, and the protagonists are completely different. Even so, Gansu insisted that the novel was too short and persaded Lin to let them use the manuscript of *Body Fluid* as the final section of *A War with Oneself*.

Obviously, the publisher's motive was to exploit the more suggestive title and explicit content of this novella to add to the sexual allure and commercial attraction of the original story. Lin Bai soon regretted her compliance with this distortion, and hoped to change it back during proofreading. But the book was published in a great rush, and she didn't have a chance to make the revisions before the novel reached the market.[21]

It happened that around the same time, a semiautobiographical novel by Hainan, *Wo de qingren men* (My Lovers), was also published with similar crude packaging and promotion.[22] This gave both moralistic and feminist critics a strong excuse to declare the birth of a new kind of women's writing, and many discussions of the two novels, in the form of reader's responses, reports of symposia, and book reviews, began to appear in the media. One such debate was conducted in *China Reading Weekly*. In December 1995, the article "Nüxing wenxue ji qita" (Women's Literature and Other Matters) criticized the feminist critic Dai Jinhua for citing *A War with Oneself* as a powerful feminist text, and claimed that the novel was actually soft porn that should be banned because the sexual awareness it displayed would have a bad influence on young people. Xu Kun then wrote an article, *Yinwei chenmo tai jiu* (Since We Have Been Quiet for Too Long), rebutting this reductive and moralistic reading. The debate was subsequently repeated and extended by various other literary journals and newspapers.[23]

This controversial reception affected the subsequent publication history of *A War with Oneself* in two ways. By the mid-1990s, as described in previous chapters, the Chinese publishing industry was rapidly transforming itself from a relatively homogeneous collection of state-owned and -sponsored public institutions into a heterogeneous group of market-oriented, financially independent enterprises. Publishers and book dealers were developing new strategies for producing, packaging, promoting, and distributing books; however, the government still exerted a certain degree of control through its policies, regulations, and book licenses, as well as through censorship. So on the one hand, high-profile and controversial books like *A War with Oneself* tempted publishers with their market potential, but on the other hand, the label "soft pornography" made such books difficult and risky ventures because of their possibly negative "social influence."

We can see the effort to balance these two aspects in the third edition of *A War with Oneself*. After Lin Bai took back the copyright from Gansu, she began looking for a new publisher to set the novel straight. She did sign a contract with one publishing house, but before the book was sent to the printers, the *China Reading Weekly* article attacking it appeared and the publisher decided to withdraw from the contract and return the manuscript. After that, she contacted seven more publishers through an agent; all seven declined to publish her work. Some responded that they had consulted with legal experts, and that unless Lin made some substantial changes, the novel could not be published. Finally, Inner Mongolia People's Publishing House (Neimenggu renmin chubanshe), located in remote northern China and famous for bringing out controversial works, accepted the novel as part of a collected edition of *Lin Bai zuopin ji* (The Collected Works of Lin Bai), with some compromises agreed to by the author. In the end, *A War with Oneself* was retained as the title of the collection, but a number of revisions and cuts were made to reduce its explicit sexual content. These included cutting the last two paragraphs of the original epigraph (quoted earlier), along with some other phrases in the text related to lesbianism and masturbation. Lin Bai agreed to these changes, since it was the only way to get the novel republished at the time; even so, she considered this edition "a bowdlerized version."[24]

A War with Oneself and her two other autobiographical novels—*Shouwang kongxin suiyue* (Watching the Empty Years Passing By) and *Shuo ba, fangjian* (Speak, My Room)—initially made Lin Bai the target of many harsh critiques and mistreatment by her editors. Yet those same novels later ensured her entry into a select group of women writers heavily courted by publishers after 1996, once the virulent attacks on women's privacy literature gradually subsided (on this, more later). In 1996, Jiangsu Art and Literature Publishing House (Jiangsu wenyi chubanshe) brought out *The Collected Works of Lin Bai* in four volumes. This project included the Inner Mongolia version of *A War with Oneself*. In 1998, Hong Kong and Taiwanese editions of the novel came out, and this spread Lin's name beyond Mainland China.[25] Around the same time, pirated editions under the title *Lin Bai zuopin jingxuan* (Selections of Lin Bai's Works) were appearing all over the country in private bookstores and at streetstalls. Pirated editions are only profitable when the books being "stolen" are extremely popular, so they serve as an informal index of the most recent best sellers in China. Thus, we can safely conclude that Lin Bai, as a result of her notorious novels, was by the late 1990s one of the best-selling contemporary Chinese authors.

As a final demonstration of changing attitudes toward Lin Bai's work, in 1999, five years after it was first published, Changjiang Art and Literature Publishing House (Changjiang wenyi chubanshe) decided to bring out an unexpurgated edition of *A War with Oneself*. Lin Bai was given complete freedom to revise the novel in any way she wished. This time, she not only added back the two most controversial paragraphs at the beginning of the first chapter, but also repeated them at the end of the novel, as she put it, "to give the book a feeling of completion."[26]

During the 1990s, the Chinese government was rushing to "marketize" its economy, and as part of that, commercial publishing was given the green light to continue its development. During this process, the poorly regulated book market was jolted repeatedly by the contradictions between socialist "spiritual civilization" and capitalist consumerism. In the publishing climate that prevailed, Lin Bai's treatment as a female writer was hardly unique. Commercializing publishers were exploiting many serious works by women, typically by distorting their contents during editing, packaging, and promotion in order to appeal to a broader market.[27]

Yet the roles of victim and victimizer were not necessarily fixed. As we have seen, Chinese women writers were among the first "victims" to be exploited by a publishing industry in transformation. Yet by the end of the 1990s, privacy literature by women had acquired a significant "marketable value," and some women writers were beginning to capitalize on their gender and private experience, and learning to exploit publishers and the literary marketplace to achieve their own highly profitable ends. In the following section, I will describe the events surrounding the publication and promotion of Wei Hui's *Shanghai Babe* as an example of how privacy literature—once a derogatory term used as a weapon against a certain kind of women's writing—began to be shamelessly exploited by publishers, and even more so by women writers themselves.

3. 'Shanghai Babe'

> My name is Nicole, but my friends all call me Coco. The famous Frenchwoman Coco Chanel is actually second on my list of icons; Henry Miller comes first, of course. Every morning, as soon as I open my eyes, I feel like doing something unusual, and I imagine that one day my fame will rise up in the sky over this city like exploding fireworks. This has become my dream, the only reason for me to live.
>
> This feeling is tied to the city where I live, Shanghai. What constantly floats in Shanghai's sky is grey fog, depressing gossip, and a feeling of superiority leftover from colonial days. This superiority stimulates and irritates a proud and sensitive girl like me. I both love and hate it.
>
> But still, I am only 25 years old. One year ago, I published a collection of my short stories, which didn't make much money but brought me some fame: one male reader

even wrote me a letter enclosing some pornographic pictures. Three months ago, I quit my job as a fashion magazine
reporter. Now I am working as a waitress in a café called
Lüdi, wearing a miniskirt that shows my bare legs.[28]

This is the opening of Wei Hui's semiautobiographical novel *Shanghai Babe*, one of the most recently banned best sellers in China. It was published in September 1999, with an initial print run of fifty thousand, two months after the manuscript was completed, by the Beijing editorial office of the Cloth Tiger series, which was affiliated with Chunfeng Art and Literature Publishing House. After that, the book went through seven reprints, selling more than 110,000 copies in just half a year—highly unusual for a literary novel. This book's sales rose sharply mainly after early April 2000, when Wei Hui visited Chengdu, the capital of Sichuan province, to promote the book by signing copies at bookstores and having her picture taken for the local women's magazine *Wutai yu rensheng* (Life on Stage). On this trip, she acted outrageously to promote her image as a spokeswoman for generation X-ers (*xin xin renlei*). Dressed in a black-lace see-through top or a pink, open-backed tank top with matching embroidered shoes, cigarette in hand, blowing kisses and screaming back at her fans, she seemed wild, chic, and decadent—exactly the image of "babe writer" portrayed in her novel.[29] Her juicy performance was immediately picked up and hyped by the local tabloids and entertainment magazines and even by a local television station. Thus, by the end of April, with the help of the sensation-hunting and high-tech–equipped media, Wei Hui's name and photo had spread rapidly all over China.[30] The main website publicizing *Shanghai Babe* had more than 140,000 visitors by May—remarkable for China, where at the time the Internet was only available to a small minority of people. Very soon after this, a government ban gave Wei Hui even greater publicity, although this had not been part of the marketing plan.

In late April of 2000, the Chinese Writers Association and state publishing houses in Beijing were informed that *Shanghai Babe* contained "filthy, pornographic content." The Beijing News and Publishing Bureau ruled that any unsold copies in bookstores would be confiscated and that the publisher must destroy the printing plates and stop business for three months to "clean its ranks." The Beijing office of Chunfeng Art and Literature Publishing House, which had produced this book, was permanently shut down.

Despite the ban, or perhaps because of it, *Shanghai Babe* and four other books by Wei Hui immediately turned into the hottest commodities on the book market. Various pirated editions of these five titles appeared in privately run bookstores and at bookstalls,[31] and even state-owned superstores like the Beijing Book Plaza (Beijing tushu dasha) ranked reprints of Wei Hui's *Hudie de jianjiao* (The Scream of a Butterfly), *Yuwang shouqiang* (Gun of

Desire), and *Xiang Weihui nayang fengkuang* (Crazy Bird)—titles that had not been banned—at the top of their best seller lists. This ironic commercial twist extended to the global book market. In Hong Kong and Taiwan, all five of Wei's books were reprinted, with the label "private fiction" (*si xiao-shuo*) and Wei Hui's picture on the covers. Eighteen foreign publishers purchased the copyright of *Shanghai Babe*, and an English translation of *Shanghai Babe* is now on its way, from Simon and Schuster. *Shanghai Babe* became the biggest Chinese literary sensation since Jia Pingwa's *Fei du* (Ruined Capital) in 1993.

Through her exhibitionism both within and beyond the text, Wei Hui had written herself into celebrity status, just as she had dreamed in the opening paragraph of her novel. Yet despite what some Western media commentators see as the book's "alternative" face, and despite the dissident aura surrounding the government ban, *Shanghai Babe* serves as an excellent illustration of Chinese-style commercialization in today's writing and publishing scene. This is mainly because its promotional campaign adopted a deliberate strategy of arousing the voyeuristic desires of readers by providing a woman's "autobiographical confession" of her private life.

Below I will show how this strategy was employed both in the text of *Shanghai Babe* and, just as much, in the book's packaging and promotion. I will argue that *Shanghai Babe*, despite its self-declared feminism and subcultural veneer, is actually just a "gender performance" in the marketplace, a masterful coproduction that has relied on the expert calculations of the writer, commercial tricks by the publisher and book dealers, sensational scandals in the tabloid press, and finally, if unwittingly, censorship by the government. The *Shanghai Babe* phenomenon thus reveals the ambiguous identity of women's semiautobiographical novels—"privacy literature"—in a marketplace where previously sincere body language has turned into sensationalistic posing.

In Lin Bai's *A War with Oneself*, the sexual experience is written about in a symbolic style. In contrast, Wei Hui's *Shanghai Babe* adopts an exhibitionist directness in presenting female desire and "embodied experience"—more so than any previous novel. At the same time, it reveals a shrewd commercial calculation: that such private details can now be marketed and consumed in China just like other commodities.

The cover of *Shanghai Babe* best exemplifies all of this. It is a simple but chic black-and-white design with Wei Hui's half-portrait in the corner. Her long black hair hardly covers her smooth, naked body, on which the characters "Shanghai Babe: A Semiautobiographical Novel" and "Wei Hui" are inscribed. Beside these larger characters, two blurbs appear in smaller script: "A physical and spiritual experience from a woman to other women," and "An

alternative love story set in the secret garden of Shanghai." This cover is perfectly suited to the kind of commodity being sold. Capitalizing cleverly on
the fashionable trends for women's writing and privacy literature, it places
the beautiful babe writer herself in the limelight. It not only emphasizes her
sexual appeal, but also underlines her ambiguous identity: she is both the
character/narrator of the novel, Coco, and the writer Wei Hui.

This market awareness and the deliberate blurring of the real and fictional
worlds are reaffirmed by the words attributed to Wei Hui on the back cover,
but which can also be found in the novel, where they are attributed to Coco:

I fell in love with myself in the novel, because in the novel, I am smarter and more
street-wise. . . . Such art can become a super commodity, something that can be sold
to the smooth-faced, radical young generation seeking pleasure in the secret garden
of Shanghai in a fin de siècle age. It is they, the generation X-ers hidden in various
corners of the city, who will applaud or attack my novel. They are carefree and ideal
friends of young novelists who are looking for something new.[32]

In the novel's postlude, the writer Wei Hui describes the process of de-
livering her own manuscript to the publisher:

This is my first novel, and I wrote it from spring to summer, often so emotional, lost
in my fictional world. As I typed the last words on my computer, a long-distance call
came in. I couldn't react immediately to the "Hello" on the other end of the phone.
The sun outside the window was fading, the ivy climbing up the window of an old
western-style building, and somewhere a child was playing "Fur Elise." I threw my
cigarette into the ashtray, and whispered down the phone in German, "I love you."

Here again, the personal life of the protagonist and that of Wei Hui herself
overlap and become difficult to distinguish, not just because they are both
writers completing similar novels, but because both have German lovers.
Cleverly and deliberately, Wei leads her reader to believe that she is Coco,
writing her own story, and that *Shanghai Babe* is that story: "This book may
be called a semi-autobiographical novel. I always wanted to hide myself a bit
better among the lines and pages, but I found that is really difficult. . . . So I
have spit out what I wanted to say, and no longer wish to conceal anything."[33]

In *Shanghai Babe*, we see an approach to writing semiautobiographical fiction that is completely different from previous women's writing: instead of
claiming its fictionality, or at least maintaining a certain ambiguity between
fiction and autobiography, Wei Hui openly declares her novel's "truthfulness."
In other words, "Wei Hui is Shanghai Babe" and "Shanghai Babe is Wei Hui."

The novel's metafictional structure and the various carefully introduced
plot details reinforce this mirror-image identification between author and
main character. The narrator/protagonist of *Shanghai Babe*, Nicole (nick-
named Coco) is a beautiful young college graduate who works as a café
waitress by day; by night, she hangs around in the most trendy cafés, bars, and

restaurants of Shanghai with her friends, who include avant-garde artists, rock musicians, nouveau riche businesspeople, and white-collar professionals who work for foreign companies. Nicole cohabits with her boyfriend, the gentle but impotent drug-addict artist Tiantian, who lives on money his mother sends him. At the same time, Coco is having a secret affair with a German businessman, Mark, who likes playing around with exotic Chinese girls. Between wild parties and sexual encounters, the ambitious Coco is writing a book, which she hopes will make her famous. This book describes herself, her friends, and "Shanghai at the fin de siècle."

The book thus unfolds along two tracks: "my life" and "my writing." Also, it ends with the boyfriend Tiantian dying of a drug overdose, Mark returning to Germany, and "I" finishing the novel and planning to leave on a trip to Europe. All of these events merge perfectly in the postlude, in which the writer finally makes it clear that fiction and reality are one.

Many other details in the book add to its autobiographical texture: these include place names—the protagonist and her friend hang out at real in-spots in Shanghai, such as the Yin-Yang Bar and Peace Hotel. Also, actual events form a backdrop to the story—for example, the American bombing of the Chinese Embassy in Yugoslavia. And most of all, Wei Hui casually but consistently plants her own actual experiences in Coco's life, including her Fudan University education, her first story collection, *Scream of a Butterfly*, and her experience of choosing to be a waitress after quitting her news reporter's job. This self-referential framework even extends to the text of *Shanghai Babe* itself—a scene in chapter 6 describes a party at which Coco's friends read a just-finished section of her (i.e., Coco's) novel; yet the careful reader will notice that this extract is a straight pull from two paragraphs in chapter 2 of Wei Hui's novel.

Of course, a full identification between writer and character cannot be achieved without the text being socially circulated. As I mentioned earlier, it was actually during her book tour that Wei Hui picked up her self-performance in the text and stepped with it into the real world. And after April 2000, the game of identification between Wei Hui and *Shanghai Babe* was no longer played by Wei alone; now it also involved the media, the government, and curious readers. Thus it had become part of a much broader identity confusion.

One demonstration of this is Wei Hui's website, which was set up only after the book was supposedly banned. On it, Wei's self-promotion is tinged with the pride she feels about being banned by the government. "I am the writer whose works are pirated most," she declares. She has become an instant celebrity in Hong Kong and in the international media. It is clear from her website that she now sees herself as a social butterfly, and as someone who can use her fame to become a "patron" for artists and musicians. Her assertion of the "Shanghai Babe" alter ego continues to strengthen: her personal photo album is placed side by side with her fictional works, and the website's "wallpaper" is a photo of Wei Hui dressed in a black Qipao with roses embroidered on the front—the very dress that Coco, the "Shanghai Babe," shows off in the novel. Her statement on the website headed "I am Wei Hui" confirms this link in the most blatant way:

> Wei Hui: To become a Shanghai Babe
> A. She is the spiritual saleswoman of "Generation X"
> B. She represents the post-'70s alienated era
> C. She is probably listening to decadent jazz or just dancing wildly in a pub in a corner of the city
> D. Her first semi-autobiographical novel is *Shanghai Babe*
> E. According to witnesses, tonight Wei Hui is just like an amazing butterfly.[34]

By this stage, the play between reality and fiction—originally an artistic innovation of the mid-1980s—has clearly become part of a textual strategy to create a best seller as well as an extratextual strategy to promote the writer's fame. Wei Hui has rapidly learned how her "true to life" appearance can help sell a fantasy, especially when this fantasy is also "private," "sensational," and "alternative."

Wei Hui describes her work as "writing of/with the body" (*shenti xiezuo*)—a provocative statement that indeed accurately describes the exhibitionist nature of *Shanghai Babe*. Throughout the book, as the half-nude photograph of Wei Hui on its cover promises, this real/fictional female writer/narrator/character reveals a "private" and "sexual" story based on "real-life experience." And this sensational reading experience climaxes with the protagonist's orgasms.

The stage Wei Hui chooses for this exhibitionist performance is the cosmopolitan city of Shanghai. In Wei Hui's view, Shanghai is a "pleasure-seeking city, which grows bubbles of pleasure, nurturing and raising the new generation on the vulgar, sentimental and mysterious moods surrounding its broad avenues and back lanes."[35] With its mix of old, Concession Era buildings and new shopping malls, nostalgic jazz and countless pubs and nightclubs, foreign investors and emerging Chinese middle classes, Shanghai is a seductive "secret garden" that promises sensational excitement and forbidden adventures.

The human face of Shanghai's intense hedonism is a group of characters whom Wei Hui calls alternative (*ling lei*). Tiantian is a pale and sensitive yet talented artist who wants nothing more than to wait on his girl and feed his drug addiction. He is supported by his mother, who had lived in Spain and married a Spaniard and who has now returned to open a luxurious Spanish restaurant in an expensive European-style building. Mark is a German businessman, ambitious, successful, superior, sexually aggressive, and always impressing "oriental beauties" with his "Nazi" coolness. Then there are two female characters: Madonna, a nouveau riche Chinese socialite, made her money as a madam and then married a rich old man on his deathbed, so that she can now afford to spend every moment conducting experiments in "sexual liberation." And finally there is Judy, the narrator's cousin, an elegant "educated beauty," who speaks fluent English. She has a high-paying job with a foreign company, but soon tires of her boring "middle-class" existence and joins this alternative group by marrying an avant-garde artist. Wei Hui sums up her characters this way: "They are like chic glow-worms living off desires and secrets, their bellies emitting seductive blue lights, lights which flash in response to the culture and carnival of city life."[36]

The book glamorizes the places where these characters hang out, the clothes they wear, the music they listen to, and the sex games they play. Even their workplaces and residences are described in a brash and self-indulgent style that prevents any of the usual ironic and critical associations of the term "alternative" from surfacing. In fact, the concept "alternative" in *Shanghai Babe* is actually a distorted synonym for a life of pleasure and high-priced commodity worship, filled with shameless desires for spiritual superiority and physical affluence. Along with its close cousins "cool" and "avant-garde," Wei Hui's so-called "alternative" is just a glossy artistic façade that barely conceals the characters' stereotypical modern lifestyle in a consumer society.

Central to this "alternative" scene is the sexy pose of "Shanghai Babe," Coco herself. She is a beautified, puffed-up self, an erotic, seductive, and outrageous self, perfect in every detail, from her family background and education to her tastes and physical appearance. Her life consists of wild house parties, cocaine addiction, mingling with foreigners, hanging out in chic bars and restaurants, and shopping in luxury malls.

But most important in the book is Coco's (or Wei Hui's) wild and carefree sex life, which comes to symbolize the decadent lifestyle and "alternative" subculture of a new generation of urban youth. In some ways, we could say that *Shanghai Babe* is an unabashedly graphic striptease that gradually reveals more and more of the writer/narrator's "private" self. She is constantly bragging about her sex appeal and her never-satisfied desires: "For many men, I am a little bitch full of desire, with big eyes like those Japanese cartoon beauties, and a long neck like Coco Chanel."[37] Since Chinese boyfriends cannot satisfy her, she develops a wild "flesh only, no love" affair with a foreign man, yet even then she often has to seek sexual release by masturbating, especially when she is writing:

Still grasping the pen in my right hand, I silently slid my left hand downwards. It was already wet down there, and it felt sticky and swollen like a jellyfish. I explored inside with one finger, then with a second. . . . Slightly nauseated by my own enthusiasm, I satisfied myself. . . . Other people are motivated to write masterworks by the destruction of their homes and their own suffering in exile, but as for me, I rub myself with expensive Opium perfume, shut myself in day and night with the destructive chords of Marilyn Manson's music, and burst through to victory all on my own![38]

In more than a dozen places in the book, the narrator graphically describes her sexual desire and subsequent satisfaction. The most provocative scenes involve sexual intercourse between Coco and her German lover: in the small washroom of a trendy rock bar, and in a spacious foreigner's apartment; in a public park close to a street, and during a fancy-dress party at a luxurious hotel. All of these scenes are exhibitionist displays of sensual, exotic, illicit, and "Nazi-influenced" sadistic sex. The compliments Mark offers her while they make love complete the tantalizing image that "Shanghai Babe" represents: she has a "wild spirit," a Henry Miller–style literary talent, a Coco Chanel sense of fashion, and a streetwise manner, and besides all this, he declares, "'You have the most delicious private parts, there are none to compete with them from Berlin to Shanghai'. . . . The fleshly pleasure bewitched my mind: winning the 'most delicious private parts award' sounded good; perhaps it could move a woman's heart more than winning an award for the best story of the year!"[39]

Clearly, *Shanghai Babe* is a sensualist's fantasy in which a woman writer is exploiting her own private life. But unlike some earlier novels by Chinese women, this exhibitionist display has nothing to do with personal growth, political protest, or rebellion against social convention; it has more to do with the writer's market calculations, which are based on an age-old assumption: sex sells, especially women's sex, especially a famous woman's sex. The only aspect of this model that is new and distinctively Chinese is the "alternative" setting of modern-day Shanghai, but as we have seen, this "Shanghai alternative" is really nothing more than stereotypical cosmopolitan hedonism, materialism, and consumerism.

The self-promotion and exhibitionism in *Shanghai Babe* was certainly neither the first nor the last case of Chinese women's writing being exploited for profit. In Chinese publishing in the 1990s, writers and publishers quickly learned a basic truth about their market: book sales are closely associated with the invisible capital of fame, publicity, media exposure, and public attention. *Shanghai Babe* was merely the culmination of the late 1990s phenomenon of babe writers, whose gender and personal stories were exploited for quick fame and big profits. I conclude this chapter by placing *Shanghai*

Babe and Wei Hui in this wider context and by contrasting babe writers with earlier women writers such as Lin Bai.

In 1997, the works of a group of young women writers including Mian Mian, Wei Hui, and Zhou Jieru began to appear frequently in literary journals such as *Xiaoshuo jie* (Fiction World), *Zuojia* (Writer), *Shanhua* (Mountain Flower), and *Furong* (Lotus). These works, many of them urban tales about wandering youth, were filled with descriptions of Shanghai bars and cafés, rock musicians, brand-name clothes, drug addicts, and "material girls" from well-off but spiritually lonely one-child families. Although artistically raw, self-indulgent, and rather generic, these works were applauded by some male editors and critics for their "innovative, decadent, and alternative" manner. Literary journal editors saw in this new trend an opportunity to pump up declining sales, so they hyped this new group with great energy. These writers were labeled the Post-70s Generation or the Babe Writers, and their "alternative" stories, along with eye-catching and photogenic portraits, began to fill the pages of many respected journals. *Writer* and *Lotus* even published special issues and established columns to promote these writers separately, and literary newspapers such as *Literature Press* ran special reports about them.[40]

In these various articles and special issues, attention focused not on the stories but rather on the young women writers themselves—on their family backgrounds, personal lives, romantic feelings, and literary ambitions, and especially on their "beautiful" looks. For instance, in the special issue of *Writer*, two entire covers (inside covers 2 and 3) were filled with photos of these dressed-up babes, and artistic portraits of them accompanied the texts of their stories. Alongside each writer's contribution, the journal ran an explanatory passage by the writer and words of praise from the journal editors or critics. All of these extra materials emphasized and confirmed the babes' "rebellious" lifestyle and identified their personal lives with those of the characters in their fiction. The words typically used to describe these writers were "sensual," "private," "alternative," "urban," and "feminine." Within two years, this special group had been so overexposed for their looks and personal lives that readers began to ask suspicious questions along the lines of "For what did they become prominent in the literary field?" (Tamen ping shenme zai wentan jueqi). But even this kind of criticism was picked up by the media to strengthen the hype around these writers.[41]

Although the label Babe Writer is ambiguous and rather patronizing, one thing is certain: it has stimulated the curiosity of readers. Many publishing houses compete to publish these writers, either individually or in a Babe Writers series. For instance, Huashan Art and Literature Publishing House (Huashan wenyi chubanshe) published a Breaking-Through series (Tuwei xilie), edited by Wang Gan, in which Wei Hui's *Shui zhong de chunü* (Virgin in the Water) appeared; Zhuhai Publishing House brought out the New Literary Generation series (Xin sheng dai), edited by Xie Youshun, which included Wei Hui's *Xiang Wei Hui nayang fengkuang* (Crazy Bird); Chinese Drama Press (Zhongguo xiju chubanshe) started an Alternative Passions of Generation X series (Xinxin renlei linglei qinggan), which included Mian Mian's *Tang* (Candy), another bad-girl writer's autobiographical account of sex, rock and roll, and drug chic. Following in the footsteps of the successful role models Wei Hui and Mian Mian, more Babe Writers are always emerging onto the literary scene. For example, Chinese Drama Press recently brought to market four new "literary beauties" (*wenxue liangnü*) in its Pink Collar romantic series (Fenling yizu qinggan xilie congshu); and the journal *Lotus* has recently introduced three new Babe Writers from Beijing, perhaps hoping to start a Beijing Babes trend to complement the Shanghai Babes coterie.[42] Pictures of these beauties and their alternative lifestyles are again featuring prominently in various promotional articles and interviews.

This public demand and publishers' enthusiasm for Babe Writers certainly encouraged Wei Hui to choose her alternative path to literary fame: commercial writing in the name of "feminism" and "alternative experience." Clearly, her success has in turn inspired even younger Babes to grasp the new opportunities offered by the market economy and to engage in a commercial writing calculated to make the most of their gender advantage.

In this chapter I have followed this commercialization process in detail. First, I have shown how publishers took advantage of the publicity and controversy surrounding privacy literature to make female authors like Lin Bai out to be much more exhibitionist and sensational than they really were, in order to sell more copies of their books. Second, I have demonstrated how a new generation of younger women writers, the Babe Writers typified by Wei Hui, learned to exploit the newly commercialized world of publishing as well as the desire of readers to pry into women's private lives. However, as I have indicated, this increasing turn toward women's privacy literature in China is, perhaps, more a function of crude market forces than it is evidence of a growing self-awareness and self-understanding among women writers in the 1990s. The developing interest in women's semiautobiographical novels and the changing meaning of the term "privacy literature"—from a pejorative slur by moralist critics to an advertising label—provide clear evidence of the material forces guiding literary production and consumption in today's China. These phenomena also show that the role women writers have played in this cultural market is not fixed—quite the opposite, it is complicated, ever-changing, and often ambiguous. The publication of *A War with Oneself* in the mid-1990s showed us how female writers and their works could become victims of the emerging commercial publishing industry and consumer-oriented market. By the spring of 2000, Babe Writers like Wei

Hui were proving that they could successfully exploit their "invisible capital" as sexualized women to profit from the increasingly commodified cultural market. These younger women writers have voluntarily embraced the marketing and publishing industries in an attempt to promote their works and themselves to the highest degree. In this new partnership, it is more and more difficult to distinguish victims from victimizers, and kitschy commercial strategy from ingenious artistic innovation.

CHAPTER 5

Translating Foreign Literature

FROM ELITISM TO POPULISM

1. Translation of Foreign Literature: 1950s to 1980s

Translating foreign literature has been an important literary and cultural enterprise in China throughout the twentieth century. The first large-scale translation of foreign philosophy and literature began in the late Qing dynasty and lasted through the early Republican period. This was a time when intellectuals were questioning Chinese tradition and promoting new cultural values based on those of the modern West.[1]

Right from the start, this translation enterprise raised varying expectations among those engaged in it. In the first place, reformers and socially engaged intellectuals saw the translation of foreign literature, along with philosophy, political tracts, and historical works, as a vehicle for promoting social reform and cultural transformation. This clearly affected which titles they chose to translate. Some titles reflected the late Qing craze for political fiction (as advocated by Liang Qichao); others focused on "the oppressed classes" of Eastern Europe and the Soviet Union. The latter were translated by Lu Xun and other leftist writers of the 1920s and 1930s.

At the same time, a newly emerging urban culture and advances in printing technology created the economic conditions for professional translators, writers, publishers, and bookstore owners to introduce foreign popular literature for mass consumption. Just like Hollywood movies and other imported foreign goods, foreign popular fiction was an easy way for the rising urban middle classes to acquaint themselves with Western lifestyles and to satisfy their curiosity about the exotic world outside. Although quite different in purpose from the serious works selected by reformers and revolutionaries, these translations did play an important role in constructing an urban Chinese modernity.[2]

Despite the different political and artistic orientations of its participants, this shared enthusiasm for translating foreign literature continued throughout the first half of the twentieth century, even through the turmoil of war and revolution. However, this relatively diverse approach narrowed considerably in the early 1950s, when China's relationship with the rest of the world changed following the Communist takeover. The translation of foreign literature in Maoist China (1949–76) was strongly influenced by the following factors.[3]

First, after the government took over the publishing industry and nationalized the culture business in the early 1950s, literary production became an integral part of the state's plan. Accordingly, the government subsidized it but at the same time regulated it. Foreign literature was controlled especially closely owing to the sensitive nature of relations between China and the West. Only a handful of "reliable" publishing houses enjoyed the privilege of translating and publishing foreign literature; these included People's Literature Publishing House (Renmin wenxue chubanshe), World Knowledge Publishing House (Shijie zhishi chubanshe), and Shanghai People's Publishing House (Shanghai renmin chubanshe). This small group effectively monopolized the publication process, from project conception, title selection, and hiring of translators to printing and distribution. Thus, other publishing houses were prevented from introducing any controversial foreign works.

Second, in terms of title selection, political considerations became paramount. Contemporary titles were clearly slanted toward works from the Soviet Union, Eastern Europe, and those many Asian, African, and Latin American countries which were friends or allies of Socialist China.[4] And the government often used these foreign works, together with revolutionary historical novels by Chinese writers, to help "engineer" the socialist revolution. In the 1950s, these books were seen as playing a central role in "socialist education," especially in schools and colleges. This explains why books about the Russian Revolution and the building of socialism, and about the Soviet struggle against Hitler during World War II, were especially prominent. Some translated titles, such as *The Tempering of Steel* (Gangtie shi zenyang lian cheng de) by Nicolay Ostrovsky, *The Young Guard* (Qingnian jinweijun) by Alexander Fadayev, and various others by Gorky and Mayakovsky became extremely popular in China, with millions of copies sold.

In contrast, there were few translations of contemporary works from North America and Western Europe. Most of the Western books chosen for translation were "classics" written before the twentieth century—in particular, "critical realist" novels of the eighteenth and nineteenth centuries that exposed the corruption and social ills of Western society. Prominent among these translated authors were Dickens, Balzac, Hugo, Stendhal, and Tolstoy. Not until the 1980s would a more representative selection of twentieth-century foreign literature begin appearing on the shelves of state book-stores.[5] At least for openly published works, cultural elitism and political engagement were clearly the dominant criteria for selecting and translating foreign literature in Socialist China, and this would remain true until the 1980s. The policies and practices of the publishing business were centralized, just as they were for other cultural institutions. This system openly served the state's overseers, and to further their ends, published works were repeatedly revised to stay in line with changing political winds. During the Cultural Revolution (1966–76), even these carefully selected examples of foreign works were denounced as poisonous, with the result that very little foreign literature was published openly.

However, during the three decades between 1949 and 1979, there were other avenues besides open publication for foreign works to enter China. Indeed, considerable numbers of "politically incorrect" Western modernist and Soviet "revisionist" works were being translated and introduced into China throughout that period, through an alternative channel known as "internal publication" (neibu faxing). This method began on a large scale in the early 1960s and would continue right up to the mid-1980s. The opening up of China in the late 1970s gradually made it superfluous.[6]

According to Quanguo neibu faxing tushu zongmu 1949–1979 (Catalogue for National Internal Distribution 1949–1979),[7] in the three decades between 1949 and 1979, more than 18,301 internal publications appeared, including nearly 9,700 titles in the humanities and social sciences. Among them were a number of modern literary works from outside China. Most of these (more than one hundred) were from the Soviet Union; American works came in second (nearly thirty). Also, there were twenty-four titles from Japan, fifteen from France, and fourteen from the United Kingdom. The kinds of works selected were in stark contrast to the openly published foreign literature of the 1950s and early 1960s.[8] For example, although works from the Soviet Union dominated the publication lists, both internal and open, the kinds of works selected were completely different. The open publications emphasized "progressive models of socialist revolution, construction and patriotic spirit," whereas the internal publications included many controversial works by dissident humanists and modernists of a younger generation, such as Ilya Ehrenburg, Konstantin Simonov, Alexander Solzhenitsyn, and Vasily Aksyonov. Ehrenberg's controversial novel The Thaw (Jiedong) was translated into Chinese as early as 1963, and four volumes of his six-volume memoir People, Years, Life (Ren, suiyue, shenghuo) appeared between 1962 and 1964,[9] doubtless because of his great influence and notoriety in both the Soviet Union and the West.

Also, many important works of Western modernism were translated very soon after they were written. These included Jean Paul Sartre's *Nausea and Other Stories* (Yanwu ji qita, translated 1965), Albert Camus's *The Stranger* (Juwairen, 1961), Samuel Beckett's *Waiting for Godot* (Dengdai geduo, 1965), Franz Kafka's *The Trial and Other Stories* (Shenpan ji qita, 1966), T. S. Eliot's *Selected Essays* (Tuo Shi Ailuete lunwen xuan, 1962), Jack Kerouac's *On the Road* (Zai lushang, 1962), and J. D. Salinger's *The Catcher in the Rye* (Maitian li de shouwangzhe, 1963).

Commissioned by the government, and translated and edited by carefully chosen intellectuals, researchers, translators, and editors from the Institute of Foreign Literature in the Chinese Academy of Social Science and the People's Literature Publishing House, these books were brought out exclusively by the handful of privileged publishers mentioned earlier. They were meant to circulate only among high-ranking officials in the Propaganda Department and government cultural bureaus and among a handful of intellectuals, to equip these people with updated knowledge of modern life and contemporary ideologies in the West and the Soviet Union. But before long, many of these works gained a much broader readership than the government intended. In the beginning, this usually happened only when the children of respected intellectuals and high cultural officials—especially those of high school and college age—gained access to their parents' books. These youths then passed the books among their friends, within their "underground salons." Most of the members were children of the elite, who thus enjoyed a somewhat unexpected intellectual enlightenment.[10]

A much broader dissemination of these internal publications occurred during the most turbulent period of the Cultural Revolution, when all boundaries and social order broke down. Beginning in 1966, the Red Guards repeatedly raided libraries and reference rooms in cultural institutions, as well as the homes of scholars, high officials, and famous writers. After confiscating many of these restricted works as evidence of wicked bourgeois influence, some guards were then tempted to read them and pass them around. The most popular of these translated works were also circulated in hand-written copies.

After 1968, most urban youth involved in the Red Guard movement were sent down to the countryside, and some took these books with them; this allowed their influence to spread even further among Chinese youth. Some of the most popular books were existentialist or beat generation works that offered some kind of meaning to the spiritual crisis these young people were experiencing. Among them were Kerouac's *On the Road*, Salinger's *The Catcher in the Rye*, and Camus's *The Stranger*. According to many of the urban youth of the early 1970s, their disillusionment with Chinese Communism found echoes in the spiritual world of alienation and loss depicted in these works.[11] The most often mentioned example is the influence of such works on the Baiyangdian poetry group[12]—the precursor to the popular Misty Poetry and *Today* poetry groups of the late 1970s.[13]

There is no doubt that these internal publications—in particular, modernist writings from the West and the Soviet Union—allowed an entire generation of literary youth to break away from the narrow intellectual perspective instilled in them by the first seventeen years of socialist education. These works taught them to think for themselves, and would strongly influence Chinese literature in the late 1970s and 1980s.

Yet at the same time, both cultural elitism and political censorship constrained the translation and distribution of foreign literature in China before 1980. For most of that period, access to foreign knowledge was heavily guarded in the name of revolution. The process of selecting and translating foreign works was treated as a serious academic or "cultural" venture with a strong political purpose, and no ideas about selling such books for profit were entertained. As late as the 1970s, bookstores in Beijing that sold "internal publications" (*neibu shudian*) were only allowed to admit customers above a certain official rank. Most people were prohibited from either possessing or reading internally published books.

When China reopened to the outside world again in the late 1970s, the situation changed completely. A flood of Western works appeared—literature, philosophy, general humanities, and social sciences. This was especially after the Fourth Congress of Writers and Artists, held in October and November 1979, where Deng Xiaoping gave a speech urging writers to modernize by learning from the West. Many of the works that suddenly came onto the market were internal publications that had once been restricted. They had been translated years earlier and only now were being reprinted in commercial editions. These works provoked vibrant discussions. They also stimulated many influential writers of the 1980s—writers such as Wang Meng, Gao Xingjian, Bei Dao, Liu Suola, and Xu Xing—to begin experimenting with modernist techniques.[14]

According to Wang Xiaoming, between 1978 and 1987, more than five thousand foreign titles were published in the humanities and social sciences—ten times the number of translations published openly in the preceding three decades.[15] Another study calculated that the average number of literary works translated annually increased from 172 per year between 1949 and 1979, to 657 per year between 1980 and 1986, and to more than 1,000 in 1988 alone.[16] There was also a much more systematic approach to introducing Western ideas, culture, and literature, in contrast to the piecemeal approach of the preceding period.[17]

Also, the works being selected for translation in the 1980s were more intellectually independent and more likely to challenge prevailing cultural and intellectual norms. In the field of literary translation, culturally elitist and avant-garde tendencies were especially noticeable. There was a systematic introduction of scholarly editions of foreign literary works, such as the influential *Xifang xiandaipai wenxue zuopin xuan* (Anthology of Western Modernist Works) edited by Yuan Kejia, and *Meiguo xiandai shi xuan* (Anthology of Modern American Poetry) edited by Zhao Yiheng. In addition to this, several literary magazines devoted to foreign literature—especially contemporary literature—were either established or reestablished. These included *Shijie wenxue* (World Literature, reestablished in 1977), *Waiguo wenyi* (Foreign Art and Literature), *Dangdai waiguo wenxue* (Contemporary Foreign Literature), and *Sulian wenxue* (Soviet Literature). These journals were often guest-edited by experts or by well-known translators, and the translations were often accompanied by critiques and scholarly introductions. These journals applied different selection criteria—for example, *Foreign Art and Literature* made a name for itself as a publisher of avant-garde experimental works—but in general terms, they all focused on serious literature translated to a high standard.

Perhaps even more significant than this rapid increase in the availability of foreign serious literature was the meteoric growth of foreign popular fiction after the late 1970s, and especially after the mid-1980s. Popular fiction had not been published in China since the early 1950s. Much of it had been proscribed—for example, the Sherlock Homes detective stories, love stories like *Gone with the Wind*, and blockbusters by Erich Segal, Arthur Hiller, and Sidney Sheldon. Yet all of these were now being published and sold to a broad and diverse audience. At the same time, restrictions on publishing foreign literature were being loosened somewhat, and many publishing houses, especially provincial ones, were rushing to participate in this profitable new sector. Some government organizations even used their political privileges and access to foreign information to profit from translations of popular fiction. For instance, in the late 1970s and early 1980s, the Masses Publishing House (Qunzhong chubanshe), run by the Ministry of Public Security, began bringing out crime novels, spy fiction, politicians' memoirs, and even some borderline pornography, offering the excuse that it was helping the Chinese people stay alert to the enemy.[18]

These kinds of books became extremely popular, some selling in the millions. With China finally opening up to the outside world after several decades of isolation, ordinary people were intensely curious about all things foreign. The government sometimes felt compelled to take administrative measures to control the numbers of popular fiction books being sold.[19]

Throughout the 1980s, a large proportion of popular fiction titles published in China were translations. According to the aptly titled *Da hongdong* (Sensation), a 1993 study of the best seller market in Mainland China, the craze for popular foreign fiction started around 1985 and reached its peak between 1987 and 1989. In the handful of months from late 1987 to early 1988, more than eighty popular foreign novels were translated with an average print run of 115,600 and an average price of 2.81 yuan; if one "adds those sold on the black market and illegally printed copies, the gross income received for these books was certainly no less than 200 million yuan."[20] This figure is even more impressive when we consider that the average price of a book at that time was only 0.99 yuan. According to their covers, these books were being published by state-run publishing houses; in fact, most were collaborations between the second channel and state publishers, and the actual producers were private book dealers (see Chapters 2 and 3).

Popular foreign fiction was treated from the beginning purely as a money-making venture. It follows that these books differed greatly from serious literature in the way they were produced. First of all, neither publishing houses nor book dealers were concerned about developing systematic translation plans; most popular titles were being published for short-term gains. Similarly, publishing houses, although happy to earn profits from these books, treated them with less respect than literary or academic works and did not view them as their main focus. In fact, they often left the job of translation to book dealers, who rushed to get the books to market, hiring college students and other less qualified translators. As a result, the quality of these books was extremely variable. Third, packaging and distribution were also down-market, since most of the titles were sold through streetstalls and private bookstores, which at that time were quite primitive operations. Fourth, in terms of title selection, since the producers sought to maximize sales by appealing to readers' baser instincts, a considerable proportion of these foreign translations were pulp fiction of the lowest kind, focusing excessively on violence, crime, and sex.[21] Also, because there was limited access to contemporary foreign literature, many book dealers and publishing houses were happy to pick up whatever they could find, regardless of quality. Some actually drew most of their titles from the paperbacks discarded by foreigners in their hotel rooms. With selection processes like these, readers inevitably got a narrow impression of Western society, as materially abundant but morally corrupt. Finally, copyright issues tended to be ignored completely.

During the 1990s, there were a number of changes relating to how foreign works—both serious and popular—were translated. These changes led to a convergence between the two extremes. Reforms in the state publishing sector—especially reductions in government funding—made these houses more aware of the bottom line and of the need to earn profits even from literary titles. As a result, many of the more progressive publishers and literary journals began packaging, marketing, and promoting foreign serious literature using techniques learned from the market for popular literature. At the same time, the overall quality of foreign popular fiction began to improve as second-channel book dealers became more professional and better educated. Instead of simply choosing pulp fiction titles at random, these dealers and the publishers with whom they cooperated took more account of trends in foreign book markets. Increasingly, they introduced foreign titles that had already proved their worth elsewhere.

To give a clearer picture of the changes that took place in the foreign literature market from the early 1980s to the mid-1990s, in the next section I introduce a case study: the magazine *Yilin* (Translations). In the 1980s and 1990s, this provincial literary magazine established a solid reputation for introducing and promoting contemporary foreign literature. In 1988, it tapped its considerable assets—a large collection of foreign literature translations—to establish a publishing house, Yilin Press (Yilin chubanshe), which published mainly foreign literature. A look at the practices and products of *Yilin* and Yilin Press will highlight several characteristics of the foreign literature market that was then developing in China: publishers were selecting a greater and greater variety of books, especially popular books; many publishing houses, especially provincial ones, were beginning to enter the market for foreign literature; and most significantly, political and artistic criteria began to lose ground to the profit motive when titles were being selected for translation and promotion.

2. *'Yilin'*

Yilin was founded in 1979 as a literary quarterly attached to Jiangsu People's Publishing House (Jiangsu renmin chubanshe). The launch of this new magazine, which intended to focus on contemporary foreign literature, coincided with the government's policy of "blooming and contending" in the cultural field. Around this time, many other literary magazines were either being established or resuming publication. But when we remember that foreign literature had until recently been a privileged field that few publishers could enter, it was exceptional that an ordinary provincial publishing house had been granted a license to produce a translation magazine. In 1979, there were only two other literary magazines publishing foreign literature exclusively: *World Literature*, founded in 1953 and recently revived, affiliated with the Chinese Academy of Social Sciences; and *Foreign Art and Literature*, founded in 1978, affiliated with Shanghai Translation Publishing House (Shanghai yiwen chubanshe), and focusing more on the southern market. However, these latter magazines tended to adopt an elitist and often academic approach when selecting and introducing foreign literature.

Yilin was the harbinger of a popularizing tendency in the publishing of foreign literature in China. This was the result of a deliberate attitude change fostered by the publisher. By the late 1970s, Jiangsu People's Publishing House was already publishing foreign literature successfully, especially contemporary works with mass appeal. In this area, along with several other provincial publishers, it was beginning to challenge the near-monopoly of People's Literature Publishing House.

The success of Jiangsu People's was partly due to its location in the provincial capital Nanjing, which had two universities with excellent foreign literature departments that could provide quality translators as well as scholars to edit the books. Jiangsu People's healthy sales of foreign literary works convinced its directors that they could launch a successful literary magazine, especially in the booming journal market of the late 1970s. They were also certain that this would improve the house's reputation as a cultural enterprise and help it make a profit. In the magazine's editorial guidelines, the directors stated their ambitious plan quite clearly: "dakai chuangkou, liaojie shijie" (Open the windows and get to know the world). Those guidelines also stated: "Yilin publishes translations that reflect contemporary foreign society (especially Western countries) and popular fiction published within the last five years."[22] This statement about welcoming foreign popular fiction, although innocuous today, was very bold for its time, when cultural elitism and political puritanism were still tightly enforced. It should be no surprise, then, that Yilin immediately found itself embroiled in controversy as a result of the the so-called Death on the Nile Incident.

In its very first issue in 1979, Yilin featured Agatha Christie's Death on the Nile (Niluohe shang de can'an). This was a clever strategy, because the film version of this detective story was being shown to packed houses at theaters all over China and millions of moviegoers were being thrilled by its plot twists and turns. The magazine's first print run of 200,000 immediately sold out; another 200,000 copies were printed but even these could not meet the demand. On the black market, the issue was selling for 2 yuan—almost twice the original price of 1.20 yuan—plus two cigarette coupons! Jiangsu People's followed up with a book edition with a first print run of 400,000.

Yilin got the public's attention with Death on the Nile; however, its huge success generated controversy among researchers and scholarly translators of foreign literature. Surprisingly, it was these elite intellectuals, not government officials, who first raised criticisms of the magazine. In early 1980, Feng Zhi, a well-known poet, scholar, and translator of German literature with the Chinese Academy of Social Sciences, wrote a letter to Hu Qiaomu, then in charge of the Propaganda Department. In it, he rebuked Yilin for publishing "decadent" works like Death on the Nile purely to satisfy readers' "low tastes" and to seek huge profits. He even declared: "The Chinese publishing field has never been so degenerate since the May Fourth Movement in 1919!" Such a reproach from a famous intellectual would have sounded the death knell for most publishers, and everyone in literary translation circles considered this a test case for the government's new policy on translating and publishing foreign literature. Yet the Publishing Bureau of Jiangsu province, to which Hu forwarded Feng's letter, stood behind *Yilin*, and *Yilin* cleverly exploited the media to air its side of the story.[23] All the media attention, along with popular support for *Yilin*, meant that China's leaders had to exercise caution over this matter. At the Conference of Literary Journals in May 1980, Wang Renzhong, Chief of the Propaganda Department, declared that *Yilin* had complied with the principles underlying the government's open-door policy and that *Death on the Nile* contained no socially harmful content. Therefore, following the recommendation of the Jiangsu Provincial Communist Party Committee, *Yilin* should be permitted to continue in business, although it should be careful to avoid publishing potentially dangerous materials in the future.

Feng Zhi's rather extreme reaction to Agatha Christie's mystery tale was taken seriously enough to become a national incident; yet it was clear from the final decision that official attitudes toward foreign popular fiction were changing. Over the following decade, it would become much easier to publish a wide range of foreign literature without government interference, except in extreme cases. *Yilin* survived, and throughout the 1980s ventured fairly freely into the market for translated popular literature. It paid close attention to recent best sellers on the Western book markets, especially in North America, and it quickly and efficiently hired people to translate those books into Chinese. Best-selling American writers such as Sidney Sheldon, Robin Cook, Michael Crichton, John Grisham, and Mario Puzo all became household names in China through *Yilin*'s efforts.

Yilin's success depended not so much on the excellence and originality of the books it selected, nor on the quality of its translations (which was often mediocre), but rather on its gift for judging what the public was curious about. Other houses in the same sector had not yet developed this skill. For example, *Yilin* advertised itself as publishing the most recent Western fiction about contemporary life—something that would certainly appeal to readers in a society that until recently had been shut tight. Also, because *Yilin* was a magazine, it was more flexible than book publishers and thus capable of faster turnaround times. This meant it was able to reach the market first with the latest foreign works. Quite often, it was able to publish Chinese translations of best sellers almost immediately after their original editions came out—for exmple, Arthur Hailey's *The Evening News* (1990) and John Grisham's *The Pelican Brief* (1992). As noted earlier, *Yilin* was also quick to capitalize on Chinese people's unprecedented enthusiasm for foreign films. In its first five issues, published in 1979 and 1980, four of the featured novels—*Death on the Nile*, *Rebecca*, *Kramer vs. Kramer*, and *Jaws*—had been made into blockbuster movies that were showing at the time in Chinese cinemas.

As a result of these business methods, despite frequent and unpredictable government campaigns against "spiritual pollution," *Yilin* became so successful during the 1980s that its owner, Jiangsu People's Publishing House, was able to bring out profitable book editions of many of the magazine's featured novels. To formalize this practice, in 1988 the foreign literature office of the house and the *Yilin* editorial office joined forces to found Yilin Press. This was the first provincial publishing house to specialize in foreign literature and translation; it was also the first to compete with the two national publishers in this field in Beijing and Shanghai (People's Literature and Shanghai Translation). That Yilin Press was founded at a time when many literary magazines were facing financial crises and shrinking subscriptions testifies to the success of *Yilin*'s popularizing approach. Yilin was making the most of its proven skill at maximizing the market potential of its literary products. Literary works could be tested by being published in the magazine; if they succeeded there, and proved to have lasting appeal for readers, they could then be published as books, quickly and relatively cheaply and with a reasonable expectation of continued healthy sales. And of course the same translations could be used.

3. Yilin's Promotion of 'Ulysses'

Yilin Press did not confine itself to translations that appeared in the sister magazine. The house had three main literary series, divided into two basic marketing categories: classics and popular best sellers. World Classics (Shijie wenxue mingzhu) collected foreign literary masterpieces published before World War II, many of them retranslations of books previously published by People's Literature or Shanghai Translation. The rationale behind this series was that Chinese readers were enthusiastic about anything "classic"; besides, copyright had expired on most of these works, so they were cheap to produce. By 2001, more than one hundred titles had appeared in this series out of a planned total of two hundred. The second series was the similarly titled World Classics: Modern and Contemporary (Shijie wenxue mingzhu: xian dang dai xilie), which focused on the postwar period and included authors such as Graham Greene, Kenzaburo Oe, and Carlos Fuentes. Over the past ten years, more than seventy titles have appeared in this series. The third and most popular series was the World Best Sellers Library (Dangdai waiguo liuxing xiaoshuo mingpian)—which consisted primarily of book editions of popular novels published in *Yilin*.

Very often, Yilin Press publishes several different editions of the same titles simultaneously. This "multiple packaging" approach demonstrates the house's propensity for marketing the same products to as many readers as possible. For instance, in its World Classics series the titles come in three different editions: "hardcover" (*jingzhuang ben*), "paperback" (*pingzhuang ben*), and "popular" (*puji ben*). Besides these, "deluxe boxed sets" (*hezhuang dian-chang ben*) are available by special order. The pocket-sized popular editions are densely printed, with the type filling the pages; the hardcover editions are generously spaced, with much wider margins. The paper quality and cover designs are also obviously different, even though the content of the books is the same. The hard covers come in a classy-looking brown, with traditional engraved cover illustrations by foreign artists and with the authors' names written in elaborate calligraphy. These editions are obviously aimed at wealthier bibliophiles. The paperback covers (aimed, perhaps, at less well-off bibliophiles) show colorful nineteenth-century oil paintings, whereas the popular editions (aimed at the general reader) feature photographs from movie versions of the books. The editions' different prices reflect these stylistic differences: in the case of Jane Austen's *Pride and Prejudice*, for instance, the hardcover costs 18 yuan, the paperback 12.50, and the popular edition 8.40. The same "multiple packaging" strategy is also used for packaging the World Classics: Modern and Contemporary series.

The World Best Sellers titles come only in regular paperback editions. Hollywood movie scenes are displayed on their covers. These books are aimed not at serious readers of "classics," but simply at those who want to be entertained. The intimate yet approachable covers of these paperback and popular editions have been a great innovation in the packaging of foreign literature in China—although doubtless strongly influenced by Western publishing techniques. Foreign literature translations in China always used to come in plain, sober covers. The use of vivid and down-to-earth photographs has certainly made readers at large much more comfortable about purchasing these "foreign" texts, since they can now easily identify with the familiar pop-culture images and associate the books with favorite movie stars. The cheap prices of these popular editions are another important selling point. Even in 2001, most were still priced under ten yuan—half the price of hardcovers. The wisdom of this business strategy became especially apparent in the 1990s, when book prices rose dramatically until many readers could no longer afford to buy regularly priced editions. Also, Yilin's dirt-cheap popular editions have made it difficult for pirated editions to compete on the market.

Like *Yilin* magazine, Yilin Press achieved strong commercial success by publishing foreign popular literature that appealed to a mass readership. However, it also went further than the magazine by using clever marketing techniques to popularize elite foreign literature, or "World Classics." This latter development deserves more detailed illustration, since it demonstrates in the clearest terms the power of marketing and promotion in creating demand among readers for unfamiliar foreign literary products. Yilin Press was a pioneer in this area, and in recent years its techniques have been embraced and refined by many other Chinese publishers. To conclude this section, I will describe how Yilin Press published and promoted a new translation of James Joyce's *Ulysses* in 1995. Then in the final section, I will show how various other publishers have adopted similar commercial methods, with varying degrees of success, in promoting translated foreign literary works in China.

The success of *Yilin* magazine and its evolution into a publishing house specializing in foreign literature could not have occurred without Li Jingduan, editor in chief of *Yilin* and president of Yilin Press until 1999. Before entering the publishing industry in 1975, Li worked in foreign trade and journalism; this gave him more commercial experience than most Chinese editors at the time. By the early 1990s, Yilin Press had built a solid reputation for publishing foreign popular literature and had become China's biggest importer of American and European best sellers. Yet Li realized that in order to really challenge the established publishing houses and increase its market share, the press would have to venture into elite literature as well. He decided to make a splash by "filling the most significant blanks in Chinese literary translation history"; to that end, he would translate two of the most influential masterpieces in modern Western literature: *Remembrance of Things Past* by Marcel Proust, and *Ulysses* by James Joyce.[24]

The translation of Proust's huge novel was carried out by fifteen translators working simultaneously on different sections, and completed in 1991. This translation, although not exactly a best seller, was reprinted four times over the following three years, selling forty thousand all told.[25] More important, this project won Yilin Press a national award for foreign literature publication, and this cemented its reputation as a top-quality literary translation house. Flushed with this success, Li Jingduan sought to strengthen the press's reputation even more by translating the notoriously difficult *Ulysses*. He was so confident that Yilin Press could produce a definitive version of this novel that he refused to abandon the project even after learning that People's Literature had already invited a famous Joycean scholar, Jin Ti, to translate the same work.

Jin Ti, a professor at Tianjin Institute of Foreign Languages, was an experienced translator who had developed his own translation theory. His involvement in the *Ulysses* translation dated from 1979, when Yuan Kejia asked him to translate the novel's second chapter for the *Anthology of Western Modernist Works*. Later, he published another section from its third chapter in *World Literature*. In 1987, the Hundred Flowers Art and Literature Publishing House (Baihua wenyi chubanshe) in Tianjin published Jin's abridged translation of *Ulysses*. People's Literature then invited him to translate the complete novel over three years. For various reasons—including the difficulty of the remaining chapters and an extended visit by Jin to the United States in the late 1980s—the project was still far from complete in 1994. By that year, only the first volume was ready for publication.

This delay made it possible for Yilin Press to preempt People's Literature with its own translation. From the start, the *Ulysses* project was given the highest priority, and time was pressing. In 1990, Li Jingduan himself took the job of executive editor, and expressed his determination to find a translator as famous as Jin Ti to carry out the work. Several of the older generation of English literature translators refused to take on such a difficult task. Among them, Xiao Qian seemed the best candidate. Xiao, who was also a famous writer, had studied stream-of-consciousness techniques and modernism while at Cambridge during the 1930s. Xiao was already in his eighties and insisted he lacked the stamina to complete this huge work; however, Li was able to convince Xiao's wife, Wen Jieruo, a foreign literature editor at People's Literature Publishing House, to do the basic translation, with Xiao as her consultant. As Li Jingduan had anticipated, once the actual translation work began, Xiao became more and more involved in the project, eventually declaring himself as cotranslator.

Now that the competition to translate *Ulysses* had begun in earnest, Li realized that a crucial factor affecting the book's profitability was going to be which version reached the market first. For this reason, he broke with the usual distant relationship between publishers and translators and extended a great deal of technical and practical support to Xiao and Wen. He helped them contact scholars and experts in China and abroad, and he bought them reference books and many editions of the novel, including translations into other languages. Yilin's original plan had been to publish the entire book at the end of 1994, less than four years after Wen and Xiao started translating it. However, early in 1994, Jiuge Press in Taiwan published the first volume of the novel using Jin Ti's translation, in complicated characters; around the same time, People's Literature announced that it would publish its own version of the first volume in May of that same year, with simplified characters. Li responded immediately, by moving up the publication date for Xiao and Wen's completed first volume. After a few months of feverish activity, during which the translating, editing, and proofreading work were all carried out simultaneously, Yilin Press succeeded in bringing the first volume to market in May as well. The first print run was eighty thousand—an impressive number, considering the profoundly challenging style of Joyce's original work and its irrelevance to most Chinese readers. Yilin brought out the other two volumes of its edition at the end of 1994, following its original schedule, and way ahead of the second volume of Jin Ti's version.

The relaxed attitude of People's Literature and Jin Ti regarding their schedule for publishing their translation of *Ulysses* was typical of established publishers and translators in China before the mid-1990s. Neither was much concerned about the project's profitability—they simply assumed that as an elite literary work, it would sell poorly. Both, however, felt a profound responsibility for ensuring a translation of high quality. This attitude was somewhat anachronistic, although it certainly would have made sense in the previous Chinese publishing system, which was a socialist monopoly built on cultural elitism. Thus, when interviewed in the spring of 1995, even while the competing Yilin Press edition of *Ulysses* was raking in profits, the editor at People's Literature in charge of Jin Ti's still incomplete version calmly explained:

I was assigned by my supervisor to take charge of this book because they needed an experienced editor. After the first volume was published [in the spring of 1994], people were looking forward to reading the second volume. However the translation was too complicated, the style varied too much, and there were many technical problems. . . . To be frank, I am not interested in this book myself, and I don't quite understand it either. But Jin Ti is an old-fashioned scholar, very strict about the translation quality, and he has emphasized again and again that he won't finish the translation in a rush just to get it published quickly. Otherwise, he would feel guilty to both the writer and his readers. So far, he still hasn't sent in one of the chapters, and because there are quite a few tables and music scores in the second part of the book, there are lots of extra technical problems still to be solved. So even I am not sure when this volume will be published.[26]

Indeed, this final volume wasn't published until March 1996, two years after the first volume. By then, Yilin's edition had already taken a large chunk of the market.

The success of the Yilin Press version of *Ulysses* did not depend solely on speed of publication. In fact, the most important factor was certainly the press's publicity campaign, which began long before the translation was completed and continued for some two years after publication. Throughout the campaign, Yilin Press demonstrated keen business instincts, emphasizing efficiency, professionalism, and reader-oriented pragmatism—all of this in stark contrast to the old-fashioned and inefficient People's Literature.

Yilin's marketing campaign included the following main strategies. First, Li promoted the Yilin translation by emphasizing the celebrity of the writer and the translators. Promotional materials circulated during the translation process offered the background of the original "masterpiece" and pointed out Joyce's centrality to literary history; they also repeatedly praised the talents of Xiao Qian as a translator and writer. Both before and after publication, Li encouraged Xiao himself to write various articles that introduced the novel, offered his own interpretation of it, and explained the original book's difficulty as a justification for his extensive notes.[27] After the book was published, Xiao Qian participated in book signings at the Xinhua bookstore in Shanghai. In May of 1995, Yilin Press organized a seminar, "Joyce and *Ulysses*," to which it invited many well-known scholars and translators as well as the Irish ambassador and the director of the Joyce Cultural Center in Dublin. This was duly reported in the literary press.[28]

Second, to arouse Chinese readers' curiosity, Yilin Press milked the notoriety surrounding the original publication of *Ulysses* in Europe. In 1993, Li Jingduan published his exchange of letters with Xiao Qian in which they discussed whether the novel—especially its controversial eighteenth chapter—would be banned for its frank depiction of the sexual psychology of the female character Molly. Xiao concluded his letter with the enticing statement: "Unlike half a century ago [in Europe], the government will not take us to court over this book."[29]

Later, Li expanded on these statements in a review article, "Yi bu qishu, tianshu, he jinshu" (A Remarkable Book, a Difficult Book, and a Banned Book). In it, he recounted the obscenity trial in Europe that followed the book's original publication, and noted its sexual content, stream-of-consciousness techniques, and modernist style. Thus, readers' appetites were well and truly whetted before the translation appeared.

Third, Yilin Press exerted great efforts to make the novel accessible and attractive to ordinary readers. Li Jingduan asked Chen Shu, a professor of Irish Literature at Beijing Foreign Languages University (Beijing waiyu xueyuan), to write *Youlixisi daodu* (Guide to *Ulysses*), aimed specifically at Chinese readers; it would be published at the same time as the translation. Advertisements emphasized the accessible qualities of the Yilin translation, especially when read side by side with Chen's guide.[30] Indeed, the Yilin edition of *Ulysses* was as reader-friendly as one could possibly expect, considering the challenging nature of the original. Xiao incorporated many more colloquialisms and Chinese idioms than Jin Ti, and his style was obviously more felicitous. The differences between the two translations were so obvious that heated debates arose in the literary press over which translation was more true to the original. Many felt that Jin preserved the spirit of the original better than Xiao.[31]

Xiao departed the most from Joyce's original in his translation of the final chapter, Molly's stream-of-consciousness soliloquy, for which Joyce provided no punctuation whatsoever. Xiao "punctuated" his translation with spaces between each sentence. According to Li Jingduan, it was he who suggested this approach, arguing less than convincingly that English has capital letters and a strict word order, and that without punctuation, Chinese would not provide any indication as to where sentences began and ended. This already difficult book would have been virtually incomprehensible had Xiao not taken this approach.[32]

The other innovation of Yilin's edition, also intended to make the book more comprehensible, was the vast number of explanatory footnotes. Xiao's translation included more than six thousand footnotes—several hundred per chapter. For example, Chapter 9 contained 555 notes, and Chapter 15 contained 984. Besides offering necessary explanations for allusions, foreign customs, special names of places and people, and the like, many of these notes were clearly intended to help readers understand the basic text. Examples: "Here he / him refers to Bloom," and "This is from the famous verse in *Hamlet* 'Frailty, thy name is woman.'" The critics agreed that Xiao had completed an enormous amount of work but were divided over whether his extensive notes violated the spirit of the novel—Joyce himself apparently disliked the idea of providing such notes. But here, and throughout this translation project, Xiao and Yilin Press decided to place Chinese readers' needs above total fidelity to the writer.

Finally, Yilin Press compiled various other reference materials in its edition, including a lengthy translator's preface and appendixes titled "Youlixisi yu aodexiu ji duizhao biao" (Table of Comparisons Between *Ulysses* and *The Odyssey*) and "Zanmusi qiaoyisi dashi ji" (Chronology of James Joyce). These, in conjunction with the notes, offered Chinese readers extensive background about this profound book, allowing them to become informed commentators rather than merely uncomprehending admirers. The press even solicited readers' reviews under the heading "Wo du You li xi si" (My Reading of *Ulysses*), and published them in *Yilin* magazine beginning in 1996. Furthermore, it organized a readers' symposium on *Ulysses*, held in 1995 in Shanghai.[33]

The "contest" between these two publishers and their translations of *Ulysses* became one of the most intensely debated media events of 1994 and 1995. Newspapers and journals hyped it as a "civil war" between North (Beijing's People's Literature) and South (Nanjing's Yilin Press).[34] The slew of reviews, the scholarly evaluations of the relative merits of the competing translations, and the translators' dismissive comments about each other's work all became grist for the media hype mill. As Yilin Press predicted when it first decided to wage this battle, the controversy provided a great deal of free advertising and significantly boosted the sales of this profoundly difficult book. With its clever marketing techniques, Yilin was able to exploit its proximity to the southern and eastern markets, selling almost seventy thousand of the first volume in one week in Shanghai, Nanjing, and Guangzhou. The publicity was also good for the first volume from People's Literature, whose initial print run of ten thousand also sold out immediately, forcing it to immediately reprint another forty thousand. But with its time advantage in producing the complete version within a year, and the accessibility of its edition for ordinary readers, Yilin soon gained the upper hand in terms of sales. In fact, *Ulysses* sold so well that in 1996, the press published a clothbound edition with a print run of forty thousand. According to a 1996 article by Li Jingduan, the total sales of the two Yilin editions had reached 150,000, planting the book firmly in best seller territory.[35]

4. *Expansion of Foreign Literature Translation*

The rise of Yilin Press illustrates the transformation that has taken place over the past two decades in the field of foreign literature. The purposes of translation, the targeted audience, title selection, packaging and marketing, and even the actual translation process all reflect this wholesale transformation. Today it is abundantly clear that, as with other areas of literary publication in China, the translation and publishing of foreign literature are increasingly dominated by market-oriented mentalities and mechanisms.

Moreover, as a result of extensive deregulation that has introduced market forces to Chinese publishing, foreign literature is no longer a heavily guarded monopoly, the preserve of a small handful of publishing houses; it is now an open field ripe for general harvesting. Many publishing houses are now venturing into the foreign literature market, from newly established specialty houses such as Yilin Press, to those which previously only published Chinese writing, such as Writers Publishing House. Now that all art and literature publishing houses are permitted to bring out foreign translations, there is increasing competition within the industry.

All of this means that publishing houses in this field have had to improve their business strategies. This has been especially urgent since 1992, when China joined the Berne World Copyright Convention; since then, it has become more difficult to publish foreign books without paying royalties. In these new circumstances, publishing houses have had to work even harder to ensure reasonable returns on their heavy investments in foreign copyrights. This is why foreign literature publishers since the 1990s have developed a number of new approaches to increase both their efficiency and their profits. In this final section, I will introduce the most important of these approaches.

First, the work of translating and marketing foreign literature in China has become more globalized, in the sense that publishing houses now track the foreign best seller lists much more closely than before and at the same time imitate Western business models in introducing these best sellers to China. A seminal text in this regard was the 1988 Chinese translation of John Sutherland's *Bestsellers: Popular Fiction of the 1970s*.[36] Sutherland's book was used as an index of best-selling titles, which every publisher then competed to bring out. It also served as a kind of bible for Chinese publishers regarding how to produce "American-style" books.

The practice of tracking foreign best seller lists has become even more common since the mid-1990s. As a result, Chinese translations of best sellers generally appear much sooner than they once did—sometimes a matter of months after original publication rather than years. Some examples of rapidly translated foreign best sellers that took the Chinese market by storm are *The Bridges of Madison County* (600,000 copies), from People's Literature Publishing House; *The Horse Whisperer* (230,000), from Writers Publishing House, and Mitch Albom's *Tuesdays with Morrie* (300,000), from Shanghai Translation Publishing House.[37] For most Chinese publishing houses today, translations of best sellers are a shortcut to huge profits. By introducing foreign best sellers, they can solve the problem of the scarcity of best-selling Chinese manuscripts and at the same time reduce the risks of publishing unfamiliar foreign writers.

The 1990s have also seen more and more contact between Chinese and foreign publishers, through exchange visits, book exhibitions, and copyright agencies within China and abroad, and much more interaction with Taiwanese and Hong Kong publishers that also produce translated Western books. This allows Chinese publishers to follow the foreign book markets even more closely. Once they hear about a potential best seller, they can offer down payments and royalties immediately in American dollars—something that required lengthy approvals before. Often there are bidding wars among Chinese publishers for the domestic copyright of foreign books.[38]

Besides all this, more and more publishers are now applying promotional strategies developed in the West to help these best sellers succeed in the Chinese market. This has certainly been helped by their greater familiarity with the Western publishing industry. One of the most noteworthy recent cases of this relates to the Chinese translation of the Harry Potter series.

As soon as J. K. Rowling's books began to take Western markets by storm, several major Chinese publishers joined in the bidding war for the Chinese copyright. People's Literature, with its established reputation and financial resources, won this battle in August 2000. The house set up a Harry Potter Project Group to oversee the translation and promotion of the books. In October, less than three months later, the first volume was brought to market. A series of promotional events followed throughout the country, including live performances at book launches in different cities and Harry Potter souvenirs offered with book purchases. By the summer of 2001, when the fourth volume came out, total sales of the first three volumes had broken 1.3 million copies—that is, 415,000 sets.[39]

This outstanding success was certainly helped by the books' cult status abroad, but it was also the result of careful planning by the new directors of People's Literature, a house that had long been notorious for its conservatism and inefficiency. The Harry Potter translations were completed at great speed by a team of female translators. The publisher chose women translators in the belief that they would be able to catch the flavor of the originals and better imitate the language of teenagers! To prevent pirated editions—the most serious problem for best seller publishers in China—the house spent a great deal on printing and design. Thus, the books came out with gilded covers, on specially colored paper, and with exquisite bookmarks attached. This meant that pirated editions would be extremely costly if not impossible to produce. With regard to distribution, besides going through state-owned Xinhua bookstore channels, People's Literature convened the country's major private book distributors at a special convention, where the books and the promotional plans were introduced to them. Finally, the house made use of a new sales tool, the Internet, contracting Chinese Internet bookstores such as BOOK800.com and Bookoo.com to advertise the titles and take orders.[40]

More recently, People's Literature has signed an exclusive merchandising agreement with Time Warner to develop Harry Potter products in China, including a Harry Potter Fun Book. This is a clear example of a Chinese publisher exploiting a single brand-name product in several different markets. And when the motion picture *Harry Potter and the Philosopher's Stone* was shown in China in 2001, an advertisement including the text "Harry Potter's Chinese Edition is Available from People's Literature Publishing House" was flashed on every cinema screen in the country before each showing, and the books were sold in the lobbies of the theaters.[41]

The success of the Harry Potter series and other Western best sellers in China clearly demonstrates that in this globalizing era, literary products are rapidly circulated and consumed in widely different parts of the world, and that the techniques for circulating and promoting them are converging.

A second aspect of foreign literature publishing in 1990s China is the overall improvement in the quality and appearance of its products, especially in the area of popular fiction. During the 1980s, when second-channel publishers were publishing mainly low-grade pulp fiction, this quality was poor. Since then, established houses such as Lijiang, Writers, Shanghai Translation, and People's Literature—not to mention new houses like Yilin and improved second-channel producers like Alpha Books—have begun bringing out foreign popular literature and standards have risen sharply. As our account of Yilin indicated, publishers of foreign literature in the 1990s increasingly adopted a middlebrow approach in packaging and promoting foreign literature. In other words, they began treating popular works more seriously while at the same time broadening the market appeal of serious literature.

This change was the result of both cultural policy reforms and market pressures. After the government's 1989–90 Campaign Against Pornography and Illegal Publication, when all publishing houses had to reregister and many unofficial publishing operations were closed down, the craze for publishing the lowest kind of foreign pulp fiction abated somewhat. The state publishing houses realized that if they hoped to keep profiting from the foreign popular literature market, and if they wanted to avoid problems with the government, they would have to improve the quality and selection of their titles. More progressive houses such as Yilin and Writers took production of popular literature titles into their own hands instead of leaving it to illicit second-channel producers, who might use the publishing houses' names to produce trash.

As for readers, once their initial curiosity about all things foreign was satisfied during the 1980s, and once they had acquired a more sophisticated knowledge of other societies through their personal experiences and through the media, they became less enthusiastic about buying crude and badly produced pulp fiction. They demanded a much greater variety of entertaining and better-produced foreign works that would open their eyes and give them new experiences.

In the previous section, I described how Yilin succeeded in popularizing *Ulysses* and turning that challenging literary work into a best seller. To illustrate the opposite movement—the raising of a foreign popular novel to the status of a "modern classic" through clever packaging and marketing—I will describe one of the first outstanding examples, the Chinese edition of *The Bridges of Madison County*.

Robert Waller's novel first topped the best seller lists in the United States in the summer of 1993. A Hollywood movie was produced soon afterwards, providing more publicity for the book. People's Literature bought the Chinese copyright that same year. The People's Literature edition was an extremely high-quality product compared to most foreign popular works that had been produced in the past. First, unlike many other translations completed in a rush, this one was beautifully executed, fluent and refined, strongly suggesting the lyrical nostalgia that suffused the original work. This was mainly owing to the translator, Meijia (penname for Zi Zhongyun), an expert in American literature at the Chinese Academy of Social Sciences, who had been carefully selected. Second, the edition was imaginatively packaged. The "cute" pocket-sized book had a light-yellow plastic cover with gold stars; the cover art showed a "weathered" oil painting of a Madison County bridge. The upper left corner provided a blurb in white characters on a blue background, which readers could easily associate with the American flag when they juxtaposed it with the stars on the cover. The blurb itself declared the book "a best seller that has taken the American market by storm." The back cover offered more enticing promotional copy: "Why do Americans love this book so much? What does it tell us about the mind of contemporary Americans? Reading it will help you find the answers!" The book's contents were designed to harmonize with the novel's overall tone, to exploit its nostalgic sentiments. For example, a separate page before each chapter gave the title in elegant brush calligraphy; also, each of these pages was accompanied by a small black-and-white photograph of a different Madison County bridge. Doubtless the American edition influenced some of these design ideas; even so, for China at the time, they were highly innovative and "tasteful."

The first print run in 1994 was 100,000—unusually high for a conservative house like People's Literature. The book was not an immediate hit, perhaps because of the publisher's lackluster marketing campaign. However, word of mouth and especially the screening of the Hollywood film starring Meryl Streep and Clint Eastwood—one of the ten imported foreign films for 1996—caused sales of the book to explode.[42] By late 1996, it had sold more than 600,000. Another important element that helped increase sales was an unexpected national debate that soon spread through the media regarding the aesthetic and moral values of this novel and the movie. Many Chinese readers felt that their deepest values of love and family loyalty were being challenged and turned upside down in this era of social transition. They longed for the kind of dignified and profound love between the main characters in the novel, and for the simplicity of their traditional resolution of an extramarital affair, and they contrasted this with the realities of contemporary Chinese society. Readers from all different social groups and backgrounds joined in the debate, in most cases praising the book as a model for elevating family values and true love.[43]

The Bridges of Madison County was a typical (if extremely successful) popular romance in the West, one that serious critics did not rate very highly; even so, its Chinese publisher was able to market it as a "classic." Chinese publishers have similarly promoted many other popular Western novels as serious literary classics, including such potboilers as *Gone with the Wind* by Margaret Mitchell and *The Thorn Birds* by Colleen McCullough. Undoubtedly, these publishers are exploiting Chinese readers' love of "classic" products and their unfamiliarity with the Western literary tradition simply to boost their sales.

One of the most interesting examples of this tendency is the series Foreign Literary Masterpieces and Their Sequels (Waiguo wenxue mingzhu ji xupian), published by Shanghai Translation Publishing house. This series mixes true classics and best sellers from different eras and countries. Titles, with sequels attached, have included *Jane Eyre*, *Pride and Prejudice*, *Les Misérables*, *Love Story* (Erich Segal), and *Gone with the Wind*. Most of the sequels have little connection with the originals, and are generally of dubious quality, since they are by completely different writers; nevertheless, they have generally sold as well as the originals in China, helped along by the "brand-name" attraction of the classic writer. Especially in the case of *Scarlet*—the sequel to *Gone with the Wind*, by Alexandra Ripley—the publisher made good use of the media hype surrounding the sequel in the West as well as the classic movie of the original. As a result, the book sold more than 160,000 after its 1996 publication, despite its high price of 25.80 yuan.

Of course, not all Western best sellers necessarily become blockbusters in China. In fact, in certain genres most foreign translations have done rather poorly. For instance, the novels of Stephen King have not taken off in the Chinese market, perhaps because China has no tradition of horror stories. Science fiction is another risky area; ordinary Chinese readers generally seem to prefer more "true to life" stories.[44]

Chinese translations of foreign literature have generally improved with regard to both variety and quality. However, the introduction of market mechanisms into foreign literature publishing has also led to many problems. Two of the most common complaints among translators and readers concern the poor quality of many translations and the so-called repetitive publishing (*chongfu chuban*). Many houses have now ventured into foreign literature; however, many do not employ qualified foreign literature editors, and furthermore, they often lack access to expert translators. The result is that despite the heartening growth in the range of available foreign literature, many translations are suspect and even misleading. Even a specialized publishing house like Yilin sometimes produces a low-quality title, especially when dealing with a difficult original. For instance, a quick flip through Yilin's edition of Anthony Burgess's *A Clockwork Orange* would leave Chinese readers completely nonplussed; the translator has simply been unable to deal with all the neologisms in the original.[45] Plagiarism of translations is also a very serious problem, for the same reasons.[46]

Repetitive publishing is a related phenomenon. Lacking qualified translators, and unable to pay too much for copyright, many publishers simply regurgitate already translated versions of older works whose copyright has expired. This tendency is most obvious in the area of "world classics"—that is, famous foreign works from before the twentieth century. Among newly established foreign literature publishers trying to spread their names quickly and cheaply, publishing collections and classics series by purchasing or simply "cutting and pasting" earlier translations has become extremely common. Old translations are simply recycled under different covers and titles by different publishing houses. This saturates the market; it also deprives readers of true choice and doubtless misleads them on occasion into purchasing books they already own.

Shakespeare provides a typical example of repetitive publication. Prior to 1995, the only publisher that had published Shakespeare in China was People's Literature, with its *Complete Collection of Shakespeare's Works* (Shashibiya quanji), published in 1978 based on the translations by Zhu Shenghao done back in the 1930s and 1940s. In 1996, fifty years after Zhu died and the translation copyright expired, many houses immediately brought out competing Shakespeare editions. In January, Chinese Drama Publishing House (Zhongguo xiju chubanshe) and Era Art and Literature Publishing House (Shidai wenyi chubanshe) both published a *Complete Collection of Shakespeare's Works* —and both were simply reprints of Zhu's translation. The only difference was that the latter was proofread and revised slightly by a group of expert translators headed by Su Fuzhong. Then in March, Inner Mongolia People's Publishing House joined the fray by importing the venerable Taiwanese edition of Liang Shiqiu's translation of Shakespeare's works; this edition included both plays and poetry in an eight-volume set, again titled *Complete Collection of Shakespeare's Works*. Then in 1997, Yilin Press brought out a four-volume *Complete Collection of Shakespeare's Works*, based on Zhu's translation but with revisions by Qiu Ke'an. At the same time, Chinese Cinema Publishing House (Zhongguo dianying chubanshe) and Masses Art and Literature Press (Dazhong wenyi chubanshe) published their own Shakespeare collections, and Zhejiang Art and Literature Publishing House (Zhejiang wenyi chubanshe) published its *Complete Poetry of Shakespeare* (Shashibiya shi quanji). These were again basically reprints of Zhu's translation for People's Literature. The only truly new translation during this frenetic period was *New Translation of Shakespeare's Works* (Xin Shashibiya quanji) from Hebei Education Publishing House, whose translator Fang Ping imaginatively experimented with Chinese verse forms to try and lend a more authentic flavor to the original works.[47]

The market for published literary translations, both popular and elite, has continued to expand over the past decade, and overall, the quality of the selections and the effectiveness of their packaging have improved enormously. Clever marketing has enabled publishers to sell elite literary works to ordinary readers in unprecedented numbers, and careful tracking of Western best-seller markets and imitations of Western publishing techniques have greatly increased the success rate of foreign books transplanted to China.

As in other areas of Chinese publishing, therefore, although many problems remain, the commercialization of the foreign literature translation market has generally had a positive impact on the availability of foreign titles and led to a great deal more choice for readers interested in learning about the world outside China.

CHAPTER 6

Literary Journals

BETWEEN A ROCK AND
A HARD PLACE

EVEN TODAY, CHINA has more literary journals than any other country in the world. After 1949, its system of state-funded literary journals played a crucial role within the socialist cultural establishment. Over the past two decades, these journals have faced unprecedented challenges as a result of sweeping economic reforms and the emerging cultural marketplace.[1] This once popular and prestigious sector has declined so sharply that it is now in crisis, and many journals now realize that each new issue could be their last. In this chapter I describe the problems facing literary journals and their stumbling efforts to become more commercially adept—efforts that mirror those in other sectors of literary publishing in China during the reform period.

I will begin by describing the crisis as it was felt by journal editors in the late 1990s. Then I will trace the causes of this crisis back to the mid-1980s, when the government began reducing funding for many cultural institutions and requiring them to "marketize" themselves. I will examine various strategies for raising capital that journal editors adopted during the late 1980s and early 1990s—strategies that included often awkward attempts to sell advertising space and to seek corporate sponsors. Finally, I will show that since the late 1990s, a few journals have tried to follow a middle course—to adopt market mechanisms while broadening their definitions of literature. Journal editors have been trying to avoid both the rock of their outdated and inefficient socialist literary legacy and the hard place of financial ruin brought about by market forces.

For the sake of continuity, I will focus on one specific journal, *Beijing wenxue* (Beijing Literature), referring to other journals when relevant. I have chosen *Beijing Literature* for two reasons. First, it is one of the most prestigious of the provincial-level literary journals affiliated with a local Writers Association or Federation of Literary and Art Circles. Founded in 1950, its very existence is associated with the unique nature of the socialist literary establishment; as a result, in recent years it has been one of the journals most heavily affected by recent systematic reforms to the artistic and literary fields (*wenyi tizhi gaige*). Unlike the top national journals such as *Renmin wenxue* (People's Literature), and unlike journals affiliated with publishing houses such as *Dangdai* (Contemporary), provincial-level journals such as *Beijing Literature* lack a countrywide reputation, with the broad subscription base this would bring; furthermore, they lack adequate outside funding from the government or publishing houses.[2] Second, because it is based in the capital, Beijing, near the center of that city's (and the country's) cultural circles, the story of *Beijing Literature* illustrates especially clearly the contradictions that arise when literary journals try to overcome their financial problems while simultaneously dealing with political directives that restrict the measures their editors can take. Unlike similar journals in the remote provinces or in the more relaxed special economic zones, such as *Foshan wenyi* (Foshan Art and Literature) in Guangdong and *Tianya* (Frontiers) on Hainan Island, *Beijing Literature* can neither completely follow the demands of the market nor test the boundaries of politically provocative content without facing immediate criticism and penalties.

1. Crisis

In the fall of 1998, the presidents and editors in chief of more than eighteen literary journals—including *People's Literature*, *Beijing Literature*, *Zhongshan* (Zhong Mountain), and other prestigious journals—met at the foot of Tian Mountain to discuss the alarming state of literary production in contemporary China.

The central issue on the conference agenda was how literary journals could adjust to the new demands of the cultural market—more precisely, how they could overcome the financial difficulties that most had been suffering since the late 1980s. With the dramatic drop in both subscriptions and government funding (some had lost their funding completely), literary journals were besieged with problems from every side. Many editors in chief spoke about how difficult it was simply to keep their journals alive, and about their uncertainty over the future. Most felt that the government had betrayed them and left them to languish in the new market economy. They had been trained to run their journals for the party, and they had been working within the state-sponsored literary world for decades. Now they were expected to compete with the tabloids, pulp novels, fashion magazines, and other popular publications that had appeared suddenly in the poorly regulated cultural market, even while concerning themselves with "social benefit" and "artistic value." How were they supposed to do all this?[3]

These editors' complaints were well founded; so were their anxieties. In 1998 alone, four literary journals closed down one after another, including the well-established full-length journal *Kunlun*. Then, at the beginning of 1999, the government announced that *People's Literature*, the premier national journal, which it had been supporting for five decades, would have its funding cut back over the following three years, and that the journal must ultimately become financially independent. This announcement added to the panic among those journals which still held out hope for government funding to allow them to survive.[4]

Similar accounts of editorial symposia, accompanied by heated discussions regarding how literary journals could survive in the market, appeared often in the Chinese media in the late 1990s.[5] The survival of the literary journals became a favorite topic in literary circles. However, this mourning over their sudden fall from privilege was merely a much-delayed and still reluctant response to the decline of the socialist literary system and the rise of a new cultural market—developments that were already two decades old.

In 1949, *Wenyi bao* (Literary Gazette) and *People's Literature* were founded as the mouthpieces of the two principal cultural associations, the China Federation of Literary and Art Circles and the Chinese Writers Association. The mandate of both was to establish the Chinese Communist Party's criteria for quality literature and to promote orthodox literary works. Over the next few years, many other literary periodicals were founded along the same lines as *People's Literature*; these newer ones were based in provincial capitals and other major cities. By 1959, there were eighty-nine literary journals in China. The editors of these journals were always government employees, and their editorial boards always included cultural officials who served as liaisons between writers and the party. Clearly, the mission of literary journals was to foster socialist writers and encourage them to publish works that supported the government and the party. As a result, besides controlling the content of available literature in Chinese society, these journals became important indicators of the party's latest policies toward literature and broader cultural and social issues.

During the harshest years of the Cultural Revolution (1966–76), all literary journals ceased publication, and most other cultural and literary activity shut down. The only journal to continue publishing during those years was *Jiefangjun wenyi* (People's Liberation Army Art and Literature). Then in the late 1970s, literary journals enjoyed a renaissance: all of the pre-Cultural Revolution journals were revived, and many new ones were established. Many of the new ones were full-length journals affiliated with publishing houses, and focused on novels and novellas. These new journals, which included *Huacheng* (established 1979), *Shiyue* (October, 1978), *Dangdai* (Contemporary, 1979), and *Zhongshan* (1978), became the most influential venues for the so-called "post-Mao" literature that emerged in the 1980s. By 1980, the number of nationally distributed literary journals had mushroomed to around two hundred; besides these, there were many others with local circulation.[6] Many of these journals achieved impressively high circulation figures. For instance, in the late 1970s and early 1980s, two journals, *People's Literature* and *Xiaoshuo yuebao* (Fiction Monthly), attracted more than a million subscribers each. Several others, such as *Contemporary*, *Xiaoshuo xuankan* (Fiction Digest), *October*, *Shouhuo* (Harvest), and *Zhongpian xiaoshuo xuankan* (Novella Digest), regularly achieved distributions of more than 400,000.[7]

The blooming of literary journals in the late 1970s and early 1980s reflected the masses' thirst for literature ("spiritual food") after the hardships of the Cultural Revolution (an ironic term, in retrospect); it also pointed to the multiple practical functions of literature in what was essentially still a prereform socialist society. Three of these functions were especially important.

First, in a national environment in which literature was essential to the fostering of morality, social cohesion, and politics at every level, literary journals, which constitute the main official outlet for writers, played a vital journalistic and public media role, both for the government and for writers and readers. "Political leaders sometimes used literary outlets to broach purely political moves," and literary magazines were a place "where both the leadership and the public were accustomed to look for significant political messages."[8] Yet so complete was the literary thaw in 1978 and 1979—one result of Deng Xiaoping's conciliation policies toward intellectuals—that intellectuals and even dissidents were able to clear their throats and begin voicing, through literature, their honest opinions on political and social issues. Similarly, after early 1980, when Deng began issuing warnings about "bourgeois liberalization," the leadership's new direction was reflected immediately in official criticisms of previously published literary works. As a result, literary journals often became a contested public sphere, one in which writers, readers, critics, and political authorities voiced their contrasting opinions about social and political issues. It often happened that a novel, a piece of literary reportage, or even a short story in a literary magazine or newspaper stirred the entire nation and sparked a national debate. This was the case with Liu Binyan's "Ren yao zhi jian" (People or Monsters; *People's Literature* 9, 1979), with Lu Xinhua's "Shanghen" (Scar; *Wenhui Bao*, August 11, 1978), and with Yu Luojin's "Yige dongtian de tonghua" (A Chinese Winter's Tale; *Huacheng* 3, 1980). Obviously, this sort of publicity worked wonders for literary journals' circulation figures.

During these years, literary journals were also one of the only available and acceptable forms of entertainment for general readers. As late as the mid-1980s, China's entertainment industry was severely underdeveloped. Almost no one owned a television or videocassette player, and for those who did, there was little to watch. And most newspapers at that time were dry official documents that neither challenged nor entertained readers. Literary journals, besides being very inexpensive, were almost the only diversion available to people when they needed to escape everyday reality and find something imaginative, outspoken, or even just pleasantly sentimental.

Furthermore, literary journals, besides being the centerpieces of socialist literary institutions, were the means at hand for promising literary youths (*wenxue qingnian*) to gain a measure of fame and career advancement. After the Cultural Revolution, many young educated Chinese found that they had lost years of formal education and the opportunities for advancement that education offered (review here the account of Tian Yanning and Tan Li in Chapter 1). Many realized that writing literature was the only path available for them to climb in society and to earn a decent and secure living.

Most literary journals were affiliated with Writers Associations or with Federations of Literary and Art Circles. They took it as their mandate to publish fiction and poetry, but also to discover and develop literary newcomers. To that end, they organized writing workshops (*peixun ban*) and writers' symposia (*bihui*) for young writers; also, many of the newer journals focused specifically on "youth literature." With all of this enthusiastic encouragement, and with rewards beckoning, plenty of neophyte writers were submitting their work to journals. According to one source, during the early 1980s, in the offices of some acclaimed journals such as *People's Literature*, *Beijing Literature*, *Harvest*, and *Contemporary*, manuscripts were piling up like mountains, with sacks more arriving every day.[9]

From the late 1970s to the early 1980s, many literary journals were able to flourish. From the perspective of intellectuals, readers, writers, and the Chinese government itself, these journals were both useful and necessary. Their circulations generally stayed extremely high, and the great majority of them received generous government funding. In effect, this funding subsidized readers' subscriptions. Unfortunately for the journals, the enormous social changes and sweeping economic reforms of the following decade would knock the legs out from under the literary journals and leave most of them struggling to survive, when not rendering them obsolete.

After the early 1980s, even more extensive economic reforms began in China, and the cumulative effect of these threatened the strong position of literary journals. Basically, the journals faced four challenges: the government was withdrawing funding; mass media and popular reading materials began to compete in the same market; readers began to matter more to editors than writers or government directives; and institutional structures fell out of date, a victim of their own inflexibility. The first two were external factors, totally beyond the journals' control; the last two were internal factors, largely a result of the journals' socialist, state-planned procedures, which caused them to drag their feet rather than adapt quickly to the new economic order.

Regarding funding reductions, signs of government abandonment appeared as early as the end of 1984, when economic reforms were first implemented in the cultural arena. The government made it clear that although a handful of publications would continue to receive favorable treatment, most literary journals would have to make efforts to become financially "self-responsible" (*zifu yingkui*).[10] As a result, over the next decade, albeit to varying degrees depending on the policies of local governments, government funding as a percentage of the total income of literary journals began to fall every year. By 1999, many journals had lost their funding completely, and others, such as *People's Literature* and *Beijing Literature*, were able to cover only one-fifth of their expenses through government finding.[11]

Moreover, literary journals could no longer look for help to the Chinese Writers Association or the Federation of Literary and Art Circles. After Deng Xiaoping's Southern Tour in 1992, a further "great leap" toward the market economy took place, and these associations, which had once been responsible for overseeing literary journals, had to face their own systematic reforms (*tizhi gaige*). They were being transformed from government and party organs (*dangzheng jiguan*) into ordinary public units (*shiye danwei*); the point of this was to force them into supporting themselves by acting more like business enterprises.[12] Lacking their own government funding and resources, these organizations had no choice but to stop "feeding" their literary journals—to use their own euphemism, they had to "set the journals free." By the early 1990s, most journals were being forced to learn how to support themselves and "swim in the business sea."

Regarding competition from other entertainment sources, the fiercest competition for literary journals came from "light-reading" materials, ranging from pulp fiction and popular romances to leisure and entertainment periodicals, such as women's fashion and lifestyle magazines and tabloid-style weekend and evening newspapers.[13] According to official statistics provided by He Chengwei, vice president of the Chinese Association of Periodicals, in 1978 there were 930 different magazines and journals of all types published in China; by 1993 there were more than 7,092.[14] Looking solely at popular fiction magazines, by the mid-1980s, there were already more than two hundred, several of them with seven-figure circulations.[15]

Thus, in 1988, there were sixteen so-called literature and art magazines with distributions greater than 400,000, but not one of these was a journal of "pure" literature. Almost all of them were popular fiction and popular culture magazines. Some of them could now claim huge readerships. Examples: *Gushi hui* (Story Session, 4,410,000) and *Dazhong dianying* (Popular Cinema, 1,650,000). This was a striking change over 1983, when fourteen literature and arts magazines had circulations higher than 400,000, and seven of these were "pure" literary journals.[16] Some critics claimed that literary journals were losing ground because people had stopped reading altogether; in fact, people were still avid readers—they were simply choosing different reading matter now that more variety was available. In the 1990s, the general trend continued toward leisure and light reading. According to the latest available statistics (from 1997), the magazines with the highest subscriptions were *Story Session* (3.92 million), *Duzhe* (Reader; 3.7 million), *Nüyou* (Girlfriend; 2.98 million), and *Jiating* (Family; 2.64 million).[17]

This problem was exacerbated by unavoidable increases in journal cover prices as a result of the deregulation of book prices and rising printing costs.[18] Let us take the high-end journal *People's Literature* as an example. Its cover price rose from 0.40 yuan in 1980 to 1.20 yuan in 1988, to 3.00 yuan in 1993, to 6.00 yuan in 1996; over the same time frame, its circulation dropped from over 1.32 million in 1980 to 452,000 in 1983, and continued plummeting to less than 200,000 in 1988.[19] The most recent figures (from 1999) give the circulation as just 50,000.[20] And *People's Literature* has been one of the *better* performers. The decline of *Beijing Literature* has been even more shocking: in the late 1970s and early 1980s, its circulation was around 250,000; currently it is 5,000 to 8,000.[21] And according to the latest available figures, the national average subscription for Chinese literary journals is now around 3,000, with some falling as low as a few hundred. At that level, it is impossible even to recover printing costs.[22]

All of these developments were clear signs that a new, consumer-oriented cultural market was forming. In that market, the economics of supply and demand were beginning to dominate. The free markets were now challenging state-planned cultural policies and regulations, with the two contending systems sometimes forced to cooperate. Businesspeople became adept at circumventing the various official restrictions so as to succeed in the new economic environment.

Most literary journals were unable to respond to the demands of the new cultural market and to profit from the new opportunities it presented. This was largely owing to a third impediment to reform—literary journals had inherited a comprehensive cultural system that was totally unsuited to survival in a competitive marketplace. Under this system, each journal was supported entirely by and responsible to a Writers Association or Federation of Literary and Art Circles, and its mandate was to showcase the "cultural work achievements" of a respective region. This meant that journals tended to be writer- and party-oriented, and that they seldom considered whether their content would appeal to readers. Likewise, there was little call for individuality in terms of editorial ideas and vision. As late as the mid-1990s, virtually all literary journals were still following the unimaginative format of "four dishes"—fiction, prose, poetry, and literary criticism—with little regard for attractive presentation. Furthermore, the complexities of the system, which was hierarchical and based on regions, led to artificial separations within the literary world. As a result, many journals printed materials that more or less duplicated what had already appeared in other journals.

Causing literary journals even greater problems in the marketplace was their remarkably inefficient distribution system. Popular reading materials were privately distributed; in contrast, state-owned literary journals were sold only through the national post office, which to this day holds a monopoly on their distribution. As a result, most journals were simply unavailable in normal bookstores or retail outlets, especially outside the cities where they were published. Thus, ordinary shoppers and impulse buyers could never see them on store shelves, and even regular readers often found it hard to obtain copies. This placed these journals at an even greater disadvantage relative to the now-ubiquitous popular magazines.

Taking *Beijing Literature* as an example, as recently as 1999, among eleven readers' letters published in the May issue, four complained about the difficulty of obtaining a retail copy of the journal even at relatively accessible locations in Shandong, Henan, and Sichuan provinces. This was something of a vicious-circle problem: unlike publishing houses, which were able to start self-marketing (*zi ban faxing*) after the late 1980s, most literary journals could not afford to organize their own marketing and distribution efforts, which might have increased their subscriptions. At the same time, private bookstores and bookstalls—an increasingly large proportion of the retailers—were reluctant to take literary journals because of their low and unstable sales figures, which were the result of poor marketing.

As noted earlier, from the 1950s to the late 1970s, this cultural system had served a useful purpose both for the government and for writers; readers stayed with these journals for lack of a better option, despite the system's disregard for their tastes and needs. Yet even after journals' readerships and incomes began to plummet during the mid-1980s, most journal editors seemed content to rely on government sponsorship to maintain their privileged positions, and saw little need for deep reforms. Newer forms of media were constantly looking outward and striving to meet the public's needs and wants; in contrast, literary journals—and their writers—tended to turn inward toward personal and individual concerns and to become more and more elitist. The journals were filled with experimental works by a new generation of writers; these works were interspersed with difficult critical articles that played intellectual games and spouted academic jargon and theory. In the second half of the 1980s, a deep split developed between popular and "serious" literature—a split that had not really existed in Socialist China up to that point—with most writers and editors viewing the market with barely concealed hostility. They saw that "market-stall literature" sold well, but they also felt that it was tasteless, that it pandered to the most vulgar desires of the masses, whereas serious literature of high artistic quality could appeal only to a small group of discriminating readers.

One can agree with such editors that quality literature is unlikely to appeal to the broader public and that literary journals ought to focus on a small, cultivated, and well-informed elite. Unfortunately, in the competitive cultural market of the late 1980s and 1990s, only a tiny number of such elite journals could survive—certainly not the hundreds left over from the socialist system.

Another mindset inherited from the socialist cultural system, and one that editors still had to contend with during the reform period, was that literary journals—like book publishers and other public institutions under the dual-track system (*shuanggui zhi*) in China—were expected to bear the standard of "socialist spiritual civilization." In other words, they were required to consider the "social benefits" of their endeavors even while carefully heeding the bottom line. Essentially, this meant keeping in lock-step with shifting and sometimes contradictory government policies and regulations.

This double-function resulted in occasional government censorship of journals, especially those journals published within easy reach of the central government. For example, in the several years after the 1989 student movement, *Beijing Literature* was punished for its radical "bourgeois liberalism" during the 1980s—in other words, for its relatively avant-garde content—and its senior editors Lin Jinlan and Li Tuo were replaced by Hao Ran, a former peasant writer who had risen to prominence during the Cultural Revolution. During his tenure, the journal adopted a strongly politicized and conservative approach, and in doing so lost many of the readers it had been able to retain until 1989. The journal's reputation plummeted, until by the early 1990s subscriptions had dropped to just a few thousand copies. A related point is that even though government supervision of literary journals has become much less strict in the 1990s, infighting in the complex bureaucracies that control these journals often leads to mutual accusations of spiritual pollution (*jingshen wuran*)—accusations that the government cannot ignore. Here, the journals are their own worst enemies.[23]

But more significant today than government censorship is the "dead hand" structural legacy of socialist cultural institutions, which continues to burden the administrative and personnel systems of journals and which inevitably results in economic inefficiencies. Income from journal sales and government funding hardly covers the operating costs of most journals—costs that include manuscript fees, printing expenditures, and editorial salaries. Yet journals incur major expenses besides these in maintaining their employees in the socialist lifestyle to which they are now accustomed. These costs include housing, medical expenses, and other benefits—and not just for present employees but for retirees as well.[24]

Faced with an impossible situation—with countless mouths to feed but huge annual deficits—many literary journals have been driven or at the very least tempted to abandon elitism and pitch themselves to the lowest common denominator of taste—in other words, reinvent themselves as popular magazines. It is here that the contradictory demands of market capitalism and welfare socialism appear in starkest relief. For example, the journal *Qingchun* (Youth; formerly *Nanjing wenyi* [Nanjing Art and Literature]) was once a highly respected "pure literature" journal that published many promising young writers in the early 1980s. By the late 1980s, having been hit by government funding cuts, this journal was in debt to the tune of around seventy thousand yuan. Its editorial board had no choice but to revamp the journal as a popular magazine that published so-called "social reportage" (*shehui jishi*), a euphemism for yellow journalism of the sort that highlights crime, sex, and strange events. In 1994, eighteen renowned local writers signed a petition to "save *Youth*," arguing eloquently that this once pure literary journal had degenerated into vulgar market-stall literature and demanding a return to the good old days. In response, the editor in chief, rejoicing that the journal was once again profitable, made it clear that the market was ruthless and that his job was to help the journal and its employees survive in the new cultural environment, even if this required some painful changes.[25]

In the 1990s, many more journals—especially those at the provincial and municipal levels—followed *Youth*'s path. These included *Tianjin wenxue* (Tianjin Literature, renamed *Qingchun yuedu* [Youth Reading]), *Hunan wenxue* (Hunan Literature, now known as *Mu yu* [Native Tongue]), *Mengya* (First Growth, from Shanghai), and *Huaxi* (Flower Creek, from Guizhou). All of these journals transformed themselves into popular magazines and selected as their target audience urban teenagers and young adults; to attract these segments, they published entertainment news, hot topical issues, fashion spreads, and sentimental romances.

Clearly, literary journals that hoped to preserve their reputations and avoid the pulp-fiction route, and still survive, would have to make drastic changes. In the second part of this chapter, I describe the often fascinating attempts made by mainstream literary journals during the past decade or so to hold on to their readers and seek alternative sources of funding. I will focus on *Beijing Literature*, which like most literary journals of similar quality has gradually and painfully learned to juggle the contradictory demands of the market, of business interests, of readers and writers, and of the government. In the process, its editors have had to rethink their very conception of "literature," as well as their social functions in a society that is markedly different from twenty years ago.

2. Flirting with the Sirens of Commerce: Initial Experiments

Like many other literary journals, *Beijing Literature* has adopted various strategies to raise money and improve its readership base. Some changes, especially the recent adoption of a new format and focus, have undoubtedly made the journal more reader-friendly, besides carving it a valuable niche in the cultural market. Others, such as the introduction of "enterprise literature" and certain ill-advised publicity gimmicks, have perhaps brought in extra revenue, but at a cost to the journal's overall quality and reputation, and besides this have blurred the distinctions between literature and naked commerce.

The first advertisement (*guanggao*) in *Beijing Literature* appeared on the back cover of the January 1988 issue: an ad for the Yixing Polyester Factory (Yixing dilun chang). Since then, almost every issue has carried similar ads, most of them promoting industrial products, from synthetic fabrics to electrical parts. These ads generally consist of a central piece of plain, dull prose introducing the company and its products, along with some uniform and often badly shot photographs. Very often a photo of the company's general manager or president takes pride of place.

At first glance, selling ad space looks like a sensible way for literary journals to raise funds. But as the above examples illustrate, most ads that *Beijing Literature* has accepted are hardly the sort to appeal to readers. Few subscribers are likely to rush out and buy industrial materials from the Fangshan Cement Plant or the Yanshan Iron and Steel Corporation. Obviously, the journal editors have been willing to run the ads of almost any company that is willing to pay for the space, no matter how incongruous. And equally clearly, the reward for buying the ad space is not greater sales of industrial products—since few readers can or would want to purchase them—but rather, kudos for the company's managers and presidents. Hence their prominently displayed photos.

There is other evidence besides that these ads are meant primarily to bolster the reputations of the industrial managers and attract their financial support. Promotional pieces have begun to appear in literary journals under the rubric "enterprise literature" (*qiye wenxue*), or "corporate alliance literature" (*lianyin wenxue*). Both terms are euphemisms. One article that discussed this trend is quoted below:

Corporate Alliance Literature refers to a marriage between writers and entrepreneurs or reformers. It is a product of the market economy. Some influential literary journals, such as *People's Literature*, *Beijing Literature* and *Zhongshan*, treat it as one of their major interests. Corporate Alliance Literature uses reportage techniques to describe the important developments taking place among enterprises, aiming to inspire other entrepreneurs to emulate their success. The writers are mostly cultural figures, some even are well known authors. Corporate Alliance Literature has already built up a valuable treasure trove of spiritual resources for enterprise culture, while at the same time helping to support serious literature. Corporate Alliance Literature differs from both ordinary advertising formats and news reports in that it ultimately remains a literary genre: it exemplifies literature moving in sync with the times.[26]

This account seems unduly optimistic about the effects of such writing on the contemporary development of the genre reportage. The reportage (*baogao wexue*) that was popular in the 1980s often exposed serious social problems and voiced ordinary people's concerns and, of course, sometimes also praised the achievements of socialism.[27] In contrast, enterprise literature focuses on glorifying model enterprises and successful entrepreneurs who "rise above the waves of economic reform." This should be no surprise, since the journals depend on such entrepreneurs for financial support. For example, the reportage "Hong liu" (Red Flood), which appeared in the September 1989 issue of *Beijing Literature*, waxed lyrical about the excellent management of the Yanshan Iron and Steel Complex, and the ad on the back cover was also for the Yanshan Iron and Steel Complex. Similar examples are easy to find, appearing as they do in almost every issue of the journal since 1989. Obviously, the ads and the "reportage" are closely linked and are designed to form a promotional whole: the manager and his firm are praised, and then the firm advertises its products.[28]

This sort of "business alliance" between literary journals and industries began as a piecemeal and occasional practice, as is evident from the initially inconsistent appearance of back-cover ads and the surreptitious placement of articles under the established genre "reportage." Gradually, however, the ads became much more regular and the reportage evolved into out-and-out promotion. Then in 1992, after Deng Xiaoping's Southern Tour and the Fourteenth Party Congress, the government began urging cultural institutions (*wenhua shiye*) to transform themselves into cultural enterprises (*wenhua chanye*) and to aim for self-sufficiency. Journals would now have to "make use of their cultural background to provide cultural services [to other industries])" and "diversify into other business ventures" in order to make a profit. They would also have to develop "management and market consciousness" and pay greater attention to "economic results."[29] Since the government looked so favorably on "alliances between enterprises and cultural institutions" (*wen qi lian yin*)—sometimes even helping arrange them—literary journals felt completely justified in greatly expanding their experiments in enterprise literature and using it as their main method for raising the money they needed to survive. Besides the promotional articles, various "symposia on enterprise literature" were co-organized by journal editorial boards and enterprises; these were often attended by cultural officials from the Propaganda Department of the local municipal government and by representatives of the Federation of Literary and Art Circles.[30]

Now journals, instead of waiting for writers and enterprises to come to them, began acting more aggressively as commercial go-betweens. For example, *Beijing Literature*, in its last two issues of 1991, ran a notice from the editorial board announcing that the journal was holding an enterprise literature contest, styled as Stars of Enterprise (qiye zhi xing). The entries would consist of reportage about the achievements of China's most promising companies. If published, both the writer and the subject of the report—represented by the entrepreneur in charge of the company—would receive a Star of Enterprise award. The notice also called for enterprises to express their willingness to be featured in this contest, and noted that if the enterprise could not produce a suitable article itself, the journal would be willing to provide a qualified writer to carry out this service.[31] After 1992, the journal began running a special section, also titled "Stars of Enterprise," to publish the best competition entries. By this stage, enterprise literature had taken over virtually all the space in the journal that had once been allotted to true reportage. In 1992, there had been only nine reportage articles; the following year, there were thirty-one enterprise literature pieces, five of them in the December issue alone. As a result of its success, this special section was revived in 1996 as a regular feature. It continues to this day, although in 1997 the section's name was changed to "Da jingjie" (Grand Views).

There is not enough space here for a complete example of enterprise literature, but to give a taste of this new genre, and to show that even in more recent issues it remains unashamedly promotional, I will quote some representative passages from the article "Chuangye zhi xing jin fengliu: ji Changchun yi qi cheshen fushu diyi fenchang changzhang Guo Xuecai" ("A Creative Star Shines Its Heart Out: A Report on Factory Manager Guo Xuecai of the Changchun No. 1 Autoworks Affiliated Autobody Branch Factory"). The piece begins:

The spring breeze of reform and opening up has blown over our whole great nation, and group after group of outstanding entrepreneurs have continuously emerged, like dazzling bright pearls, or like bamboo shoots after spring rains. These "bright pearly" entrepreneurs are a precious resource for our Party and people, and Comrade Guo Xuecai of the Changchun No. 1 Autoworks Affiliated Autobody Branch Factory is one of their most brilliant representatives.[32]

The writer next offers some background about the company, and then relates a "moving" experience:

The perceptive Guo Xuecai, noticing my excitement, said, "The weather is good today: it's not windy or raining. I'll give you a tour of the factory." I followed Guo into the workshop, and immediately I was completely dazzled: I stared with my mouth wide open and feasted my eyes. The whole workshop was totally outfitted with top quality modern equipment . . . and was extremely clean; there was no noise except for the quiet humming of machines, which the workers were operating in a relaxed but methodical manner.[33]

The piece then proceeds for several more pages in the same "purple prose" manner, offering a rags-to-riches account of Guo Xuecai's life and his determined struggle to overcome all kinds of difficulties, until he eventually set up a collective rural factory (*xiangban qiye*), perfected its operations, and was showered with various entrepreneurial awards and accolades from the government.

Presumably, such fulsome flattery disguised as reportage attracts very few readers, apart from employees of the featured enterprises themselves. Yet enterprise literature has been a constant feature of many literary journals for what is now more than a decade, so it must be profitable. Editors are doubtless willing to sacrifice some space for these articles in order to raise the money to continue publishing serious literature in the other sections of their journals—a practice the editor of *Beijing Literature* justified with this vivid phrase: "On the stage that money builds, literature can sing its song" (jinji datai, wenxue changxi).

There are many other ways besides enterprise literature that literary journals have tried to develop their corporate relations and improve their finances. These have included various activities organized by journals but sponsored by enterprises, such as symposia on certain writers or literary works, excursions for staff and writers to scenic retreats to "broaden their life experience," and especially literary competitions and awards, generally named after the sponsors. For example, in 1993, *Beijing Literature* set up a Suburban Tourism Cup (Jingjiao luyou bei), named after a travel company, for the best piece of fiction submitted to the journal; and in 1996 it announced the Shenhua Cup (Shenhua bei) for fiction and the Jiumuwang Cup (Jiumuwang bei) for lyric prose, each named after its respective corporate sponsor.

These efforts to formalize relationships between journals and enterprises have been most obvious in the establishment of Boards of Corporate Directors (Dongshi hui, or Lishi hui). For instance, since 1994, page one of every issue of *Beijing Literature* has listed the members of the journal's Board of Corporate Directors; this board comprises more than twenty entrepreneurs from all kinds of businesses, along with a few government officials and public figures. The members of this board change about once a year. According to an announcement in the April 1994 issue, the board's purpose is "to build a bridge between writers and entrepreneurs" that will "provide writers with broader opportunities to gain real life experience of ongoing economic reforms" as well as "help enterprises to build up their enterprise culture." Despite these high-sounding words, far from being a group of business specialists who offer advice to the journal's editors on how best to improve their economic performance—as one might expect from the term Board of Corporate Directors—these boards are apparently just another strategy that journals have resorted to in order to attract sponsors; they are used in conjunction with advertising and enterprise literature. In other words, a hefty financial contribution to the journal is the only criterion for joining the board. Evidence for this comes from the random and constantly changing selection of enterprises that supply the board members. Most of the leaders of these enterprises have no knowledge of or experience with cultural ventures. Also, when one compares the back-cover ads and promotional pieces in relevant issues with the names of the directors on the board, there is considerable overlap. Clearly, the journal must be offering entrepreneurs "packages" in return for their generosity—that is, in return for financial support, they are offering full-page ads on a number of issue covers, a glowing reportage article, one-year membership on the board, and the company name displayed prominently inside the journal's front cover.

Sometimes, as part of the deal, the journal even includes poems and other short pieces composed by the sponsoring entrepreneurs themselves. This is an especially effective strategy for a company manager or director who once considered himself a "literary youth" and whose creative aspirations had been frustrated. For example, in the January 1999 issue of *Beijing Literature*, the back cover offers a full-page ad for Beijing Badaling Tourism Corporation (Beijing badaling luyou fazhan youxian gongsi), with a photo of General Manager Qiao Yu prominently positioned. On the inside back cover is another picture of Qiao along with one of his poems in classical style, and a short curriculum vitae stating that he belongs to the Beijing Writers Association and once published a collection of poetry. Not surprisingly, Qiao Yu's name also appears at the top of the list of board members as Chairman of the Board of Corporate Directors for 1999.

Boards of Corporate Directors are lucrative, and have been adopted by a number of literary journals. They have turned into a quite common method for attracting financial sponsors.

A related phenomenon, and even more peculiar, has been "coeditorships." The term is misleading, however. Instead of constantly begging for money from several sponsors, a journal can (with luck) find a single sponsoring enterprise willing to donate tens or hundreds of thousands of yuan. As a reward for such outstanding magnanimity, this sponsor is named journal "coeditor"—the front cover says so. For instance, the journal *Zhongshan* was at one point being "coedited" by the Jiangsu Writers Association and the Xuzhou Tobacco Company; *Dajia* (Master), by Yunnan People's Publishing House and the Red River Tobacco Company; and *Shanhua* (Mountain Flower), by Guizhou Writers Association and the Huang Guoshu Business Group. Many of these "coeditors" are tobacco companies, which are highly profitable businesses with few places to spend their advertising money because of restrictions on promoting tobacco. As with the Boards of Corporate Directors, there is no evidence that these "coeditors" play any direct role in deciding the journals' content or editorial policy, or even its business practices. They are simply being acknowledged for their generosity.

Certainly, not all sponsors and coeditors of literary journals are engaged in completely unrelated businesses. Some are cultural institutions themselves, or they are media companies such as newspapers or televsion stations, which actually make money in the burgeoning cultural market and have been encouraged by local governments to help out their poor literary cousins. For example, *Shanghai Literature* has been sponsored by *Laodong bao* (Shanghai Worker's News), and *Yuhua* (Raindrops) has been assisted by Jiangsu Television Station. But generally speaking, there is little evidence of corporate synergy between most literary journals and their sponsors.

Part of the reason for the hands-off approach of sponsoring enterprises is the ambiguous identity of cultural institutions such as literary journals under the contradictory demands of the present "dual-track system" in China. Although the government has been encouraging these institutions to become self-supporting, it still refuses to give up actual ownership, and it continues to maintain tight control over the publishing industry, even since the Fifteenth Party Congress in 1997, when a bold plan was announced to convert state-owned enterprises into shareholding ones. This control is exerted through the strict license-number system, which covers both journals and books, and through various subsequent campaigns against illegal publishing and the selling of book-license numbers (see Chapter 3). This situation has discouraged further privatization of the kind that has taken place in some other areas of business.

Also, most of these corporate relationships have not been built on the foundations of real mutual interest; this is indicated by their generally short-lived nature. Often, the sponsoring entrepreneur plays the role of a cultural philanthropist, in some cases acting out of a sense of obligation to the journal president or editor in chief. So if the entrepreneur's company runs into difficulties and begins to lose money, or if there is a change of personnel on either the company's or the journal's side, the sponsorship deal normally falls by the wayside. And as we noted, the commercial returns of advertising in literary journals are generally negligible owing to their small readership and the fact that readers of literature were not necessarily the target customers of the sponsor. Overall, therefore, these experimental alliances between literary journals and randomly selected enterprises are more like one-night stands than serious relationships: they fail to benefit the sponsors in any tangible economic way; and they do not lead to any permanent changes in the management practices of the journals of the sort that would make them more efficient, profitable, and independent.

Besides allying themselves with enterprises, journal editors have dreamed up many other ideas, some of them quite ludicrous, in their efforts to transform their journals into profitable businesses. For instance, once the government began encouraging cultural institutions to offer various social services and to develop culture-related businesses, the journal *Mengya* (First Growth) tried to develop its own "service empire," which involved retailing books and magazines, investing in the stock market, and entering the restaurant business.[34] Often these sorts of desperate moneymaking ventures, far from improving journals' finances, greatly damaged the collective image of journals without really stemming their financial losses.

This was especially evident when journals began trying to exploit the reputation and appeal of literature among those ordinary people who still saw publication in a literary journal as a great honor. For example, journals arranged various correspondence classes (*chuangzuo hanshou ban*), where, for a high fee, students could learn creative writing; they also organized symposia or training sessions, administered literary competitions and awards, and published collections of winning works. These kinds of practices had been introduced in the late 1980s by prestigious journals and institutions such as *People's Literature* and the Lu Xun Literary Academy (Lu Xun wenxueyuan), for the serious purpose of training young writers. Gradually they deteriorated into shady cultural business ventures, as nothing more than bilking schemes.

Some editors were even willing to publish contributors' writings for a fee—although they disguised the fact that this was simply vanity publishing by referring to these fees as tuition, registration, or sales costs. For example, in the March 17, 1993, issue of *Literature Press*, there was an ad for the Correspondence Center of *Chunfeng* (Spring Breeze), a monthly literary journal based in Liaoning province. It stated that the tuition fee for their advanced class was one hundred yuan, and that students in that class would send ten pieces of writing for tutorial comments; the best of those pieces would then be selected for publication in the journal. The center also advertised a "popular fiction" class, again with a hundred-yuan tuition fee. Students would submit one piece of fiction at the end of the class, and the journal would arrange to publish a special collection of these pieces.

These practices were so poorly regulated that they soon attracted the attention of individual charlatans, who made money by inventing fake literary organizations or journals, then hoodwinking contributors from far-flung regions by promising to publish their writings for a fee. For example, in 1993, one obscure group advertised a "Contest to Discover One Hundred Chinese Poet Laureates." Each entrant would pay a fee of 18.5 yuan; when the contest was over, they would receive a copy of the "Encyclopedia of Modern Chinese Poetry," in which the poems of these "poet laureates" would be collected. The contest turned out to be a scam; and no such "encyclopedia" was ever published. The situation became so serious that in 1994 a forum, "Weinai haishi chouxue" (Feeding or Exploiting), initiated by letters from a group of angry readers deceived by such practices, was held under the auspices of *Literature Press* to expose the scams of various literary organizations and journals.[35]

The negative publicity surrounding shady ventures such as these did little to help the circulation figures of the more reputable journals. At best, it was perhaps the last straw, the one that persuaded many editors that a more rational approach to reform was necessary.

3. A More Businesslike Approach to Literary Journal Publishing

By the late 1990s, after several disheartening years spent begging for money from rich entrepreneurs, and after taking stock of the increasing commercialization of literature and of the development of a cultural market in China, the editors of most literary journals were forced to rethink their piecemeal approaches to economic reform. Many concluded that in order to solve their root problems and compete with other products on the cultural market, they would have to engage themselves much more closely with that market and with the radical structural changes it was undergoing. More specifically, they realized that as editors, they would have to develop a more business-oriented attitude and thoroughly overhaul their management practices. In this final section, I outline some of these changes.

These changes fall under four main categories: broadening the definition of literature; marketing to a target readership (in other words, becoming more "reader friendly"); improving the appearance and packaging of journals; and developing synergistic alliances with businesses in related sectors.

The first noticeable change was that editors abandoned their narrow and conventional definitions of literature, and instead embraced the concept of "literature broadly defined" (*da wenxue*). This approach allowed them to include more general, culture-oriented content that would appeal to a wider audience, and to promote new genres that were marginal, mixed, or undefined. The rationale behind this change was that since 1989, although popular culture circles seemed to have adopted an unwritten "contract" with the government to avoid political subjects—a development that allowed nonthreatening, profit-seeking press media such as entertainment newspapers and sensationalist magazines to bloom—there was still much debate among educated people about intellectual and social issues. This debate sometimes indirectly challenged the political status quo. Literary journals picked up on this debate by including more articles on such issues. This trend was launched by *Tianya* (Frontiers), a literary journal from the remote southern special economic zone of Hainan Island, masterminded by two well-known writers, Han Shaogong and Jiang Zidan.

Since changing its format in 1996, *Frontiers* has developed various "brandname" columns such as "Minjian yuwen" (Folk Speech) and "Zuojia lichang" (Writer's Position). The former column prints offerings (letters, diary extracts, and the like) from nonprofessional writers that deal with everyday life. The latter publishes various writers' views on social and cultural issues and current affairs. The issues raised in these columns are relevant to readers' lives and often raise politically sensitive questions, or pressing cultural issues. The opinions presented are often insightful and positive, and the journal editors lead the discussions in a serious and careful way, always emphasizing the need to communicate with a mass audience, not just with a narrow circle of literati. With these innovations, *Frontiers* quickly attracted readers from many social groups and established a cutting-edge reputation in literary publishing.

Inspired by the success of *Frontiers*, many other journals ventured out from their narrow, fenced-in definitions of literature and staked their claims over the latest cultural trends; their hope was to develop brand recognition and loyalty among readers. For example, in 1999, *Beijing Literature* began running radical debates on intellectual history and cultural/political issues; these included pieces of incisive cultural criticism by controversial young scholars such as Yu Jie and Mo Luo, whose works have often been banned by the government. The contents page in the February 1999 issue of *Beijing Literature* gave a good sense of the broad cultural exploration the journal was now encouraging. There were regular sections titled "Voices" (Shengyin), "Thought" (Sixiang), "Today's Writing" (Jinri xiezuo), "Contending Ideas" (Baijia zhengyan), "Reinterpreting the Classics" (Jiuwen xindu), "Memories" (Jiyi), and "Observing the Century" (Shiji guancha). Among these, only "Today's Writing" included short stories or fictional prose; the other sections all amounted to intellectual debates, many of which presented strong challenges to communist totalitarianism. A representative article in the "Voices" section, "Xiaoming de maotouying" (The Unpleasant Sound of the Owl), discussed the role of intellectuals as cultural critics—specifically, as critics of the power hierarchy. In a similar vein, three articles on the Czech dissident writer and statesman Vaclav Havel appeared in the section "Thought"; one of these was a translation of Havel's 1978 essay, "Power of the Powerless," which discussed the value of resisting totalitarian regimes. A controversial article, "Shui wujie le makesi" (Who Misunderstood Marx) appeared in "Contending Ideas"; and a similarly suggestive piece, "Weixian six-iang yu yanlun ziyou" (Dangerous Minds and Free Speech), appeared in the section "Reinterpreting the Classics."

Other journals have experimented with similarly broadened concepts of literature—for example, with nonfiction texts and hybridized genres (*kua wenti*), and sometimes even with visual art and critical articles on painting and music. Some examples: since 1999, *Huanghe* (Yellow River) in Shanxi province and *Xiaoshuo jia* (Storyteller) in Tianjin have shifted their focus almost entirely to literary and cultural history and social criticism. Both often dig out little-known historical facts and controversial issues; according to the editors, the point of all this is to attract "all intellectuals whose education is above secondary school level." Similarly, *Mountain Flower* from Guizhou and *Lotus* from Hunan are venturing into areas beyond pure literature. The front pages of *Mountain Flower* now constitute a gallery of contemporary avant-garde art; the same journal also publishes a regular section on art criticism. For its part, *Lotus* is developing a section, "Arts Frontiers" (Yishu qianyan), to cover the unofficial arts scene, from rock music and fringe plays to independent films.

These content changes reflect a new awareness among editors that they must target specific social groups and promote specific kinds of writers. For instance, *Mountain Flower* claims to be the voice of the generation of writers born since the 1960s (*wan sheng dai*) especially those from Nanjing; and *Lotus* has started a section called "Remodeling the Post-70s Generation" (Chongsu qishi niandai hou), which features young women writers from Shanghai and Beijing. Both journals are trying to appeal to "Generation X" readers through more lively and fashion-conscious presentations.

One of the most interesting examples of successful targeting is the recently remodeled *Writer*. This once elite literary journal from Changchun now pitches itself exclusively to young urban professionals. Beginning with the first issue of 2000, the journal's editors altered their stated mission from "*Writer* for writers" to "*Writer* for readers and the market," and created a fresh "yuppie" look for the journal—a blatant imitation of *The New Yorker*.[36] Indeed, the journal's promotions brazenly announced that their product was "the new *Writer*, a magazine which deserves the name '*Chinese New Yorker*.'" Besides offering carefully selected fiction and poetry in sections headed

"Golden Short Stories" (Jin duanpian) and "Poet's Space" (Shiren kongjian), the journal now includes a new column, "Material Life" (Wuzhi shenghuo), which reports on trendy places and recent parties in Shanghai, as well as various sections surveying the latest literary and artistic trends on the international scene, with catchy titles such as "New Yorker Miscellany" (Niuyueke zahui), "On the Banks of the River Seine" (Sainahe pan), and "Non-Native Speaker" (Fei muyu). Readers' survey forms are now being inserted between the pages so that the editors can find out which kinds of articles and features the readers like and dislike, and which features of the journal attract them.

Many editors also realized that besides developing more attractive content, they would have to improve the appearance and packaging of their journals. "Serious" literary journals had seldom showed much concern about their appearance. The design of almost all journals was simple to the point of monotony; moreover, paper quality was poor and there were hardly any pictures. Over the past several years, many journals have been working hard to improve these product aspects and to develop a more refined and even glossy style, the goal being to retain readers who might otherwise switch to fashion and style magazines and color tabloids. Besides resorting to the innovative cover designs and attention-grabbing section heads noted earlier, many journals now print in full color on glossy imported paper, and liven their pages with plenty of eye-catching art and photographs. *Master*, published by Yunnan People's Publishing House, was one of the first (in 1994) to revolutionize formatting in this way. It replaced the Chinese 16mo size that was uniform among literary journals with International 16mo, and it began printing its product on high-density paper. Its new format was also innovative, with wide margins filled with notes and summaries, and with elegant and unique art for both the covers and the contents. Following the example of *Master*, other journals such as *Mountain Flower*, *Lotus*, and *Writer* began competing to "change their faces." *Writer* now begins and ends with several beautifully presented full-page advertisements for Eastern and Western commodities, most of these expensive fashion accessories and luxury products that appeal to upwardly mobile urban readers. The professional graphic design and glossy full-color printing could compete with even top imported fashion magazines like *Vogue* (Chinese name, *Shishang*). Also, the journal hires its graphic artists and prints the journal in southern cities such as Shanghai and Shenzhen, where printing technology is more advanced.

Of course, these impressive changes could not have been made without plenty of outside investment and the support of related businesses such as advertising and media companies. This points to the third way that the more progressive journals have been trying to adapt to the market. *Writer* has transformed itself successfully in large part by forging synergistic alliances with businesses; in the near future, other journals will probably do the same.

In *Writer's* case, the editors developed a partnership with Panorama Cultural Development Corp. (Quanjing wenhua fazhan youxian gongsi), an advertising company in Shanghai, whose owner Xia Shang is a writer and artist himself. Panorama uses its specialist expertise and business contacts to look after the graphic design and the later-stage production of the journal; it also serves as the journal's advertising agent, which leaves the editors free to focus on content. This cooperation has sharply improved the quality of the ads and the journal's overall look. Also, the partner company has taken charge of retail distribution in southern China. Thus, although the journal is still distributed mainly through the post office system, readers can now obtain it directly from retail outlets such as supermarkets, grocery stores, bookstores, and magazine racks.

A final step that literary journal editors have taken—one that borrows from more popular publishing and cultural enterprises—involves drastically improving their promotion methods. In particular, they have invented or imitated various hyping techniques and publicity gimmicks to market their journals and create excitement among potential readers. For instance, one of the problems facing many literary journals today is a shortage of quality manuscripts. This is a result of the relatively low manuscript fees they can afford to pay (books and television screenplays are more lucrative in this regard). Some journals have now established literary competitions with huge awards to attract famous writers, whose works then pull in more readers. In this way, in 1995–96, *Master* called for manuscripts for the Red River Literary Award, sponsored by Red River Tobacco Company. It paid out what at the time was the highest literary award ever—100,000 yuan—to Mo Yan's novel *Fengru feitun* (Big Breasts and Wide Hips). Since then, many other journals have been giving out "monster awards" (*ju jiang*), or they have been offering high manuscript fees. In this vein, as far back as 1993, *Guangzhou Art and Literature* had increased its regular manuscript payments to 100 yuan per thousand characters, at a time when the national average was 30 yuan. Clearly, this magazine had set out to become the highest-paying journal in the country, the point being to attract the best writers.[37] Even *Contemporary*, a prestigious journal affiliated with People's Literature Publishing House, joined this game. In 2000, it advertised a Contemporary Literary Award of 100,000 yuan. This "relay award" (*jieli sai*) is given out each year to a writer whose work has been published in *Contemporary* and who is judged the best among six finalists in that year's bimonthly contests. Journals are claiming that these literary prizes and high manuscript fees are intended "to show the value of quality literature"; however, it is clear that they are mainly trying to take advantage of the enormous publicity surrounding these gimmicks to advertise for their sponsoring companies while attracting both writers and readers. Perhaps the most blatant illustration of the connection between such contests and journal fund-raising is *Beijing Literature*'s Stars of Enterprise Competition, described earlier. Here, the quality of the literature obviously matters less than the support offered by the enterprises in question.

Another common promotional technique is for editors to claim that they have "discovered" hot new authors and the latest trends in writing. For example, in 1994 and 1995 alone, *Beijing Literature* promoted "new experience" fiction (*xin tiyan xiaoshuo*), *Shanghai Literature* advocated "new urban fiction" (*xin shimin xiaoshuo*), *Zhongshan* raved about "new state literature" (*xin zhuang-tai wenxue*), *Spring Breeze* coined the term "journalistic fiction" (*xinwen xiao-shuo*), and *Fiction World* claimed to be introducing the new genre of "television fiction"(TV *xiaoshuo*). These vivid-sounding but vaguely defined labels were much more effective at promoting the journals, making them sound cutting edge, than at bringing to light actual changes in literary styles.

Finally, a publicity gimmick favored by virtually all of these journals is, of course, to make a big noise in the media trumpeting all their radical format and content changes, in the hope of grabbing new readers. Many of the "reports" and "news stories" about these changes are actually written by the journal editors themselves and then published in other magazines or newspapers. This practice, known as "soft advertising," is also common in book promotion today (see the account of An Boshun in Chapter 2). The result has been a dramatic expansion of newspaper supplements and book review papers. To give just one example, the first issue of *Lotus* in 2000 included an entire section offering fulsome media praise from the past year for the recent format changes made to *Lotus*, drawn from twenty-seven different newspapers and magazines. In just two weeks at the end of June and beginning of July, more than a dozen articles were published in major newspapers such as *Guangming Daily*, *China Reading Weekly*, *Literature Press*, *Chinese Cultural Press*, and *Chinese Book Business Review*. Many of these had virtually identical wording.[38]

How effective will these various format and content changes be in preserving literary journals from extinction? Much will depend on how well "literature"—a concept that itself keeps changing—sells in the new cultural market, and on how much leeway journal editors will be allowed in pushing through their reforms. Journals such as *Foshan wenyi* (Foshan Art and Literature), a popular Guangdong literary magazine with a circulation of some 500,000 over the past several years, are able to run themselves completely as businesses, from management to artistic conception, printing, and distribution.[39] However, other journals closer to the central government, such as *Beijing Literature*, have to be careful not to overstep the boundaries, even when desperate to stem their losses. For example, after *Beijing Literature*'s fifth issue of 1999 was recalled and all copies were confiscated, because of a radical article extolling democracy, the editorial board had to engage in self-criticism—a bitter reminder that the magazine was still living in the nation's capital, "at the feet of the emperor" (zai tianzi jiao xia). In later issues, some of the journal's more radical sections, such as "Voices" and "Thought," disappeared entirely.

Thus, Zhong Renfa, current president and editor in chief of *Writer*, was able to brag about *Writer*'s soaring sales figures: after its much-publicized changes, its circulation had jumped from eight thousand to eighteen thousand in just the first three months of 2000, despite its "handsome" cover-price hike from 6.00 to 14.80 yuan. Yet at the same time, Li Jingze, a veteran editor at *People's Literature*, was declaring cynically that "this was just the last leap before the fall" (miewang qian de changhuang yi tiao), and expressing doubt that such figures could be sustained once the initial surge of curiosity for the new product had subsided. Having witnessed so many waves of prosperity and decline over the past two decades, Li painted a gloomy future for literary journals on the market: "Where will the market economy bring literary journals? To their deathbed! In the end, at most two or three literary journals will manage to survive. A huge dinosaur is expiring."[40]

Yet perhaps Li is being too pessimistic, at least for journals like *Beijing Literature*, which are still fighting hard to adapt to the new realities. After its run-in with the government, and after deep discussions about how to jump-start its stalled circulation, the journal has apparently found a treadable path between politics and the market. Literature is once again its focus, rather than cultural criticism; however, it is also redoubling its efforts to appeal to more readers. These efforts are reflected in the journal's new format, launched in 2001—most notably in sections such as "Readable Fiction" (Haokan xiaoshuo) and "Bestselling Writers" (Zuojia renqi bang). The former follows on the heels of a successful, year-long forum titled "How to Make Fiction Readable" (Xiaoshuo ruhe cai neng haokan), which invited writers, critics, and readers to give their opinions on how more appealing literary works could be produced. The latter section obviously hopes to capitalize on the pull of popular writers by including their recent work and making them the focus of opinion pieces. The new format also includes a series of short pieces under the heading "Marvelous Writings from the Internet" (Wangluo qiwen); these consist of humorous and entertaining comments on a wide range of topics, from Chinese football to public figures, freshly "downloaded" from the Internet.

Yet *Beijing Literature* has not totally abandoned its controversial stance on contemporary political and social issues. Although careful to avoid the kinds of sensitive national topics that would lead to government reprisals, the journal has been trying to include more journalism features. For example, its new "Reportage" section imitates recent high-quality investigative reports in newspapers, such as Guangzhou's *Nanfang zhoumo* (Southern Weekend) and television programs like *Jiaodian fangtan* (Focus and Investigation) on Chinese Central TV; both of these have attracted a loyal following for their coverage of pressing social problems. *Beijing Literature*'s first issue of 2001 included a feature article with the promising title "The Latest Report on Upright Party Secretary Jiang Ruifeng's Anti-Corruption Measures" (Heilian shuji Jiang Ruifeng fan fubai zui xin baogao). Recently the journal has also published a series of investigative reports on reforms in high school education. Issues like these, although controversial, accord with the central government's current policies, so there is little risk that the journal will be penalized for covering them.

Beijing Literature has borrowed from its competitors by paying more attention to its readers. It now includes a Reader's Satisfaction Survey on the last page of every issue, and it runs a regular column, "Paper Exchange" (Zhishang jiaoliu), where readers' letters are published. Many readers have commented on the form and content of the journal itself. There is also a so-called "Hotline" (Re xian) column on page one, where readers can direct questions to the journal's contributors and receive responses.

Finally, *Beijing Literature*'s editorial board is adopting a much more businesslike and sensible attitude toward its contributors and sponsors. It promises that every submission will receive a response within one or two months, with comments and suggested revisions from the editors. In July 2001, the journal ran a notice inviting applications from distribution agents and retailers—a tacit admission that the journal would need to rationalize its marketing and distribution efforts in order to keep pace with its competitors.

One might conclude, then, that far from landing a deathblow on the journal's efforts at reform, *Beijing Literature*'s problems have compelled its editors to adopt a much more effective business model, but to do so in a way that does not sacrifice its reputation as a site for meaningful and incisive social commentary. We must wait to see whether these changes will result in corresponding improvements in the journal's circulation figures.

As is clear from this discussion, commercialization has had complex and unpredictable consequences for literary journals in China, and the results have been both positive and negative. Many "pure" literary journals have been forced to recast themselves as tabloids, but others have been able to thrive in the new environment, and to attract respectable numbers of regular readers. One thing is very clear: just as with the state-run publishing houses, no literary journal can ignore the changes in China's new cultural market and hope to survive. Almost every journal in China has had to overhaul itself with regard to both content and operating practices. As the example of *Beijing Literature* demonstrates, most have also had to adjust their marketing vision to factor in their duty to socialist ideals.

Only time will tell whether the creaking "dinosaur" of the socialist literary journal system will be able to soar like a bird in the cultural marketplace. Yet we can be sure that in the coming years, the concept of literature itself will be constantly reinvented in journals, just as it has been over the past decade throughout the publishing industry, in response to the far-reaching social transformations taking place in today's China.

Conclusion

LITERATURE IN A
MULTIMEDIA MILLENNIUM

THE 1990S IN CHINA were a time of rapid development in the mass media and entertainment industries, a result of the country's technical modernization and the growing commercialization of its society. Media and entertainment outlets exploded in number, with the resulting wave reaching newspapers, lifestyle magazines, karaoke bars, dance halls, and video arcades. Especially noticeable was the exponential growth in the television industry. According to official statistics, by 1999 there were 653 television stations in China, supplying programs to more than 350 million sets with over a billion viewers.[1] And all the provincial-level stations (more than forty of them) were now broadcasting nationally via satellite. In the 1980s there had been only a handful of stations in China. There is little doubt that television has become the most important medium in the lives of ordinary Chinese; it shapes their ideas and the popular culture as a whole. More and more television programs are being produced—especially entertainment shows and dramas—and their hosts and actors have become instant celebrities. Furthermore, television has become the most important platform for advertising and promoting products, be they everyday commodities such as soft drinks and washing powder or cultural products such as compact discs, films, and even books.

The growth of television during the 1990s was phenomenal. However, since 1997, and especially since 1999, the fastest-growing entertainment medium has been the Internet.[2] Personal computers and the Internet are quite new to China, and both are still considered luxuries available only to urban dwellers; that said, both have been spreading at an astonishing rate. By 2001, there were already twenty-six million Internet users in China—an increase of 56.8 percent in just one year.[3] Many users log on, if not using their home computers, in one of the countless Internet cafés that have sprung up recently in every Chinese city. Transnational telecommunications companies have been investing heavily in China, and as a result, that country's high-tech infrastructure, including its cable and broadband networks, has been developing rapidly. China is quickly becoming a member of the global telecommunications family. With its e-mail, Internet shopping, chat rooms, bulletin boards, and countless other capacities, the Internet has already begun altering ordinary Chinese lives and influencing cultural production and consumption.

All of these new media developments have inevitably changed how the Chinese, including Chinese writers, express their ideas and communicate with one another. They have also begun to challenge the traditional word-based print culture, which has long valued permanence and introspection. Visual images seem to be supplanting words as the basic building blocks of meaning, and as a result, people are shifting their focus away from "stable" printed books toward flickering television and computer screens.

Yet despite the obvious attractions of television, the Internet, and other new media, literary production in China continues to thrive to a remarkable degree. Indeed, as I have demonstrated throughout this study, the "marketization" of China has resulted in much greater variety, and better overall quality, of literary products compared to twenty years ago. Instead of being wiped out by the competing new media, the Chinese literary industry has learned to exploit these new media for its own purposes—namely, to promote and market literature through these media. At the same time, writers and publishers are constantly having to adjust their working methods in order to keep up with rapid developments in the media and entertainment industries and to continue profiting from that interaction. One result has been much closer partnerships among the various players in literary production and the new entertainment media.

In this final chapter of my study, I briefly describe some of the significant interactions between literature and other media, focusing especially on the two fastest-growing entertainment vehicles: television and the Internet. I will show how the new media have affected how literature is produced. Then I will show how writers, publishers, and others in the literature "business" have been exploiting the vast new markets and promotional avenues opened up by these new media. Central to all of this is the recently developed concept of multidimensional literary products (*duo wei chanpin*)—the idea that a single piece of writing can be repackaged and adapted to appeal to many different markets through a variety of media. I will argue that these products are, for many Chinese cultural entrepreneurs, a natural outgrowth of the commercializing reforms to literary production over the past two decades. Some critics wonder whether these products are literature at all, and such questions are valid. Yet because these multidimensional literary products represent the ultimate form of interaction between literature and the market, a look at these products may give us some idea of the future of literary production in a globalized China.

1. Television / Film Literature

National and local television stations mushroomed during the 1980s and 1990s, and this generated enormous demand for new entertainment programming. Especially popular were television series (*dianshi ju*), such as soap operas, multiepisode dramas, and situation comedies. These had been produced in the past;[4] for example, adaptations of classic Chinese novels such as *Honglou meng* (Dream of the Red Chamber, 1987) and *Xiyou ji* (Journey to the West, 1988) had been extremely popular in the mid-1980s. Other dramas had dealt with more contemporary topics, such as economic reform (in *Xin xing* [New Star]) and crime and policing (in *Bianyi jingcha* [Plainclothes Police]). Also highly popular were films and television series imported from Hong Kong, and television dramas from Japan, Singapore, and Latin America.[5] National awards were established to honor the best visual productions: the Fairy Awards became the Chinese equivalent of the Emmys, and the Golden Roosters emulated the Oscars.

But the real explosion in Chinese television production came in the 1990s, when, inspired by the huge commercial potential of the rapidly growing audience, private and state-owned cultural companies or film / television production companies, without actually running stations, began financing and producing television dramas and syndicating them for big profits to all the new national and local stations. The most successful of these cultural companies in the early 1990s was Beijing Television Art Center, which produced several blockbuster series that showed this market's huge potential. Among its biggest hits were the soap opera *Kewang* (Yearning, 1990), a family story set against the backdrop of the social upheaval of the past few decades; the sitcom *Bianjibu de gushi* (Stories from the Editorial Board, 1991), which satirized current social issues; and *Beijingren zai niuyue* (Beijing Sojourner in New York, 1993), a drama about recent Chinese immigrants to North America. For the rest of the 1990s, Beijing Television Art Center served as the model for many other production companies. According to statistics collected by Sheldon Lu, in 1994, more than 6,000 television episodes of soaps and sitcoms were produced; in 1995, more than 7,000; and in 1996, more than 10,000. This compares with just over 400 in 1984.[6]

Some have argued that exponential growth in the television sector has led to a decline in reading, with many serious books published today selling only a few thousand copies and many publishing houses suffering losses. Yet for many Chinese writers, the boom in television production was an unexpected opportunity for them to earn more money and boost their reputations. By the early 1990s, the demand for television products was causing a serious shortage of competent scriptwriters. Many respected writers of literature were being persuaded to write for television either full-time, or occasionally—that is, as a means to "subsidize" their serious work. Most of them could write one episode per week and receive eight to ten thousand yuan for it. In sharp contrast, a short story for a journal usually required much more labor and earned, at most, several hundred yuan.[7] Movies were also highly lucrative, although so few were being produced that finding work in filmscript writing was difficult.

As we saw in Chapter 1, Wang Shuo was a pacesetter, especially in television writing. After the success of *Yearning*, for which he was one of the scriptwriters, he cowrote the sitcom *Stories from the Editorial Board* with director Feng Xiaogang. Later, he adapted both into novellas. After this, he set up Sea Horse Film/TV Creative Studio to write and produce several television serials, as well as a cultural consultancy corporation that acted as an agent for television writers. He says he established these companies so that writers would be able to bargain collectively with producers for higher fees and other rights, and also to persuade more writers to involve themselves in this emerging industry.[8]

The vast majority of Chinese writers were slower than Wang Shuo to realize just how greatly television could benefit their careers. At first, many viewed writing for television (and film) as an inferior business, something to be done purely for money, unlike creating "pure literature." This attitude had its roots in the past hierarchical relationship between visual media and literature in which film and television had always been the stepchildren. Many writers especially disliked the idea that a director or producer could order them to rewrite their work. Some also feared that writing for television would destroy their creativity. They referred to film and television writing as "getting electrocuted" (*chudian*), a play on the fact that *dian*, "electricity," is part of the Chinese words for both television, *dianshi*, and films, *dianying*. In other words, television would be the death of their real work. However, this attitude gradually changed over the 1990s. More and more writers discovered that participating in this powerful new medium would bring them not only money but also much greater audience recognition—something they would never have gained just from writing. They could then transfer their invisible capital to other markets, including the market for their more "serious" literary works.

This change in attitude among writers has been strongly influenced by the work of the famous director Zhang Yimou, who according to some commentators single-handedly "saved Chinese literature"—or at least certain fortunate writers—from obscurity. Several writers suddenly attained international fame, and the sales of their books soared after being "touched" by

Zhang's "golden finger." Among them were Su Tong, from whose story "Qiqie chengqun" (Wives and Concubines) was filmed as *Da hong denglong gao gao gua* (Raise the Red Lantern); Liu Heng, whose novella "Fuxi Fuxi" (The Obsessed) was filmed as *Judou*; Yu Hua, whose novel *Huozhe* (To Live) was turned into an award-winning film; Chen Binyuan, whose "Wanjia su-song" (Qiuju's Lawsuit) became *Qiuju da guansi* (The Story of Qiuju); and of course, Mo Yan, whose novellas "Hong gaoliang" (Red Sorghum) and "Shifu yuelaiyue youmo" (Shifu, You'll Do Anything for a Laugh) were turned into the popular films *Red Sorghum* and *Xingfu shiguang* (Happy Times). Many writers now dream of being discovered by Zhang's "talent scouts"—it is said that he subscribes to several literary journals and has several assistants who regularly keep him up-to-date on the most recent writers. Some have even claimed, slightly tongue-in-cheek, that the renowned fifth-generation director has since the mid-1980s helped sell more "pure" literature than any Chinese Writers Association.

In light of the above developments, the past subservience of film and television to literature has been reversed. Some writers have succeeded in getting their fiction adapted as television series or films either by selling the rights for adaptation or by producing scripts themselves. This is a highly lucrative way to kill two birds with one stone. Others have reversed this process, having found that a successful television script can easily be turned into a best-selling novel or simply sold verbatim as a script in book form. By combining their earnings from the publishing and entertainment industries—in other words, by exploiting a single literary product in more than one market—many writers became millionaires during the 1990s.

The most outstanding example of television's power to elevate a writer is undoubtedly that of the Henan writer Ling Jiefang, better known by his pen name, Eryuehe. He worked for years in virtual anonymity on a historical novel based on court politics during the Qing dynasty (1644–1911). Then in 1999, he became a household name overnight, when the series *Yongzheng wangchao* (Yongzheng Dynasty), based on his 1991 novel *Yongzheng Huangdi* (The Emperor Yongzheng), was broadcast on China Central TV (CCTV). The novel had sold around 600,000 sets by 2001—one-third of them in 1999 alone.[9] Owing to the success of *Yongzheng Dynasty*, the two other novels in Eryuehe's Qing Emperor trilogy, *Kangxi dadi* (The Emperor Kangxi) and *Qianlong huangdi* (The Emperor Qianlong), also became hot properties and were purchased for television adaptation. Reports say he earned at least one million yuan for the television rights.[10] This kind of success tempted many other writers to jump on the scriptwriting bandwagon in the hope of garnering fame and fortune. By 2001, almost all Chinese writers, young and old, established and upcoming, were doing at least some script work, or were planning to do so when they had the chance.

Literary works are now often closely tied up with the television and film industries. As a result, developing the multimedia potential of one product—that is, recycling literary works for various reading and viewing audiences—has become a common practice among writers. Many have planned their multimedia projects before they even start writing. Ever since his series *Plainclothes Police* became a national hit in the late 1980s, Haiyan, a popular writer and businessman, has been developing a kind of production line in both the television market and the literature market. The scripts he writes are filmed by his own company, Hairun Film and Television Production Limited (Hairun yingshi zhizuo youxiangongsi) and made into television series. To capitalize on the popularity of the television versions, a complete collection of his six television novels (*dianshi xiaoshuo*) was brought out in 2001, jointly by Writers Publishing House and the Masses Publishing House (Qunzhong chubanshe).[11] Chi Li was famous for describing the lives of urban dwellers in Wuhan and for insisting on not "getting electrocuted." Yet even she changed her mind after her novel *Lailai wangwang* (Coming and Going) was successfully adapted as a series in 1999. At that point, she became one of the most sought-after writers of the 1990s. In 2000, she wrote a series script, *Kouhong* (Lipstick), and after it was broadcast rewrote it as a novel, which sold more than 200,000 within a year.[12]

It is not just writers who have learned to exploit television and film. Publishers have also been keen to associate themselves with these media. To that end, literary publishers have developed the concept of "television and film literature" (*yingshi wenxue*) to help package, advertise, and promote books, and have become highly adept at relating their products to the latest visual blockbusters.

Television and film literature is a loose term, one that includes virtually any printed literary work with some connection to television or film. It encompasses original novels and stories from which dramas and films have been adapted, television and film scripts, and postproduction novels based on popular series and films. Although these genres had been available earlier, only recently have they become prominent, with publishers gaining more commercial sense and realizing the selling power of the mass media and entertainment businesses. By 1999, there were 13 such works among the top 50 literary best sellers; in 2000, there were 7; in 2001, there were another 15.[13] Most of these books stayed on the best seller lists for only a short time—usually only for the duration of the particular series or film—but while they were on those lists, their sales were huge, often in the hundreds of thousands of copies.

This probably explains why many of the most reputable literary publishers now keep close track of the most recent series and films. Often, they will ask either the original scriptwriter or a ghostwriter to produce novels based on popular series, or they will simply publish the screenplay. In fact, for many publishers, "chasing film and television" has become a short-cut to creating best sellers. And since good best-seller manuscripts are still quite scarce, and since this approach is easy and almost guaranteed to succeed, publishers have even agreed to publish adaptations of the same series in two separate editions, but sharing the profits.[14] Even the once staid and snobbish People's Literature Publishing House has been unable to resist competing fiercely with other publishers in this newly discovered form of publishing. In 1999, it brought out a novel adaptation of the series *Qianshou* (Holding Hands) by the original scriptwriter, Wang Hailing. Benefiting from the popularity of the series, about the love lives of a typical middle-class urban family, the novel was a huge success, easily selling 250,000 in one year, and reprinted twenty times.[15] Struck by the potential of this new market, People's Literature later produced several other scripts from popular CCTV dramas, including *Da ming gong ci* (Lyrics from Daming Palace), *Juzi hong le* (Oranges are Ripe), and *Dazhaimen* (Noble House). The script from *Noble House* sold very well even though it appeared on the shelves twenty days after Writers Publishing House brought out a novel adaptation of the same series.[16]

Some literary publishers have gone a step further than this by capitalizing on the synergy between books and television and film products. Instead of simply waiting passively for scripts to adapt, they have commissioned their own scripts and financed series themselves. For example, Jiangsu Art and Literature Publishing House invested in the drama *Yuese liaoren* (Moonstruck), commissioning the script from the well-known Nanjing woman writer Huang Peijia. According to the house, it hoped to "to maximize the benefits from its publishing resources, using literary resources to fill the demand in the TV/film industry, and using TV and films as an advertising platform to promote its literary works."[17] It is very likely that more and more publishers will adopt a similar business model, developing multidimensional literary products that can be sold in diverse publishing and entertainment contexts, and creating alliances with multimedia cultural and entertainment companies to smooth the processes of adaptation and commercial exploitation.

2. Lit.com: A New Literary Space?

As we noted, television and film are not the only cultural sectors that have grown rapidly in China over the past few years. The Internet, a much more recent phenomenon, took off at the turn of the new millennium and is beginning to affect literary production in a number of conspicuous ways. A large proportion of the many Chinese websites that have recently sprouted like mushrooms after rain are literature-related. Journals, literary organizations, writers, and countless literary works of all kinds (in both authorized and unauthorized versions) have suddenly appeared on the Internet. And almost every conceivable literary activity can now be carried out using a computer keyboard and a few clicks of a mouse. One can post creative writing, read and download old and new literary works, browse the home pages of journals and writers, even buy and sell manuscripts online.[18]

"E-books" are a good example of such recent approaches to distributing literary works online. Bookoo, a Silicon Valley–based international company, is responsible for introducing the concept of e-books to China.[19] Unlike most online bookstores, which so far have simply used the Internet as a promotional platform for advertising and distributing regular printed books, e-books are books in digitized form purchased from a virtual bookstore and downloaded to the buyer's home computer, without any printed version ever being produced. Since such digitized copies enjoy much lower production costs; prices for e-books are much lower than for regular books (often just two or three yuan, compared to an average price of twenty yuan for a regular contemporary literature title). Touting both the convenience and the reasonable prices of its e-books, Bookoo claims that it will bring about a "reading revolution" (*yuedu geming*) in China.[20]

A "literary writing revolution" is also in the cards with the recent enthusiastic promotion of "Internet literature" (*wangluo wenxue*). This term encompasses any creative writing "published" on the Internet or somehow related to the Internet, and has since the turn of the millennium become a buzzword circulating among publishers, amateur writers, and various online agents. Already in 2000 and 2001, several dozen literary books (including anthologies and series) were published under the rubric of Internet literature.[21] When Netease (Wangyi), one of the largest online search engines in China, announced the establishment of its Chinese Internet Literary Awards (Zhongguo wangluo wenxuejiang), the company's promotional blurb declared that "Internet literature is the true literature of humanity. It has completely broken free from the confinement of institutions and commercialization. In cyberspace, writers do not pursue manuscript fees but only freedom, appreciation, understanding and tolerance. Sharing is the essence of Internet literature."[22] Even some established writers of conventional literature, such as Wang Shuo and Wang Meng, have become loud advocates of Internet literature, declaring that the Internet "provides people with unprecedented opportunities to express themselves freely,"[23] and that it has "altered the whole process of literary production and communication."[24]

The recent hyping of Internet literature is closely related to the global marketing of computer and Internet technology, backed by venture capital from California and Beijing. It is also tightly linked to the general commercialization of cultural production at the turn of the twenty-first century. An examination of some of the notable developments in Chinese Internet literature through case studies will further demonstrate the interactions among new media technologies, literary writing, and commercial activity and at the same time point to some of the future trends in literary production in China in the new millennium.

On its home page, Under the Banyan Tree (www.rongshu.com, hereafter Banyan Tree) claims with some justification to be "the most popular website publishing original literature in Chinese." Examining this site and its commercial underpinnings will give us some idea of how Internet literature works and why it excites so many people, especially younger readers.

Created in January 1998 by William Zhu, a young American Chinese advertising executive based in Shanghai, this site was originally a simple home page where all who wished could freely post their creative writing. Helped by Zhu's marketing talents and a series of promotional activities, Banyan Tree quickly attracted more and more contributors. On an average day in May 2001, there were some 3,500 pieces posted and 5.5 million page hits. With these impressive figures, and with its enormous archive of some 370,000 pieces, it had become the largest and best-known of the nearly eight thousand literary websites in China.[25]

Prominently displayed on the home page of Banyan Tree is a flashing icon that reads "Click here to submit your work" (an ci tou gao). This sign demonstrates the Internet's most obvious attraction for literature enthusiasts and budding writers: easy and immediate access to publication. With just a few clicks, you can post your writing on the site and have it viewed by an international audience. And you can receive an instant and unmediated response from readers. The number of "readers" (in this context, those who click a particular piece of writing) is listed at the end of each piece. Readers can also post comments about the piece, and these comments will also be posted instantly.

The ease with which writings and messages can be posted explains the astonishing amount of traffic this site has generated. Although its several thousand pieces posted every day are placed in three broad categories (fiction, poetry, and prose), there are no traditional style editors to control the site—the website manager is responsible only for technical maintenance. This welcoming environment has inspired many 'net addicts to venture into the once carefully guarded "sacred space" of literary publication to satisfy their creative impulses (and vanity). As writers, they need not reveal their true identities; in fact, most Internet writers prefer to use a net name. Furthermore, they need not censor their feelings: they can simply record their most mundane or private impressions and send them into cyberspace. But as is not the case with most other media, their words will immediately reach a huge potential audience, especially if posted on popular websites such Banyan Tree, which has millions of daily viewers. Most tempting of all is that, being a publishing platform, pieces that prove their broad appeal on the Internet may even be selected for awards, recommended to publishers, and published as books, allowing the writer to reap large financial rewards.

At first glance, Banyan Tree appears to be simply a convenient and extremely popular venue for contributors, not a commercial venture; the site does not even run commercials as such. But its remarkable growth and sustained success stem from the fact that it is one of the few Internet literary sites to make a profit. Taking advantage of its huge "literary resources" contributed by site visitors and its sustained popularity among netizens, Banyan Tree has managed to transform itself rapidly from an amateur writers' community into a market testing-ground and copyright-trading platform useful for both publishers and writers alike.

This commercial exploitation of Banyan Tree began in July 1999, when Zhu established a twelve-member editorial board to select the best submissions for publication. He then began organizing a series of promotional activities to attract more writers and readers. *Literature Press* agreed to run a special column reprinting selected works from the site. Then, starting in the winter of 1999, the site launched the First Internet Literature Award Contest (Shou jie wangluo yuanchuang wenxue jiang). Initiated by Shanghai writer Chen Cun, the chief art officer of Banyan Tree, this contest has become an annual event. Its juries include both established writers, such as Wang Anyi, Yu Hua, Ah Cheng, and Wang Shuo, and popular Internet writers, such as Ann Baby (Anni Baobei) and Ning the God of Wealth (Ning Caishen). Prizewinning works are collected in three-volume anthologies, Wangluo zhi xing congshu (Internet Literature Award Winners series), and published by Huacheng Publishing House. Besides these prizewinners, since 1999 more than a dozen anthologies of selected works pulled from the website have been published by various presses under the name "Rongshu xia: Wangluo yuanchuang wenxue congshu" (Under the Banyan Tree: Original Internet Work Series). For its most recent Internet Literature Award in 2001, Banyan Tree teamed up with the multinational publisher Bertelsmann in a lucrative sponsorship deal.

To increase and diversify its appeal, Banyan Tree has also contracted with radio stations, including Shanghai Radio and Shanghai Eastern Radio, and with influential websites such as Netease (www.163.com) and Hong Kong's Tom.com. In 2001, Banyan also purchased Xiakele (Class Over), a popular website for college students, and opened offices in Beijing, Chongqing, and Guangzhou to expand the reach of its Shanghai office to publishers and sponsors throughout the country. The prestigious Lu Xun Literary Academy set up distance learning courses using Banyan Tree's site as its base.

According to Zhu's own figures, by September 2001, he had signed alliances and contracts with 37 publishing houses, 46 radio stations, 521 "media units," and 2,011 writers. By then, Banyan Tree was already behind 117 published books with total sales of 2,350,000. Zhu claimed that by selling its Internet resources, Banyan Tree had already become profitable, with a gross income in 2001 of around four million yuan, 40 percent of which came from book publishing. Other business ventures included collaborating with radio stations and other media, charging agent's fees for recommending literary works to publishers, and publishing a regular hardcopy literary magazine, *Rongshu wenzhai* (Banyan Tree Digest).[26]

Notwithstanding its noncommercial beginnings, Banyan Tree has evolved into the base for a sprawling multimedia business that uses the most advanced technology to fully exploit the literary resources provided by writers. Internet literature has clearly become a new label full of potential, one through which regular publishers, ambitious amateur writers, and IT businesses such as Banyan Tree can collectively hype and market their cultural products.

Yet apart from exploiting the commercial ends of writing and publishing, has Internet literature actually led to any noticeable changes in literary forms, styles, and concepts, and has cyberspace managed to expand the horizons of the Chinese literary imagination?

On the surface, the Internet promises a democratic zone where everyone has the right to freely produce and publish, ignoring literary conventions, political censorship, and not least the prolonged and cumbersome publishing process. However, most objective observers would conclude that up until now, cyberspace has remained a huge virgin territory untouched by deep passion, originality, and talent. Anyone who browses through the gigantic database of literary works stored on Banyan Tree's site would agree with those critics who decry Internet literature as, at best, simply a form of "literary karaoke" for self-entertainment and, at worst, "literary detritus" freely and copiously discharged onto the screen.[27] The subject and style of these works tends to be narrow, trite, and monotonous, full of conventional and clichéd expressions of predictable personal sentiments. Although traces of unique style and language can be found in certain individual works of Internet literature, in general one must search hard to find any literary innovation. Rarely are the new technological possibilities of the medium, such as the potential for interaction between visual images and words, and the ability to link back and forward between pages, fully explored.

To illustrate these observations, I will now examine one of the best-selling Internet literature works of the past two years and the events surrounding its sudden rise to prominence.

Di yi ci de qinmi jiechu (The First Intimate Contact) is a love story by a Taiwanese 'net surfer originally posted as a series of short segments on a BBS board. Its huge popularity among Internet readers brought the novel to the attention of a regular publishing house, which published a wildly successful Taiwanese book edition. A film adaptation was also produced. At the end of 1999, the book's Mainland Chinese rights were purchased by Knowledge Publishing House (Zhishi chubanshe). After that, it remained on the best seller lists for over two years (December 1999 to December 2001). For three months it was the number-one literary best seller in Mainland China. The writer, Cai Zhiheng, visited the mainland from Taiwan to promote his book and has since published two other books, which apparently also came out first on the Internet. These two, as well, stayed on the Chinese best seller lists for extended periods.[28]

The main difference between *The First Intimate Contact* and "traditional" literary work is its style: the language is very concise and colloquial, and the sentences are short, with new ideas being thrown out in quick succession. The effect is fluid but also random. When printed in book form, the text's appearance is almost like verse, with each section broken down into many short paragraphs of uneven line lengths. This style is clearly influenced by the special restrictions of writing on the Internet. In particular, because of the time limitations enforced by the high cost of Internet access, Cai Zhiheng had to finish each section as quickly as possible and post his contributions in serial form. For the same reason, Internet readers also prefer concise and clear phrases that stick to the point rather than long, complicated sentences and drawn-out character development. In this way, Internet literature brings out a language that emphasizes speed and also simplicity, a fluid and random quality.

Another feature common to much Internet literature is that the novel's plot has a strong Internet focus: its hero is a 'net surfer named Pizi Cai (Bad Boy Cai), who falls in love with a girl 'net surfer named Qingwu feiyang (Dancing Wind). Unfortunately, she soon dies of an incurable disease. The story thus contains all of the typical romantic clichés of popular fiction that would appeal to the fantasies of young readers—love at first sight, unfulfilled desires, beautiful tragedy. However, the fresh setting of the Internet gives these tired old themes a new twist. Even the communications between the two main characters are all in the form of exchanged e-mail messages. Thus, the novel cleverly combines two concepts that have obvious appeal for millions of young Chinese readers: traditional romance and contemporary curiosity about the high-tech world of cyberspace. *The First Intimate Contact* utilizes some interesting formal features and is written in a fluent and readable style; however, its content differs little from countless popular romances produced in book form.

One noticeable difference between Internet literature like *The First Intimate Contact* and regular print-based literature is that the former offers readers a chance to become publicly involved with the work. While Cai was posting his serial novel online, many "reader's responses" were published on the same page, which doubtless attracted still other readers to discover what the commotion was about. These responses and Cai's replies to them became such an integrated part of the whole writing and publishing process that when the novel was published in book form it actually retained some of the exchanges between Cai and his readers. This seems to underscore the point that with regular literature, editors and critics must first give their approval for a work to be published; with Internet literature, in contrast, the reading masses decide whether the work deserves a more permanent form in print.

Indeed, this "mass approval" nature of Internet literature is where many publishers and writers see the new medium's commercial power. In other words, the Internet can be used as an inexpensive platform to advertise or test the popularity of a certain product. Publishing houses can purchase rights to the most popular works on the Internet, thereby lessening some of the risks and work of creating best sellers. They simply package their products with the marketable label of Internet literature and indicate on the cover page how many people have visited the website where the piece was originally posted. Likewise, unknown writers who may never have been taken seriously by publishers in the past can now prove their broad reader base and commercial potential by pointing to their Internet following, and thereby gain lucrative contracts with regular publishing houses.[29]

Of course, we need more time to evaluate the influence of the Internet on literature and literary production in China. However, some preliminary conclusions can be drawn from the materials we have examined. On the one hand, the Internet has already been used very effectively as a new medium for exploiting the commercial potential of writing, but to a lesser degree for exploring the creative potential of electronic writing. Also, there are signs that the literary language is beginning to be influenced by this fast-developing new medium, especially among the younger generation. It is likely, therefore, that the traditional artistic merits associated with printed culture, characterized by Alvin Kernan as "the intricacy of structure, complexity of meaning, irony, ambiguity, multivalency and indeterminacy,"[30] will become more and more difficult to sustain on the quick-flashing, ephemeral computer screens and websites of the future.

Clearly, the large-scale invasion of mass media and technology into literary production and consumption has coincided nicely with the marketization of cultural products in China. The television and film industries and the Internet have provided new channels through which Chinese writers can communicate with mass readers and the market. At the same time, under the influence of other forms of media, some far-reaching changes in the nature of literary production and writing are taking place. No longer separate entities with their own independent existence, literary works are now written and read as simply a part or stage in a multimedia and multidimensional production process. Where Chinese literary production was once dominated by political guidelines and elitist criteria, it is now increasingly being infiltrated by commercial considerations. With mass media and global markets emerging as two of the most important forces reshaping the cultural field in twenty-first-century China, there is little doubt that Chinese writers, publishers, and book distributors will become still more attuned to the need to adjust to principles of supply and demand and more aware of the need to adjust and transform literature to meet the needs of their consumer–readers.

Reference Matter

All translations in this book are the author's, unless otherwise indicated.

INTRODUCTION

1. Wang Xiaoming, "Kuangye shang de feixu," 27–41.

2. Wang Meng, "Duobi chonggao," 10–17.

3. The change in social environment for women writers can be seen most clearly in the case of Yu Luojin in the early 1980s. According to Wang Lingzhen, the personal voice and descriptions of a woman's private experience in Yu's *Chinese Winter's Tale* and *Springtime Tale* not only "were reframed, expurgated, and appropriated into dominant trends through the editorial activities in the process of publication," but also "were limited, used, erased or ignored by literary criticism and the public reception after publication." As soon as Yu tried to go further in expressing personal ideals and liberation, both in her texts and her life, she and her writings were immediately denounced, and she was completely removed from public view. For details, see Wang Lingzhen, 396–438.

4. The lament in literary circles over the "death of poetry" in the late 1980s and early 1990s, accompanied by the sudden deaths of several poets and novelists in that period, was symptomatic of what many writers and critics felt at first toward the prevailing social changes. The Beijing critic / scholar Zhang Yiwu's "Yige tonghua de zhongjie" is representative of these views. Throughout the 1990s, the "death of poetry" increasingly became a cultural reality, not just a literary metaphor. Nevertheless, as the market economy gradually changed social and cultural norms and conventions, many of these writers and critics "softened" their negative attitude toward commercialization. A recent dialogue between two formerly radical and elite critics, Chen Xiaoming and Zhang Yiwu, on literature and the market indicates this change in attitude. See Chen and Zhang, 116–27.

5. Of course, best sellers are not totally new in modern Chinese literary history. In fact, with the introduction of Western commercial publishing in urban areas in the early twentieth century, many best sellers were produced. But in strict commercial terms, best sellers did disappear for almost four decades—that is, from the 1950s to the late 1980s, owing to obvious social and political factors. For a convenient survey of best sellers throughout the twentieth century, refer to Xu Lifang et al.

6. Huang Jiwei; Chen Ding.

7. In the case of the film industry, after years of opening up to private and foreign investment and turning a blind eye to many "underground" productions by individuals and corporations, the government finally deregulated film production and
abandoned the former studio license system in early 2002. Any individual or company can now apply to produce a film, and will in theory be approved as long as it
has the financial resources. In the case of newspapers and magazines, the last two
decades witnessed an uneasy tension between state ownership/ideological control
and various reforms and experiments within the media industry, which turned the
government news regulation system into a moneymaking venture. Finally, the State
Press and Publication Administration issued new regulations in the summer of 2003
to "wean" all the previously government-affiliated newspapers and magazines, except
for a tiny handful that remained under state control (three major newspapers and
one magazine at the national level, and one newspaper and one magazine for each
province or region). All the others were offered up completely to the market.

8. In the rapidly changing literary publishing field of the 1990s, many of the
most interesting innovations and developments have occurred in a gray area at the
boundaries of official government policies. This means they are either not documented in written sources or are merely attacked as illicit practices by the official
press. The whole area of second-channel publishing is a case in point. To ignore
these developments would be to distort the realities of the current literary production industry in China. Also, even in those areas of literary publishing for which apparently objective written materials are available, such as best seller lists, literary criticism, and the like, I found that such materials were often less helpful than they
appeared. See note 9 for a description of best seller lists. In order to interpret these
materials properly, therefore, one must look more carefully at the hidden context
that produced them; and to do this, only detailed case studies based on extensive interviews and following the whole production process of books from writing through
publication and promotion to distribution will allow one to gain an accurate idea of
the reality behind the "objective" statistics.

Thus the most practical way to compensate for the lack of documented source
material has been to carry out extensive interviews with some of the most representative players in the field of literary production, including writers, editors, publishers,
agents, critics, and booksellers. For those whom I could not interview personally, I
consulted the available written documents that most closely record the realities the
people involved have been experiencing; these materials include memoirs, autobiographical and reportage literature, and other sources such as journals and newspapers.
Although such sources are often subjective and unsubstantiated, when used with
caution, they give a good sense of the broader context for the information I obtained from my interviews. Overall, these materials lend themselves more readily to
individual case studies than to statistical surveys.

Besides being the only practical way to deal with such an amorphous and ill-
documented realities, case studies provide an extremely vivid impression of both the
resounding successes and abject failures of writers, publishers, and distributors in their
attempts to negotiate the new and often unforgiving economic landscape in China.
Following selected individuals or enterprises through their ups and downs over the

past decade gives us a clearer idea than bare statistics of the drastic and exciting ways in which economic reforms have affected peoples' lives in the Chinese literary world.

9. China still lacks authoritative book trade databases and best seller selection systems like those of the *New York Times Book Review* and Bookwatch Ltd. in the United Kingdom. Various best seller lists and surveys have been available since the early 1990s. One of the earliest and most influential was the "Bi-monthly Popular Book List" (Banyue remenshu paihangbang) from *Wenhui dushu zhoubao* (Wenhui Reading Weekly), which started in 1991. Since the late 1990s, many book trade and review newspapers and magazines as well as bookstores have established their own best seller lists. However, these are often extremely limited in scope and unsystematic in collecting their data for analysis. Sometimes they are just another advertising gimmick; thus, they often give contradictory and inconsistent results and do not accurately reflect true sales figures. One such example is "National Outstanding Best Sellers" (Quanguo youxiu changxiaoshu), an annual event organized by the Chinese Book and Magazine Distribution Association (Zhongguo shukan faxingye xiehui). This national and official best seller list still bears the marks of a bygone era, in that its selection criteria do not follow scientific statistical methods, nor are they based on actual market figures. Instead, state-owned publishing houses nominate titles from their own publications, and the association then consults with the distribution sector for the sales of these titles and decides the final list based on principle of "excellence based on popularity, and popularity based on excellence" (zai changxiao jichu shang de youxiu, zai youxiu jichu shang de changxiao). So it is no more objective than any of the other unofficial lists. For the selection of National Outstanding Best Sellers in 2001, see a report in *Zhongguo tushu shangbao*, January 8, 2002. But I'd like to point out that with the gradual establishment of best seller mechanisms in China, more attention is now being paid to objective methods of producing best seller lists. In this regard, a more recent literary best seller list published monthly in *Zhongguo tushu shangbao* since 1999 seems to be more reliable and to reflect the national market better than other lists. The statistics are collected by the Beijing Kaijuan Book Market Research Centre (Beijing kaijuan tushu shichang yanjiusuo), which claims to collect data from about one hundred different centers throughout the country. This list also gives more detailed analysis of sales figures and number of months on the best seller list.

Thus, when using these best seller lists and sales figures, I try to give the context, the source, and any explanation if necessary.

10. The case of poetry in 1990s is very complicated, and in many ways symbolizes the challenge that pure literature faces in a commercialized society. To discuss poetry in detail is beyond the scope of this book, but suffice it to say that poetry now "has a lower social visibility" and is much more marginalized than in past decades; and that compared to the frenzied development of the publishing industry as a whole —especially the publication of prose works—poetry publication simply seems unable to thrive in the consumer market.

However, a fair evaluation of contemporary poetry cannot ignore unofficial poetry circles, which have existed since the early 1970s and have become an important cultural force with their own underground publishing network. Although it has become difficult to find a state publisher for poetry and even more difficult to produce a poetry best seller, the vitality of unofficial poetry publications (including both poetry journals and individual collections, and the newly emerging area of online publishing) is still noteworthy. Also worth mentioning is that recent debates within poetry circles on the use of language, literary craft, and the position of poetry in a consumer society have raised many serious artistic and aesthetic issues, which are seldom discussed in other areas any more.

Regarding the current situation of Chinese poets and poetry, Maghiel van Crevel ("The Horror of Being Ignored") makes some vivid observations. For a more comprehensive picture of the groups and debates within contemporary Chinese poetry, see Zan Zhou, 72–129.

11. Likewise, I am well aware that a certain degree of commercialization of literary production did occur in prerevolutionary China, especially from the 1910s to 1940s. However, there is little evidence that Chinese publishers and booksellers today are at all influenced by their prerevolutionary forebears, and to discuss that period would simply distract readers from the central focus of this book, namely, the effects of recent economic reforms on literary production in Socialist China.

CHAPTER I

1. Barmé, 9.

2. Link, 119. Link's book gives a comprehensive and detailed account of various aspects of the socialist literary system. My brief analysis of writers in Socialist China is largely based on his study.

3. Ragvald, 152–79, offers some good examples of the training and education of new socialist writers in the 1950s, which can be extended to illustrate one aspect of the general system of literary control over the succeeding four decades in Socialist China. Cf. Link for the general context.

4. According to Sun Dequan of the Chinese Writers Association, 80 percent of the more than 5,800 members of CWA are working in state institutes in the fields of journalism, publishing, culture, and education. See Wang Hong and Chen Jie.

5. At least two generations of Chinese writers—those whose literary formative years were in the 1950s, including Wang Meng and Zhang Xianliang, and those whose youth was wasted in the Cultural Revolution, such as Wang Anyi, Liang Xiaosheng, and Zhang Kangkang—have to different degrees embraced the state and enjoyed the lucrative rewards of becoming state-supported writers—rewards that include political power, material benefits, and social status. Despite occasional periods of frustration and exile, due to political infighting and campaigns that affect all intellectuals, many of these writers have risen to high positions in the political power structure. Wang Meng, for instance, served as Minister of Culture from 1986 to 1989.

Regarding the cooperative relationship that developed between writers and the socialist state, see Barmé, 1–19.

6. For example, in 1999–2000, the government allocated a one-time payment of eight to nine million yuan to the Writers Association. This amount seems substantial, but was actually hardly sufficient when one realizes that it had to cover all the Association's various expenses, including the following: literary publishing, conferences and seminars, salaries for office and editorial staff, and professional writers' salaries. The financial pressures on the Chinese Writers Association resulting from

reduced government funding can also be seen in the association's efforts to find other sources of support. In 1986, the Chinese Literature Foundation (Zhongghua wenxue jijin hui) was established as a unofficial charity to raise money through various means, including business ventures. It has raised more than five million yuan by 2000. The source for this is my interview with Li Chaoquan, secretary of the Chinese Writers Association, May 21, 2000.

7. Zhang Yigong.

8. See Chapter 6 for a detailed survey of the problems facing literary journals.

9. *Wenxue bao*, December 15, 1994, 739.

10. See *Wenxue bao*, February 8, 1996, for a report on the Guangdong case. In 1996 the Nanjing Federation and Guangxi Writers Association also contracted writers to produce either a novel or a television series script. See *Wenxue bao*, March 7, 1996, for the Guangxi case, and *Wenxue bao*, April 18, 1996, for the Nanjing case.

11. The issues of *Wenxue bao* and *Wenyi Bao* from the second half of 1992 are filled with reports and articles about reforming the professional writers' system. *Wenxue bao* even hosted a symposium, "Where Will the Commercial Tide Take Literature?" (Shangpin jingji dachao, wenxue xiang hechu qu). Some writers, including Wang Meng and Feng Jicai, supported the reforms, contending that many professional writers lived on the present system without producing quality works and that the Writers Association had become a bureaucracy that did not really serve writers. However, many writers were suspicious of reforms, arguing that literature is different from other commodities, that China was lacking an established legal framework for intellectual property protection, and (especially) that payments in royalties were still not a common practice. See *Wenxue bao*, September 10, October 22, and November 5, 1992.

12. In my interview with Li Chaoquan of the Chinese Writers Association (May 21, 2000), Li disclosed that the present approach of the Writers Association for coping with the transition is to maintain the tenured status, salaries, and benefits of established older professional writers, but to adopt the new contract-based system for young up-and-coming writers. Thus, once the surviving tenured professional writers die off, the tenure system itself will disappear.

13. Regarding the blooming of popular literature in the 1980s, see Kaikkonen, "From Knights to Nudes," 85–110; and "Stories and Legends," 134–60.

14. The phrase "second channel" is used now to refer to unofficial publishing and distribution. Originally it referred to individual book distributors operating outside the Xinhua bookstore system (the "first" or "main" channel). For more details, see Chapter 3.

15. Xue Mili did return to the literary scene in 1991. Many more pulp fiction and martial arts titles were produced, but these did not have the same impact on readers, and new titles stopped being produced around the mid-1990s. Tian Yanning still writes popular fiction, under the name "Yan Ning." Ironically, the response from society and publishers toward the original Xue Mili series has become much kinder over recent years. In 1998, Sichuan Art and Literature Publishing House (Sichuan wenyi chubanshe), which until then had refused to publish Xue Mili, brought out a four-volume selection, *Xue Mili Zhenpin ji* (Xue Mili: Collected Gems). And in 1999, the same house and Xinhua Bookstore cohosted a book-signing ceremony in Shanghai. Some even claimed that "Xue Mili is now a successful literary brand name

that represents the commercial consciousness of new era literature." See Tian Yanning and Tan Li, inside cover.

16. In 1999, Tian and Tan published a tell-all book (referenced in the previous note). In this book, they recalled bitterly the events surrounding the Xue Mili series and explained why they followed the pulp-fiction route. Clearly, they were trying belatedly to challenge the literary crusade against them of the late 1980s and to crown themselves as literary heroes who were simply ahead of their time.

17. Tian and Tan, 220–24. Yan Ning's complaint is generally true of the Chinese Writers Association as a whole. Many aspects of its corruption and bureaucracy have been revealed in recent years. See survey titled "Breaking Away," discussed below, and note 11 in Chapter 1. Even as late as 1995, a serious tendency toward "seniority first" (*lunzipaibei*) still existed in the Writers Association. In this respect, statistics of the ages of members of the Writers Association are revealing: in the mid-1990s, among the 5,200 national members, only 8 percent were "young" (that is, under thirty). In Beijing, the ages of the members were as follows: around 80 were over eighty, 200 were over seventy, 600 were over sixty, and fewer than 10 were under thirty. Statistics from *Wenxue bao*, December 14, 1995.

18. Tian and Tan, 47.

19. Link, 5.

20. Another indication of the low morale of Chinese writers in the late 1980s and early 1990s was the sudden premature death of several "serious writers," including several young poets such as Haizi, Luo Yihe, Ge Mai, and Gu Cheng, and a number of middle-aged provincial writers such as Lu Yao and Zhou Zhi'an. The latter group obviously suffered from poor health owing to hard work, family burdens, and poor nutrition caused by poverty. This caused great concern among Chinese writers, who around that time were generally experiencing both financial hardship and a loss of social status. For many Chinese writers, the often heard lament in literary circles about the "death of poetry" and the "crisis of literature" had both a literal and a material basis.

21. This comment is from the famous critic/scholar Xie Mian, professor at Peking University, as quoted in Wang Shuo, *Wuzhizhe wuwei*, 15.

22. Barmé, 69.

23. Some studies analyze in depth the literary experimentation and cultural meaning of Wang Shuo's works; see, for example, Barmé, 62–98; Jing Wang, 261–86; and Benjamin Liebman. A recent published dialogue between Wang Shuo and Lao Xia about the ambivalent relationship between Wang's work and popular culture is also very illuminating; see Wang Shuo and Lao Xia, 11–30. So there is no need for me to elaborate on these textual analyses here.

24. Wang Shuo, *Wo shi Wang Shuo*, 20.

25. Wang Shuo, *Wuzhizhe wuwei*, 24–26.

26. Ibid., 17.

27. See the account from Jin Lihong and Li Bo, two key editors and managers at Huayi Publishing House, on the publishing of Wang's *Collected Works*. Lei, 28–39.

28. The print-run payment was calculated as a percentage of the basic payment, and depended on the number of copies printed. As Link points out, print-run payments were quite different from royalties in that, first, the author's share went down

rather than up with continued printings, and second, the author's share was calculated not on the basis of the number of copies sold but by the number printed, and decisions on the size of print runs were essentially political. Thus, there was little incentive to sell more copies. See Link, 131–32.

29. Huot, 50.

30. Barmé, 97.

31. Wang Shuo, *Wuzhizhe wuwei*, 18.

32. Ibid.

33. In the summer of 2002, over ten years since its first broadcast, a local station, Heilongjiang TV, was still showing reruns of *Stories from the Editorial Board*. Wang Shuo and Feng Xiaogang also published a book entitled *Bianjibu de gushi jingcai duihua xuan* (The Best Selected Dialogues from the Stories from the Editorial Board).

The studio also produced two movies "Guozhe langbei bukan de shenghuo" (Leading A Miserable Life) and "Yueliang Beimian" (The Far Side of the Moon), but these were banned and never publicly shown.

34. Wang Shuo, *Wuzhizhe wuwei*, 15–19.

35. Barmé, 97.

36. At the turn of the new millennium, Wang Shuo made a comeback after over six years with the novel *Kan shang qu hen mei* (Looking Beautiful) and several collections of cultural criticism, *Wazhizhe wuwei* (The Ignorant Fear Nothing) *Meiren zeng wo menghanyao* (She Put Me to Sleep with a Potion). Although the novel was an artistic failure, in his criticism Wang revealed another aspect of his talent: his keen observation and razor-sharp criticism of Chinese intellectuals, the modern literary tradition, and contemporary popular culture. Again, his reputation guaranteed high print runs—in this case, 200,000 a book. The promotional campaign for *Looking Beautiful* by Huayi Publishing House included unique packaging with a CD-Rom attached, and the by now obligatory advertisements in major newspapers.

37. Both Sea Horse Creative Studio and Current Affairs Cultural Consultancy were cultural agencies funded by venture capital with Wang Shuo as the actual manager. Their original purpose was to buy works with high market potential and "recommend" them to publishers or television and film producers. See Wang Shuo, *Wuzhizhe wuwei*, 23–33.

38. Zhou Yan. According to this report, Wang Shuo himself—one of the hottest writers—was able to negotiate the enormous fee of ten thousand yuan for each series episode he wrote.

39. *Wenxue bao*, December 2 and 23, 1993.

40. This refers to the Beijing writer Huo Da, who won the Mao Dun Literary Award for her novel *Musilin de zangli* (Muslim Funeral) in 1991. At the Shenzhen auction, Huo asked for one million yuan for her film script *Qin huang fuzi* (The Qin Emperors). The "resignation" of the advisory committee members, including Li Guowen, Zhang Jie, Cong Weixi, Liu Xinwu, and Liang Xiaosheng, most of whom were from Beijing, placed political pressure on the auction. So the organizers asked other members, such as the Shanghai writer Ye Yonglie, to write statements in support of the auction. This episode showed that public opinion on this sort of marketing event was still deeply divided at the time. The controversy also explains why the auction was just a one-off event instead of becoming an annual one. For details, see

Ye. Interestingly enough, Huo's work was sold for a million yuan at the auction, the purchaser being a company in Shenzhen. *Wenxue bao*, October 21, 1993.

41. Ye.

42. Ye.

43. Zha Jiaying gives a sharply observed account of the publishing controversy surrounding *Ruined Capital*, the writer Jia Pingwa, and the broader social context of the novel. Zha, 129–64.

44. This comment, from Yiwu Zhang, is quuoted in Zha, 130.

45. Sheldon H. Lu, 243.

46. "Zhou Hong" was the pen name of two editors from the literary journal *Dangdai* who became famous for their essays on current cultural issues. Often published in newspaper columns, these essays were published as collections, including *Jinggao zhongguoren* (Warning the Chinese People) and *Zhouhong shuohua* (Zhou Hong Speaks), which became best sellers.

47. Zi.

48. See "Writers Bank a Million for Novel Lives," *China Daily*, January 7, 2002. (www1.chinadaily.com.cn/cndy/2002–01–07/50769.html). Another article, "Zuojia yi ben shu shouru er bai wan" (One Book Earns Two Million for the Author), *Wenhui dushu zhoubao*, April 28, 2001, reported that according to editors at People's Literature Publishing House, the novel *Bai lu yuan* (White Deer Plain), first published in 1993, had sold over 940,000 copies by 2001, and that the author Chen Zhongshi thus received royalties of nearly two million yuan. The book still sells at a rate of around fifty thousand copies a year. *Chen'ai luo ding* (After the Dust Settles), another best seller from People's Literature, also sold more than 320,000 in three years, with the author Ah Lai receiving royalties of 700,000 yuan plus USD$150,000 for its English copyright.

49. Liang, 274. Liang's book is an imitation of a famous article of the 1920s by Mao Zedong. Ironically, in the original piece the revolutionary Mao uses the problems caused by class conflict and social injustice to call for a socialist revolution aimed at putting an end to class differences and exploitation. Yet Liang's book reveals the reestablishment of social classes in postrevolutionary society mainly based on their financial resources.

50. Since most of these writers were born after the late 1950s, and began writing in the 1990s, they are often labeled "new generation" writers (*xin sheng dai or wan sheng dai*). Because they have only a loose relationship with state institutions, they are also known as freelance writers (*ziyou zuojia*). For more information about these writers and the events surrounding the questionnaire, see the series of interviews by Wang Jifang. Cf. Zhang Jun. For the actual questionnaires and responses, as well as the organizers' analysis, see *Beijing wenxue* (Beijing Literature) 10 (1998).

51. See a special report on the controversy in *Nanfang zhoumo* (South China Weekend), August 21, 1998.

52. Among other topics singled out for criticism were writers such as Lu Xun, Chinese and foreign critics, and authoritative journals such as *Xiaoshuo xuankan* (Fiction Digest) and *Shouhuo* (Harvest), which still "follow outdated criteria in selecting their contributors." See Han Dong.

53. Ibid.

54. Han Shishan.

55. Standaert.

56. Wang Hong and Chen Jie.

57. Crevel.

58. See "Avant-garde Writers Take a Step Back," *China Daily* (English), December 18, 2002. When I interviewed Li Feng and Zhu Wen in May 2000, both had left their work units in provincial cities and moved to Beijing in the late 1990s, and they held similar views of the practice of writing in China today.

59. Although many serious writers have turned to the "popular," there are still a few writers, such as Zhang Chengzhi and Zhang Wei, who claim that they will never associate with "evil" market forces, and who prefer to continue pursuing their "pure" literary ideals. Owing to space constraints and the focus of my study, I will not discuss this group and other alternative approaches to writing here; I would simply point out the fact that by no means all Chinese writers have jumped on the commercial bandwagon.

CHAPTER 2

1. Zhang Hongwei.

2. For a detailed study of the literary system in Socialist China, in which publishing played a very important role, see Link.

3. Link, 220.

4. Hong Zicheng, 106–24, offers a detailed account of how some of these novels were written collectively and how they were used in the late 1950s and early 1960s.

5. Pei, 155. Zhao Yuezhi also discusses in detail the causes and effects of media reform. Many of these factors are relevant to literary publishing.

6. Pei, 158.

7. In April 1984, pressured by the actual practices of many research institutes, which sponsored their researchers to publish scholarly books on science and technology when they had been declined by publishing houses for their small readership, the Press and Publication Administration and the Propaganda Department issued "Some Opinions On Current Publishing Reforms" (Guanyu dangqian chuban gaige de ruogan yijian), which stated clearly: "[Publishing houses] should open many different channels, make use of social resources, expand their capital, and become involved in cooperative publishing arrangements and subcontracting of printing and distribution [*xiezuo chuban, daiyin daifa*] in order to publish more good books quickly." See Yang Aixiang, 223–24.

8. For more discussion of private or second-channel publishing and its links with state-owned publishing houses, see Chapter 3.

9. Zhang Hongwei, 128.

10. Propaganda Department and Press and Publications Administration, 38–40.

11. Ibid., 36–38.

12. To "build socialist spiritual civilization," especially in a market economy, the Chinese government established various awards to promote "mainstream works" (*zhuxuanlu zuopin*) and "high-quality books" (*youxiu tushu*) that disseminated socialist ideas. The Five Ones Project started in 1991. This annual award is organized by

the Propaganda Department. It covers mainly the arts and is divided into several categories: books, drama, television drama, films, songs, and so on. It is a typical political campaign disguised as an arts award, and each province and work unit can win
collective awards, with individuals being eligible for certificates—and handsome
prizes as well. The National Book Award is adjudicated by the State Press and Publication Administration.

13. Long Yin.

14. Fang Wenyu. My examination of the copyright page of this book confirms
the number. Since in China the copyright page often provides information regarding reprints and the number of total copies, I have found it very useful in learning
how well a book has sold. However, this method also must be used with caution,
since it is a badly kept secret that many publishers record false numbers of copies
printed on the copyright page—usually smaller than the actual ones—to avoid taxes
and royalties.

15. The numbers of sales and print runs given here and later in this chapter are
from Zhang Shengyou unless otherwise stated. They indicate the sales figures of the
books up to the spring of 2001. The statistics from the bestseller lists are from Liu
Yongjun's articles, "Cong changxiaoshu paihangbang kan shichang zhoushi, 2000
nian tongji fenxi," 41–46; and "Cong changxiaoshu paihangbang kan shichang
zhoushi, 1999 nian tongji fenxi." Liu's data and analyses are based on the statistics of
monthly best sellers collected by Jiang Xilian, from the Beijing Kaijuan Book Market Research Center (Beijing kaijuan tushu shichang yanjiusuo), which have been
published monthly in *Zhongguo tushu shang bao* since 1999.

16. Zhou Huimin, 13.

17. Most of the information about Zhang's reform measures is from my inter-
view with Bai Bing, vice president of Writers, in May 2000. See also Zhang
Shengyou; Li and Tang; and Ah Zheng (interview with An Boshun and Zhang
Shengyou).

18. Zhang Shengyou.

19. My interview with Wang Shuli, June 14, 2001. She also gave me a copy of
her original draft sales proposal for *Frost on the Long River* (Xuanti yingxiao cehua
an), dated December 1998; it consisted of "Measures against Piracy," "Marketing
Strategies," "Distribution Strategy," and "Promotion and Advertising."

20. Another similar case is *Xiao yanzi: Nüsheng Zhao Wei* (Little Swallow—A Girl
named Zhao Wei) by the starlet Zhao Wei, who became famous overnight in 1999
with the broadcast of the television series *Huanzhu gege* (Princess Pearl), a joint venture among China, Taiwan, and Hong Kong, and based on a popular novel by Taiwanese writer Qiong Yao. Zhao is typical of the stars produced by today's transnational entertainment industry. After being "packaged" in Taiwan and Hong Kong,
she was reimported back to China to become a youth icon and fantasy figure for
millions of Chinese teenagers with her mischievous, restless look and "all round talents"—television and film, advertisements, a music CD, and a book. With her fans
mainly high school students—one of the biggest market segments for book purchases—Zhao's book also sold extremely well.

21. Li and Tang.

22. Zhang Shengyou.

23. Ibid. The story of Han Han is well documented by Han's father, including both the controversy and Han's success; see Han Renjun.

24. "Teen Writers Popular," *Beijing Review* 26 (2001).

25. From my May 18, 2000, interview with Bai Bing, vice president of Writers Publishing House.

26. Ibid.; see also Ah Zheng.

27. In May 2000, An Boshun was forced to leave Chunfeng as a result of the *Shanghai Babe* controversy. By then, there were altogether sixteen titles in the original Cloth Tiger series, including *Kujie* (Bitter World) by Hong Feng, *Wu yu zhi cheng* (City of No Rain) by Tie Ning, *Lang yuan* (Lang Garden) by Zhao Mei, *Zhi xianglian* (Paper Necklace) by Cui Jingsheng, *Minmie* (Vanishing) by Gao Xiaosheng, *Zaohua* (Good Fortune) by Lu Tao, *Ansha san san er er* (Assassination—3322) by Wang Meng, *Zoujin yewan* (Into the Night) by Ye Zhaoyan, *Qing'ai hualang* (Gallery of Passion and Love) by Zhang Kangkang, *Lie sha er hao* (No. 2 Shark Hunter) by Pan Maoqun, *Tu men* (Earth Gate) by Jia Pingwa, *Kewang jiqing* (Thirst for Passion) by Pipi; *Wo ai yangguang* (I Love Sunshine) by Xu Jia, *Yue huo yue mingbai* (The More I Live the More I Understand) by Yang Zhengguang, *Biru nüren* (Such As Women) by Pipi, and *Da yu nü* (Bathing Woman) by Tie Ning.

28. The Chinese translation of Harlequin titles—a joint venture between Harlequin and several publishing houses—started as early as 1995. But it was not until January 2000, when the alliance with Chunfeng was formed, that Harlequin romances were promoted as paperback fiction on a large scale, using many promotional features common to the original Harlequins. For example, every other month, five pocket paperbacks came on the market simultaneously, each with a first print run of twenty thousand. A market research questionnaire was included with each book, along with a preview of the next series of new titles. The joint project came to a halt owing to the *Shanghai Babe* incident, which led to the suspension of the publishing house and closing of its Beijing office in September 2001. By 2002, Harlequin had found a new partner, Writers Publishing House, and was planning to take on the Chinese market again. See Wang Yun; and Hong Fei. Some information on Harlequin's promotion of its paperback romances is from my interview with Zhao Suping, Chief Representative of the Beijing Office of Harlequin International Limited in June 2001.

29. For a detailed discussion of the *Shanghai Babe* incident, see Chapter 4. After a short hiatus in late 2000, the Cloth Tiger novel series resumed publication in 2001, and it is still being used as a brand name by Chunfeng at various book fairs and exhibitions. Its romantic conventions, familiar writers, and distinctive cover design have all been retained.

30. Liang Shanbo and Zhu Yingtai were the main characters in a popular folk story that has been passed down for hundreds of years in China through various artistic forms, including opera, music, and film. In the original story, the lovers are to be separated as a result of various social barriers. In the end they choose to die for love, and their bodies are transformed into a pair of butterflies that remain together for eternity.

31. Ah Zheng, "Changxiao shu," 163; Zhao Yuntang; and Su Jinyu.

32. *Wenyi bao*, December 7, 1991.

33. Ah Zheng, "Changxiao shu," 141.
34. An Boshun, "Chuangzao pinpai," 30.
35. From my May 2000 interview with An Boshun.
36. Ah Zheng, "Changxiao shu," 148, 152; An, "Chuangzao pinpai," 29.
37. *Zhonghua dushu bao*, November 12, 1997, 4.
38. An Boshun, "Bu laohu," 5–6.
39. Ibid.
40. Advertisement, *Zhonghua dushu bao*, November 12, 1997.
41. Ah Zheng, "Changxiao shu," 150–51, 161–62.
42. For example, a piece by An himself on Jia Pingwa's *Earth Gate*, "Bufang zou-jin *tumen*" (Why Not Enter the "Earth Gate"), November 6, 1996; a report on Jia Pingwa and Zhang Kangkang signing their new books in Shenzhen, April 23, 1997; a report on a symposium about Pipi and Wen Xi's new works, April 9, 1997; a substantial piece on the business and products of Cloth Tiger Cultural Enterprises, An's new enterprise (although not identified as such), November 5, 1997. It has become a common practice for publishing houses to sponsor a column or pay for a certain number of copies, which are then sent free to colleges or scholars. In return, the publishers are given advertising space in these newspapers.
43. *Zhonghua dushu bao*, April 9, 1997. This kind of symposium has also become a common forum for book advertising and promotion in the name of criticism. These are often coorganized by the publishing house; research institutes, critics, editors, and writers as well as the media are invited, often with fees ("expenses") and dinner provided. The reports, speeches, and papers arising from the symposium are later published in literary journals or book review newspapers.
44. See the report of the symposium in a special edition for the novel, *Xiaoshuo xuankan: Changpian xiaoshuo te kan* 1 (2000).
45. Guo Yujie.
46. Zhang Shenyou.
47. Ibid.
48. Pei, 86.

CHAPTER 3

1. Shen Changwen, 24.
2. Driver.
3. Although originally only referring to private book distributors, as opposed to the main channel of the Xinhua bookstore system, the "second channel," a loosely defined term that indicates anything not "mainstream" or official, now includes both private distribution and unofficial publishing. This is because it was private booksellers who first branched into unofficial publishing and who constitute the main influence in this area of publishing. Another term often used in relation to the second channel is "book dealer," which also includes private, unofficial distributors and publishers.
4. For example, recently a book titled *Feifa chuban huodong yanjiu* (Studies on Illegal Publishing Activities) was published as part of a state-sponsored social science research project. This book, though certainly a systematic study of the social and economic origins of "illegal publishing"—and other problems in the publishing sys-

tem—continues to maintain the official view that the second channel is completely "illegal" and depicts it as a "troubling element" in the publishing industry. See Zhang Zhiqiang.

5. Another two fictional works worth mentioning here are *Huangwu zhi lü* (Road to Ruin) by Hunan writer He Dun and *Yinse youhuo* (Tempted by Silver) by Jiangsu writer Lu Xingsheng. He Dun's book depicts a Balzacian hero, a hard-working book dealer whose business starts in Changsha's Yellow Mud Street (Huangni jie), a once notorious national base for unofficial and illegal book publishing (both retail and wholesale) in the 1980s and early 1990s, and subsequently expands to Beijing, the national political and cultural capital. He's book depicts well an individual's degeneration and inner struggles; Lu's work gives a broader picture of the underground illegal media industry and the various social forces that shaped it. The book bears strong traces of real-life events, as it is largely based on the experience of the author, who is an officer of the "Anti-Pornography and Illegal Publications Office" of Jiangsu province and actively involved in investigating the once notorious "September 18 Illicit Publication Criminal Ring" (see note 15).

6. The ghost figure expresses the resentment felt by virtually all unofficial publishers in China—even those who have found ways around the restrictions—at the irrational disparities of the publishing system. Inefficient state publishing houses still have exclusive access to book licenses, despite their frequent lack of business sense, whereas experienced and highly competent second-channel publishers must use risky and underhanded methods to obtain every single book license (methods that could easily land them in prison, or worse, on death row).

7. Yang, *Zhongguo shushang*, 120.

8. According to the book, Zhou chose the name "otter" because traditionally, otters were thought to spread the plague, and he saw book dealers like himself as a kind of plague that would cause the demise of the weak official publishing industry.

9. Yang, *Zhongguo shushang*, 219.

10. In December 1980, the State Publishing Administration (Guojia chuban ju) issued a notice, "Suggestions on Steadily Developing Collective and Individually Owned Bookstores, Booths, Stalls, and Book Dealer Operations" (Jianyi you jihua you buzhou de fazhan jiti suoyouzhi he geti suoyouzhi de shudian shuting shutan he shufan). In June 1982, the Ministry of Culture convened a symposium on the reform of book distribution and later issued a formal decision to supplement the former monopoly of Xinhua bookstore with a book distribution system using multiple channels of distribution and multiple ownership. See Zhang Hongwei, 14.

11. Pei, 155.

12. For more on the government's policy regarding "cooperative publishing arrangements," see the relevant parts of Chapter 2, especially note 7.

13. Since its establishment in the late 1980s by the newly formed State Press and Publication Administration, the book license system had been meant "to license publications by granting their publishing houses book numbers (ISBNs and ISSNS) as an official way to control book publication." But as Lynch notes, "the buying and selling of book license numbers became common as publishing houses were made responsible for profits and losses," and thus "by the early 1990s, the proliferation of print media was out of central state control and has basically remained so ever since"

(159). This out-of-control situation is especially serious at the lower provincial and municipal levels.

14. Pei, 160.

15. Ibid., 160. This event is known as the *jiu yaoba feifa chuban an* (September 18 Illicit Publication Case), named after the date of the crackdown. The group was headed by Cao Zhixin, who was based in Jiangsu province. Cao was executed in 1992.

16. *Cehua* is a term often used in today's publishing circles. Originally referring to the curating of art exhibitions and displays or other kinds of planning and organizational work related to arts projects, in publishing this word is now commonly used to refer to conceiving a publishing project *and* carrying out the work to put it into practice, including finding investors, employing or contracting staff, and finally, doing marketing and sales work. Hence the term has a quite elastic meaning, convenient for the gray area of second-channel publishing.

17. He did keep a position at the Beijing Federation of Literary and Art Circles, but this was basically a sinecure.

18. From my December 1999 interview with Xing An.

19. Zhang Li.

20. From my May 15, 2000, interview with book dealer Chen Liu.

21. Wang Lei, "Huozhe zaoyu liangzhong shichang mingyun." The novel was also included in the second volume of *Yuhua zuopin ji* (Yu Hua's Collected Works), published by Social Sciences Publishing House (Shehui kexue chubanshe) in 1995, but the print run was just five thousand—an average number for literary works at that time.

22. As a result of pressure arising from the controversy surrounding Mian Mian's novel *Candy*—another novel produced by Ding Xiaohe that was banned by the government after *Shanghai Babe*—it was extremely difficult to find Ding for an interview. The information about Ding Xiaohe that I use here was collected from several editors I met in Beijing in May 2000, especially Gu Jianping, editor of the literary journal *Shiyue* (October).

23. Another book agent who is devoted to producing such quality books is Hu Yanhua. Having established professional contract relations with Guangxi Education Publishing House (Guangxi jiaoyu chubanshe), he deserves credit for "edition upgrading" many previously published scholarly books and works of high literature, such as *Mei de licheng* (The Pilgrimage of Beauty) by Li Zehou, on ancient Chinese art, and *Niuniu: yi ge fuqin de shouji* (Niuniu—Notes from a Father), by the essayist and scholar Zhou Guoping. The elegant designs, with many illustrations throughout the text and high-quality proofreading and printing, have all contributed to the new trend for quality books in literature publishing.

24. The information and data I collected for this section are based on the following interviews, unless otherwise indicated: interview with Guan Bo, general manager of Guolinfeng bookstore, May 22, 2001; interview with Xin Jiping, general manager of Alpha Books, May 31, 2001; interview with Miao Hong, project manager of Alpha Books, in charge of title selection and book production, May 31 and June 5, 2001.

25. The phrase in Chinese, *zheng ben qing yuan*, abbreviated, provides Alpha Books' Chinese name Zhengyuan.

26. Liu Cuiping.

27. For the popular response to *Class*, see Yang Xueping.

28. Zhang Fu.

29. Shi Kang, "Preface."

30. Rosenthal.

31. Ibid.

32. Yang Zhijun, 327–28.

33. Wu Peihua, 16.

34. Of course, Xinhua does now have a handful of flagship superstores in big cities like Beijing and Shanghai. These have greatly improved their selection and service; however, such stores are still in the minority.

35. Xi, 157–74.

36. According to a recent survey on online bookstores, Xishu Bookstore is the most efficient in locating rare titles, and in its ordering service and delivery. "Yifen wangshang goushu de ceshi baogao" (Survey on online bookstores), *Zhonghua dushu bao*, April 19, 2000.

37. Liu Nan.

38. He explains the name of the studio and series as follows: "Horses live in the wilderness, and Wilderness Tribe is the breeding ground for Dark Horses." Yu Jie, "Preface," 4.

39. Yu Jie (back cover).

40. Several of the publishers who were regulated were collaborators of He Xiongfei. Their editors were disciplined or replaced. Yu Jie, the dark-horse writer, was asked to leave his job at the Modern Literature Gallery. See Lin and Wu, "Beijing Cracks Down on 'Politically Incorrect' Publishers."

41. I personally witnessed the difficulty private publishers face collecting money from retailers when I interviewed Chen Liu (see note 20). According to Chen, this remains a very common headache for private publishers.

42. See the program produced by Hong Kong's Phoenix Satellite TV about the piracy suffered by Yu Qiuyu's works: "Zhushu zhe de fannao" (The Worries of a Writer), broadcast May 14, 2000.

43. This subgenre derives its name and tradition from the great late-Qing vernacular novel *Guanchang xianxingji* (Officialdom Unmasked) by Li Boyuan, which depicts the corruption of government officials and scholars. The contemporary "guanchang xiaoshuo" often combines the traditions of Chinese vernacular with Western realism. It exposes the deeply rooted official corruption at different levels of government and in society in general through the experiences of a rising young hero beginning his career as a public official.

44. He and Wu, 22–23.

45. Xu Linzheng, 160–66, 216–19.

46. When I interviewed Chen Liu, a private book dealer (May 15, 2000), he condemned the book license system and criticized the present discrimination against private publishers. He claimed that even though many private book dealers had been contributing to the prosperity of the book market, they were usually the first targets of government campaigns against illicit publishing. He argued that a registration system would encourage healthier competition. In a recent article, "Tushu chubanye

gaige zhong de zhiheng zhanlue," Zhang Shengyou, the president of Writers, drew a similar conclusion. See Chapter 2.

47. For details about the loosening of control over the film industry, and for more recent newspapers and magazines, see the Introduction.

48. Another example of how the second channel has undermined the state's ideological control is provided by He Guimei in her research into books on the Anti-Rightist Movement (*fanyou shuji*). According to He, the second channel played a very active role in breaking into the "forbidden zone" of publishing books on the Anti-Rightist Movement and even the Cultural Revolution: "The majority of books on the Anti-Rightist movement published before 1998 were circulated within the second channel." He contends that it was the second channel's decade-long practice of bringing out such books that led to official publishers' "self-liberation" in 1998, when several of them also began to publish formerly "banned books" on the Anti-Rightist Movement, although of course the real incentive for publishing these books was "their market value due to their obvious ideological taboo." See He Guimei.

CHAPTER 4

1. Xu Kun, *Shuangdiao yexing chuan*, 7.
2. Xu Kun, "Cong ci yue lai yue mingliang," 17. The following information related to the Red Poppy publishing incident is from Xu's writing, unless otherwise stated.
3. *Qianjiang wanbao*, August 23, 1995.
4. Xu Kun, "Cong ci yue lai yue mingliang," 6.
5. Wang Meng.
6. Niu Suqin, 21–22.
7. Xu, "Cong ci yue lai yue mingliang," 17–18.
8. This term was used to refer to prose works, often first published as special columns in women's magazines or evening newspapers, by women writers from Shanghai and Canton, represented by Huang Ai, Dong Xi, Zhang Mei, and others. Many are feuilletons about women's daily life—about shopping, makeup, fashion, love, and sexual experiences. The style is heavily influenced by women writers from the 1940s, such as Zhang Ailing and Su Qing, as well as some contemporary Hong Kong and Taiwanese women writers. In the following pages, I discuss some examples of "privacy literature" and "alternative writing," and so need not explain these terms here.
9. Xu, "Cong ci yue lai yue mingliang," 17.
10. Dai Jinhua, 4.
11. Lan, 6.
12. The obvious discrepancies are easy to detect in the titles, the covers, and the serious original preface from Lan Lizhi, which is still retained at the beginning of each book. See Lan, 4–7.
13. Dai Jinhua, 8.
14. Han Xiaohui.
15. The three novels are *Qingtai* (Moss, 1995), *Shouwang kongxin suiyue* (Watch-

ing the Empty Years Passing By, 1995), and *Shuo ba, fangjian* (Speak, My Room, 1997).

16. For more discussion about personal writing and the recent changes in themes and narrative styles in contemporary novels, see Shuyu Kong, "Journey Within: The Inward Turn of the Contemporary Chinese Novel" (Ph.D. dissertation, University of British Columbia, 1997). Many novels published around the same time, such as *Zai xiyu zhong huhan* (Crying in the Fine Rain) by Yu Hua and *Bianyuan* (On the Margins) by Ge Fei, share similar thematic concerns and narrative innovations.

17. My interviews with Lin Bai in December 1999 and May 2000 confirmed these personal experiences.

18. Lin, *Yi ge ren de zhanzheng*, 1–2.

19. A dozen years ago, Huacheng published another novel by a woman writer, Yu Luojin's autobiographical *Yige dongtian de tonghua* (A Chinese Winter's Tale). This novel caused much controversy and suffered editorial cuts, and the writer was eventually exiled. See note 3 in "Introduction." This is in marked contrast with the enthusiastic reception for Lin's works, although they too were "edited" without the author's consent. The two cases illuminate separately the influence of politics and commerce on literary production in the early 1980s and late 1990s.

20. Lin, "Guanyu yi ge ren de zhanzheng," 228.

21. Ibid., 228–29. But according to Chen Xiaoming, the Beijing critic who helped Lin Bai contact the Gansu publishing house, the facts were more complicated. Chen recalled that Lin Bai was eager to get her novel published since she had just been laid off and needed income to support herself and her young daughter. So Chen contended that Lin was not a complete innocent in this matter. And Chen later agreed to compensate her by offering to help her publish another novel, *Qingtai* (Moss) in 1995. From my June 12, 2001, interview with Chen Xiaoming.

22. The cover shows a photograph of a woman (the writer herself) surrounded by men's naked legs and various sadomasochistic paraphernalia. See Hai Nan (cover).

23. "Nüxing wenxue ji qita" and "Yinwei chenmo tai jiu" were published separately in *Zhonghua dushu bao* on December 20, 1995, and January 10, 1996.

24. Lin, "Guanyu yi ge ren de zhanzheng," 229.

25. *Yi ge ren de zhanzheng* (Hong Kong: Tiandi tushu, 1998); *Yi ge ren de zhanzheng* (Taipei: Maitian, 1998).

26. Lin, "Guangyu yi ge ren de zhenzheng," 229.

27. There have been many cases of women being mistreated and mispackaged. One of the most serious involved the extensive "revising" and vulgar packaging of Chi Zijian's *Chenzhong Xiangche huanghun* (Morning Bell Rings through Evening) at the hands of Shenyang Publishing House (Shenyang chubanshe). It led to a lawsuit in 1996 that Chi, supported by public opinion, won. See Chi's letter to *Wenxue Bao*. See also Shi, "Chi Zijian wei chenzhong taohui shuofa."

28. Wei, *Shanghai baobei*, 1–2. The English translation here is mine. Bruce Humes translated the book into English as *Shanghai Baby* (London: Robinson, 2001).

29. The women's magazine *Wutai yu rensheng* (Life On Stage) ran a special cover story on Wei Hui, which included the original media coverage of her Chengdu tour. See *Life on Stage* 5 (2000).

30. Worth noting is that much of the publicity surrounding Wei was actually generated by a notorious literary "catfight" between Wei and another Shanghai writer, Mian Mian. The "fight" was started by Mian Mian, who claimed that Wei Hui's so-called cool and alternative writing was only kitsch, a shameless and insincere exploitation of the painful experiences of real alternatives such as Mian Mian herself. This cultural brawl has spread through the Internet and inspired a heated debate over what constitutes a true or false "alternative."

31. By my own observation (at bookstalls in Zhongguancun, Beijing, in mid-May 2000—admittedly a random survey), at least a dozen collections of Wei Hui's works had been published as of May 2000. According to Wei, her works topped the pirate best seller lists. She proudly estimated that there were no less than three or four million pirated copies in circulation; see Wei's personal webpage (goldnets.myrice.com/wh).

32. Wei, *Shanghai baobei* (back cover).

33. Ibid., "Postlude."

34. See Wei Hui's personal website, goldnets.myrice.com/wh.

35. Wei, *Shanghai Baobei*, 24.

36. Ibid., 38.

37. Ibid., 16.

38. Ibid., 168.

39. Ibid., 212.

40. *Zuojia* published a special issue, "Qishiniandai chusheng de nü zuojia xiao-shuo zhuanhao" (Women Writers Born After the 1970s) (No. 7, 1998). *Wenxue Bao* also dedicated special issues to them on September 3, 1998, and March 16, 2000. For more about the commercialization of literary journals, see Chapter 6.

41. A reader's letter, "Tamen ping shenme zai wentan jueqi" (For What Did They Become Prominent in Literary Field), was published in *Wenxue Bao*, September 3, 1998.

42. See "Beijing nü zuojia zhuanji" ("Special Collection of Beijing Women Writers"), which included Ah Mei, Hou Bei, and Liu Yu, *Furong* 3 (2000).

CHAPTER 5

1. A typical example is Yan Fu, an early modern Chinese thinker and translator, who introduced Spencer, Huxley, and Adam Smith to Chinese readers at the turn of the twentieth century; see Schwartz.

2. One important point that both Leo Ou-fan Lee and Shih Shu-mei make is that in 1930s and 1940s Shanghai, the introduction of literary modernism was closely related to other forms of popular culture, such as fashion and cinema, rather than highbrow. In fact, many urban Chinese literati got to know contemporary Western literary works through popular literary and general interest magazines such as *Vanity Fair, Esquire, The New Yorker,* and *Saturday Review*. See Lee and Shih, both of whom discuss in more detail how Chinese writers imported foreign ideas and lifestyles.

3. Although here I am describing the general situation over three decades, my account is more valid for the years 1949 to 1966 and for after the early 1970s. This is because from 1966 to 1972, there was very little official publication of foreign literature.

4. The observations in the following section are based mainly on statistics collected from *Waiguo wenxue tushu mulu (1951–1990)*, from People's Literature Publishing House, which has been the most important and representative publisher in foreign literature over the past five decades. I also refer to Xiao Xiao.

5. For example, the titles of three major projects initiated in 1959 by People's Literature Publishing House in collaboration with the Institute of Foreign Literature of the Chinese Academy of Social Science and Shanghai Translation Publishing House (Shanghai yiwen) indicate the kinds of selective criteria adopted during this period. They were: the Foreign Masterpieces series (Waiguo wenxue mingzhu xilie) and the Foreign Literary Theory series (Waiguo wenxue lilun xilie), which focused strongly on pre-twentieth-century "progressive" (mainly critical realist, literary, and theoretical) works, and the Marxist Literary and Art Theory series (Makesi zhuyi jingdian zhuzuo).

6. For more details on internal publication of foreign literature, including its origins, titles, and distribution, see Kong, "For Reference Only," 76–85.

7. See *Quanguo neibu faxing tushu zongmu (1949–1979)*, ed. Zhongguo banben tushuguan (Zhonghua shuju, 1980).

8. Virtually no foreign literature was openly published during the ten years of the Cultural Revolution (1966–76). In contrast, many internal publications were produced in the early 1970s.

9. The fifth and sixth volumes had also been translated by the summer of 1966; however, these were not printed until 1979 due to the chaos caused by the Cultural Revolution. My interview with Qin Sunxin, one of the translators. Qin is also former Associate Editor in Chief in charge of foreign literature of People's Literature Publishing House.

10. Before 1966, small circles of children from the elite governing classes—mainly literary youth who wrote poems and loved the arts—would often form cultural salons that met in their homes. The most famous underground salons in the early 1960s were the "Sun Brigade" (Taiyang zongdui), hosted by Zhang Langlang, son of the famous artist and art critic Zhang Ding and a student at the Central Academy of Arts, and the "X Poetry Society" (X shishe), hosted by Guo Shiying, son of Guo Moruo and a student of philosophy at Peking University. Zhang Langlang recalls that around that time, many internal books were being privately circulated among the literary youth of Beijing; these works were so popular that some young people even hand-copied them. See Zhang Langlang, 30–52. These underground salons enjoyed a revival in the early 1970s among the young elite in Beijing. For example, the one hosted by Xu Haoyuan, located in the staff residences of the State Council and Ministry of Transportation, forged close relations with the Baiyangdian poetry group. See Duoduo, 195–202. Another was the famous "Peiduofei Club" hosted by He Jingjie, the daughter of the famous poet He Qifang. See Ge, 96–100.

11. Xiao Xiao, 4–16.

12. The name comes from the place where these young poets—most of them Beijing youth, including Duoduo and Mang Ke—stayed during their "sent down" years. It is a rural area in Hebei province famous for its Baiyangdian Lake.

13. See Liao, 221, 219, 287, 292.

14. Gao Xingjian, the 2000 Nobel Prize winner, is representative in this respect. He was among the first Chinese writers of the 1980s to read, advocate, and apply to his own writing Western modernist literary techniques. His *Xiandai xiaoshuo jiqiao chu tan* (Preliminary Exploration on the Techniques of Modern Fiction) inspired much controversy and enthusiasm for Western modernism.

15. Wang Xiaoming, "Fanyi de zhengzhi," 219.

16. Li, "Fanyi 'huai xiang' liu zhong," 30–31.

17. In the culture and philosophy fields, many translation series also appeared. Three of these were especially influential: the Aesthetics in Translation series (Meixue yiwen congshu) edited by Li Zehou, the Into the Future series (Zou xiang weilai congshu) edited by Jin Guantao, and the Culture: China and the World series (Wenhua: Zhongguo yu shijie congshu) edited by Gan Yang.

18. Link, 184.

19. Ibid.

20. Wu Xusheng, 41–42.

21. In the summer of 1988, this trend toward publishing violent stories and erotic fiction led to a broad campaign against illegal publishing by the Press and Publication Administration. During this time, two "notorious" pornographic works—*Meigui meng* (Rosy Dream) and *Qingchang dutu* (Gambler in the Tournament of Love)—were banned. All copies of both were confiscated, and the two publishing houses—Yanbian Publishing House (Yanbian chubanshe) and Workers Publishing House (Gongren chubanshe)—were fined and suspended.

22. Li, "Dakai chuangkou chu kaifang," 46–48.

23. The account of this "incident" is based on Li, "Dakai chuangkou chu kaifang" (see preceding note) and on Qie Shi. The latter mentions that *Yilin* invited a Xinhua journalist to produce a special report on this incident for an internally published newsletter, *Guonei dong tai* (Domestic Developments).

24. Li, *Botao shang de zhuji*, 270. This book records Li's personal experience working as editor in chief of *Yilin* and later as president and editor in chief of Yilin Press. This book includes a special section, "About Ulysses" (Guanyu youlixisi), in which Li provides much inside information about this publishing event. Some of my understanding of this event is based on his account. I also refer to Wang and Zhao, "Yilin ban Youlixisi yuan he changxiao."

25. Li, *Botao shang de zhuji*, 270.

26. Wang and Zhao, "Renwen ban Youlixisi jie mi."

27. See, for instance, Xiao Qian, which includes an editor's note introducing Yilin's translation.

28. See for example, the special edition "Youlixisi, tianshu poyi" (Deciphering Ulysses), *Zhonghua dushu bao*, May 10, 1995.

29. See *Xinmin wanbao*, September 22, 1993.

30. See Chen Shu's promotional article.

31. See the special edition of *Zhonghua dushu bao*, May 10, 1995. See also Feng Yidai and Liu Junping for two examples of the many scholarly articles comparing the two translations. There was also some argument between the two translators regarding who had been more loyal to the original; see Wang Zhenping; Xiao, Wen and Xu; and Wen Jieruo.

32. Li, "Guanyu youlixisi," in *Botao shang de zhuji*, 267.

33. See *Yilin* 5 (1995), inside cover 3.

34. See Yu, for example.

35. Li, *Botao shang de zhuji*, 264. Besides healthy sales, the Yilin edition of *Ulysses* also won First Prize in the National Outstanding Foreign Literature Book Awards (Quanguo youxiu waiguo wenxue tushu jiang) in 1995 and was nominated for the National Book Prize.

36. The Chinese edition of Sutherland's book, *Changxiao shu*, was a volume in the then popular Five Dime series (Wujiao congshu) from Shanghai Cultural Publishing House (Shanghai wenhua chubanshe).

37. Figures from Su.

38. Typically, Chinese publishing houses buy the copyright by paying an 8 to 9 percent royalty (a marked increase from the earlier 4 to 5 percent), often with an advance of several thousand dollars. However, it is common to pay the translator a fixed manuscript fee of a certain amount per thousand characters. See "Liaokai banshui fu chou de miansha."

39. See "Harry Potter Sales."

40. Yang Jing. Most of the information was confirmed during my June 2001 interview with Nie Zhenning, president of People's Literature.

41. Ibid. See also Meng.

42. Since 1994, China has allowed in ten foreign films annually—most of them Hollywood blockbusters—to boost the declining domestic film market. According to Mark O'Neil, these ten films account for about 60 percent of national film ticket sales. See O'Neil.

43. A review by Zhang Fuhai typifies the enthusiastic response of Chinese readers to *The Bridges of Madison County*: "*Bridges of Madison County* can't avoid becoming a bestseller because it solves the emotional problems of Americans, Chinese, even the whole universe today." See Zhang, "Zua zhu meng de shou."

44. Su.

45. See *Fatiaocheng; Mozhate yu liangqun* (A Clockwork Orange), trans. Wang Zhiguang and Pu Long (Nanjing: Yilin chubanshe, 2001).

46. Regarding the poor quality and plagiarism of translations, see Li, "Chuban ye yao dajia" in *Botao shang de zhuji*, 234–38; and "Fanyi 'huai xiang' liu zhong."

47. See Zhao Wuping. Another flagrant example of repetitive publication was Stendhal's *Rouge et Noir* (Hong yu hei), of which more than twenty Chinese editions were produced by the end of the 1990s. Almost all copied one of three reliable translations: those by Shanghai Translation, Yilin Press, and Zhejiang Art and Literature. See Li, "Fanyi 'huai xiang' liu zhong."

CHAPTER 6

1. Here I focus on so-called "pure" or "serious" literary journals (*chun wenxue*, or *yansu wenxue qikan*). Although the concept of pure literature is of course controversial, there was until recently quite a clear demarcation in China between pure, serious journals and popular ones. The vast majority of officially published literary journals after 1949 were "serious" journals, and still conceive themselves as such, owing

to government efforts to eliminate popular entertainment literature and to promote a kind of moralistic literature supporting its revolutionary course.

2. The situation of provincial journals is especially instructive because they are in the awkward position of being neither "highbrow" enough nor "lowbrow" enough. The top national journals have long-established reputations and loyal readers; this is considerable "invisible capital"—enough for them to keep running. For instance, even in recent years, *Shouhuo*'s sales have been healthy enough that it can avoid running ads or publishing enterprise reportage. Moreover, some of these larger journals are associated with publishing houses and therefore face fewer financial pressures and distribution problems than journals attached to the Writers Associations or to the Federation of Literary and Artistic Circles system. For instance, *Huacheng*, affiliated with Huacheng Publishing House in Guangzhou, can afford not to advertise for other companies or publish enterprise literature. These top journals see little need to drastically alter their approaches.

3. Guo Xiaoli.

4. Liu Ying.

5. See for example, Zhu; also He Long.

6. From *Zhongguo chuban nianjian*, 1989; also from Hong Zicheng, 24.

7. *Zhongguo chuban nianjian*, 1981; 1984.

8. Link, 14–15.

9. Song and Zhou.

10. "The State Council's Announcement, 1869–70."

11. From my December 1999 interview with Li Jingze and Zhang Dening.

12. See Chapter 1 for more details on the reform of the CWA.

13. Regarding the growth of the mass media and popular literature in China and the impact of both on contemporary culture, see Chapters 1, 2, and 3 of this book. See also Zha; Barmé.

14. Jiang Zhenxin.

15. Marja Kaikkonen, "Stories and Legends," 134–60.

16. *Zhongguo chuban nianjian*, 1984, 680.

17. "Woguo xikan jishen . . . "

18. Jiang Zhenxin.

19. *Zhongguo chuban nianjian*, 1981, 635; 1984, 680; 1989, 59.

20. From my December 1999 interview with Li Jingze.

21. From my December 1999 interview with Zhang Dening.

22. Xiao Yuan. My personal research, including interviews with editors, seems to confirm that these basic figures, although imprecise, reflect the reality of literary journal subscriptions today. For example, *Beijing wenxue* presently sells around five thousand a month (from my December 1999 interview with its president, Zhang Dening). *Writer* sold eight thousand a month in 1999 (from my May 2000 interview with president and editor in chief Zong Renfa); and *Lotus* regularly sells seven thousand, according to Xiao Yuan, its editor in chief. Because this information is so recent, I haven't been able to find more precise statistics. There is a joke in Chinese literary circles: Don't ask a lady her age, and don't ask the editor of a literary journal about its subscription! Other factors besides these make it difficult to find out true

subscription figures. For instance, a journal might print more copies than the real subscription because printing houses won't do a print run if the number is too small.

23. From my December 1999 interviews with Li Jingze, editor of *Renmin Wenxue*, and Zhang Dening, president of *Beijing wenxue*.

24. This same problem was discussed in Chapter 2 in the context of state-run publishing houses.

25. Xie.

26. Ding.

27. For a detailed study on contemporary Chinese reportage, see Moran.

28. This kind of promotional reportage actually originated with newspapers, where "all-expenses-paid news reporting" emerged as early as the mid-1980s. For a more detailed account of how this practice developed, see Zhao Yuezhi, Chapter 4. By the late 1980s, the practice had spread to other print media, including literary journals. The authors included journalists, professional and amateur writers, and even college students (whoever had access to potential sponsors and was willing and able to write a flattering piece). The host company would introduce its "achievements" to the writer and provide free transportation, meals, and accommodation during the visit. The writer would then receive a fat commission on completion of the article; the journal or newspaper in which the piece was published was also handsomely rewarded through advertising fees.

29. See the report of the speech given by Gao Zhanxiang, then Vice Minister of Culture, in *Literature Press*, September 17, 1992. Gao's speech reflected the official attitude toward reform of cultural institutions after Deng Xiaoping's Southern Tour. It called for deepening market reforms.

30. One such example in the founding meeting of the Beijing Literature Board of Directors on December 11, 2003, when many of these cultural officials at the municipal level attended the meeting. See *Beijing wenxue* 2 (1994) (inside cover).

31. See the notice for the Star of Enterprise reportage contest in *Beijing wenxue* 11 (1991).

32. Sun, 110.

33. Ibid.

34. Dou.

35. See a series of readers' responses and discussion in issues from April 28 to June 16, 1994; see also Gu.

36. This and the following information regarding *Writer*'s reform is from my May 2000 interview with Zhong Renfa, president and editor in chief of *Writer*, unless otherwise indicated.

37. Jiang Xun.

38. See the editor's note in *Lotus* 1 (2000), 173–75.

39. Although it claims to be the "No. 1 Literature and Art magazine in circulation," there is controversy about whether *Foshan Art and Literature* can be counted as a literary magazine at all, considering its populist slant and hybrid content. This controversy demonstrates that the whole idea of the "literary journal" is undergoing a significant conceptual shift, and perhaps is no longer even loosely definable.

40. From my December 1999 interview with Li Jingze.

CONCLUSION

1. The number of television stations comes from "To Thoroughly Carry Out President Jiang's Instructions and Bring About a New Era for Chinese TV and Radio Work," by an unnamed special columnist of *Dianshi yanjiu* 2 (2001), 6. The other figures are from Zhang Changming, 9.

2. According to Daniel Lynch, the spread of computerized telecommunication networks and the Internet throughout China dates back to 1994–95, after the Ministry of Post and Telecommunications lost its monopoly and started developing a marketing plan including the promotion of Internet services. But the number of Internet subscribers was very small at first: in mid-1995 it was only 1000 nationwide. Even as recently as 1997, only about 620,000 people had access to the Internet in China. See Lynch, 108–9.

3. "State Bureau Examines Internet Cafés" (english.peopledaily.com.cn/200108/20/eng20010820_75430.html).

4. The mid-1980s saw the first major increase in television series. According to Sheldon Lu, in 1983, 428 episodes were produced; in 1984, 740; and in 1985, 1,300. See Sheldon H. Lu, 165.

5. Lynch notes that many television stations "turned to the international market to buy or otherwise acquire programming." One 1993 survey found that 74 percent of programs broadcast at the provincial level and below originated abroad. Lynch, 110. Lynch discusses TV globalization further in his sections on "Legal and Semilegal Importation of Television Programs" and "Satellite TV."

6. Sheldon H. Lu, 213.

7. These numbers are based on my interviews with several writers who have written scripts for television dramas—in particular, my December 1999 interview with Li Jingze. They are confirmed by written materials. For example, Liang Xiaosheng revealed that around the mid-1990s he received a fee of ten thousand yuan per episode for writing scripts for two series based on his own novels. See Liang, 286.

8. Wang Shuo, *Wuzhizhe wuwei*, 23–33.

9. See Zhou Baiyi, 31–32.

10. "Writers Bank a Million for Novel Lives," *China Daily*, January 7, 2002.

11. This collection, titled "The Hai Yan TV Novel Series" (Hai Yan dianshi xiaoshuo shu xi), included *Bianyi jingcha* (Plainclothes Police), *Yong bu ming mu* (Die with Regret), and *Yu guanyin* (Jade Bodhisattva), among others. All three were produced as television dramas and became immediate hits.

12. See Chi Li.

13. This information is from Liu Yongjun's articles on best sellers and market trends. Liu's data and analysis are based on the monthly statistics for best sellers collected by the Beijing Kaijuan Book Market Research Centre. See Liu Yongjun, *Chuban guangjiao* 4 (2000) and 4 (2001).

14. Su, "Yingshi hong."

15. See Wang Hailing, *Qianshou*.

16. One example of the competition between publishers in producing television and film literature is the bidding war between People's Literature and Writers for *Noble House*. The series was broadcast on CCTV during prime time in the summer

of 2001. The media had hyped it in advance as "a modern-day *Dream of the Red Chamber*." Both Writers and People's Literature raced to publish book versions. The Writers edition was a novel adaptation based on the series, whereas the People's Literature edition was simply the original screenplay by director/screenwriter Guo Baochang. Writers managed to get its product to market twenty days before the People's Literature edition was ready, and sold some 200,000 during that short period. Despite the delays, the People's Literature edition also sold very well. This episode demonstrates the enormous potential for publishers who move quickly enough to bring out television scripts and adaptations while the program is still fresh in viewers' memories. This information is collected from my June 2001 interview with Nie Zhenning, president of People's Literature.

17. Wang Lei, "Yingshi yu tushu hudong de dianxing ge'an," 59–60.

18. See, for instance, the Writers Association's official website, www.chinawriter. org (Jinri zuojia wang); the Chinese Literary Journals Internet Alliance website www.nethong.com; and Golden Bookhouse (huangjin shuwu) (wenxue.lycos.com. cn), which has the most comprehensive collection of modern/contemporary literary works with electronic copyrights.

19. Unlike private websites, which offer downloading "service" for fellow enthusiasts, Bookoo is attempting to prove that selling copyright-authorized e-books can be a viable business. After opening its Beijing office in April 2001, Bookoo began furiously buying up the electronic rights for many contemporary writers' works and displaying them on its e-bookstore site with fancy and professional editing. It also tried to familiarize Chinese readers with e-books through an extensive promotional campaign in various media. See bookoo's website: www.bookoo.com.cn; see also my interview with Bookoo's Alex Cai (Cai xuejun).

20. Unfortunately, a serious cash flow crisis for Bookoo at the end of 2001 forced it to leave its modern, spacious Beijing offices and downsize its operations. Like many dot.com firms, Bookoo seems to have expanded too rapidly. It relied on overoptimistic venture capital and did not properly test the market demand for its products. Chinese consumers had grown used to obtaining Internet literature for free, and when they wished to buy a literary work, they preferred to have a real book in their hands rather than a virtual one on a screen, despite the marked difference in price. Also, the lack of a proper credit card system in China made it difficult for Bookoo to collect fees. The company had to spend a great deal to establish its own Bookoo Card system, on top of its huge investment in purchasing copyright from writers.

21. Based on my own observations, in the spring of 2000, there were more than two dozen Internet literature titles available in Beijing bookstores. Many of them were in the form of series. Here are just a few of the titles: the Internet Book Series (Wangluo shuxi; Beijing: Zhishi chubanshe, 2000); the Internet Literature series (Wangluo wencong; Beijing: Zhongguo shehui kexue chubanshe, 2000); Selection of the Best Internet Literature (Zhongguo wangluo yuanchuang zuopin jingxuan; Changchun: Shidai wenyi chubanshe, 2000); Under the Banyan Tree: Original Internet Works series (Rongshu xia: Wangluo yuanchuang wenxue congshu; Shanghai: Shanghai wenhua chubanshe, 2000); and Stars of the Internet series (Wangluo zhi xing congshu; Guangzhou: Huacheng chubanshe, 2000).

22. Zhao and Jiang.

23. Wang Shuo, "Zhe zhihou yiqie jiang bian," in Chen Cun, *Wo ai shang*, 291.

24. Wang Meng, preface to *Zhongguo wangluo yuanchuang zuopin jingxuan*.

25. These figures are up to date as of May 31, 2001, from www.rongshu.com.

26. See Zhang Yizhen's article "Rongshu xia: ba suoyou lirun chi tou," in which the information and data are based on the author's interview with William Zhu. The accuracy of the figures is questionable; I am using this information to suggest the business strategies and structure of this e-commerce company, not to provide exact statistics.

27. Mo Yan and the Taiwanese writer Li Ao are among those writers who distrust the quality and even the whole idea of Internet literature. Li Ao calls Internet literature "toilet literature" (*cesuo wenxue*) and "literary froth" (*wenxue paomo*). Wang Haijuan, 27.

28. *Yuyi* (Raincoat) and *Lovepost aierlan kafei* (Lovepost: Irish Coffee) both remained on the best seller list for over a year after being published, in 2000 and 2001, respectively. The latter was actually a collection of Internet pieces by various contributors from Taiwan and the Mainland. Cai's piece "Irish Coffee" was included to act as a promotional "face" for the collection.

29. One of the clearest examples of the Internet proving the salable potential of an unknown author is *Wukong zhan* (Monkey's Biography), a comic fantasy by Jin Hezai (a pen name meaning "Where is he now?"). Based loosely on the classic Chinese novel *Xi you ji* (Journey to the West) and its most popular character, Monkey (Sun Wukong), this Internet rewriting of the story of Monkey focuses on the newly invented love affairs of Monkey, Pigsy (Tianpeng/Zhu ba jie), and two female demons. The content and style of *Monkey's Biography* are influenced by Hong Kong comedian Zhou Zingchi and his film *Dahua xiyou* (Ranting to the West), with wild comic dialogue and wordplay incorporating many present-day colloquialisms.

Monkey's Biography was first posted in installments on the popular website Sina.com (xing lang wang, www.sina.com.cn) in the spring of 2000, and soon began to attract a huge number of hits. Apparently, young netizens found this "subversive" (or ludicrous) text clever and humorous. In 2001, the completed work won an award in the Second National Internet Literature Contest, and in the same year Guangming Daily Publishing House (Guangming ribao chubanshe) agreed to produce a book edition, which also sold extremely well. Attracted by this success, China Film Conglomerate (Zhongguo dianying jituan gongsi) then purchased the movie and television rights from the author for an undisclosed but "very high" price. Currently, China Film is investing more than 10 million yuan on an animated movie and a fifty-two-episode animated series of the work, with Jin Hezai agreeing to write the preliminary script and screenplay. See Chen Hua.

30. Alvin Kernan, 150.

Glossary

Ah Lai   阿来
Ah Zheng   阿正
Ai ni mei shangliang   爱你没商量
An Boshun   安波舜
Anni baobei   安妮宝贝
Bai Bing   白冰
Baihua wenyi chubanshe   百花文藝出版社
bailing jieceng   白领阶层
Bai lu yuan   白鹿原
Baiwanzhuang shushi   百万庄书市
Bai Ye   白烨
banben shengji   版本升级
ban quan   版权
ban shui   版税
ban zizuan ti xiaoshuo   半自传体小说
baogao wenxue   报告文学
baozhuang chaozuo   包装炒作
Bashan wenxue   巴山文学
Beijing chubanshe   北京出版社
Beijing dianshi yishu zhongxin   北京电视艺术中心
Beijing kaijuan tushu shichang yanjiusuo   北京开卷图书市场研究所
Beijingren zai niuyue   北京人在纽约
Beijing tushu dasha   北京图书大厦
Beijing wenxue   北京文学
Beijing xinwen chuban ju   北京新闻出版局
Bianjibu de gushi   编辑部的故事
bianlian   变脸
bi hui   笔会
Bing yu huo: yige beida guaijie de chouti wenxue   冰与火：一个北大怪杰的抽屉文学
Biru nüren   比如女人
bi shang liangshan   逼上梁山
Bo ku   博库
Bo ku shu ye   博库书业

Bu laohu congshu   布老虎丛书
Cai Zhiheng   蔡智恒
Caoyuan buluo chuangzuoshi   草原部落创作室
ce hua   策划
cehua bianji   策划编辑
Chang hen ge   长恨歌
Changjiang wenyi chubanshe   长江文艺出版社
changxiao shu   畅销书
changxiao shu bang   畅销书榜
chanye hua   产业化
Chenai luodi   尘埃落地
Chen Binyuan   陈斌源
Chen Danyan   陈丹燕
chengbao   承包
Chen Liu   陈柳
Chenlun de shengdian: zhongguo ershi shiji qishi niandai dixia shige yizhao   沉沦
     的圣殿:中国二十世纪七十年代地下诗歌遗照
Chen Ran   陈染
Chen Xiaoming   陈晓明
Chen Zhongshi   陈忠实
Chi Li   池莉
Chiruzhe shouji: yi ge minjian sixiangzhe de shengming tiyan   耻辱者手记:一个民间
     思想者的生命体验
Chi Zijian   迟子建
chuangzuo hanshou ban   创作函授班
chuangzuo shi   创作室
Chuban guang jiao   出版广角
chu dian   触电
Chunfeng   春风
Chunfeng wenyi chubanshe   春风文艺出版社
chun wenxue   纯文学
chun wenxue qikan   纯文学期刊
Cong ci yuelai yue mingliang   从此越来越明亮
Cong dianying mingxing dao yiwan fu jie   从电影明星到亿万富姐
Cun Zien   崔子恩
Da chuanqi   大喘气
Da hong denglong gaogao gua   大红灯笼高高挂
Da hua xiyou   大话西游
Dajia   大家
Daming gong ci   大明官词
Dang dai   当代
Dangdai nüxing wenxue shuxi   当代女性文学书系
Dangdai zuojia pinglun   當代作家評論
dang zheng jiguan   党政机关
dao ban   盗版
dao yin   盗印

dazhong chuanmei 大众传媒
Dazhong dianying 大众电影
dazhong wenhua 大众文化
Dazhong wenyi chubanshe 大眾文藝出版社
da wenxue 大文学
Da yu nü 大浴女
Da zai men 大宅门
deng ji zhi 登记制
dianshi lianxu ju 电视连续剧
di er qudao 第二渠道
Ding Xiaohe 丁晓禾
ditan wenxue 地摊文学
Di yi ci de qinmi jiechu 第一次的亲密接触
Donwu xiongmeng 动物凶猛
duanlie 断裂
duan nai 断奶
duo wei chanpin 多维产品
duo ye zhu wen 多业助文
dushi xiaoshuo 都市小说
Dushu 读书
Duzhe 读者
Er yue he 二月河
Erzi Han Han 儿子韩寒
Fatiao cheng:Mozhate yu langqun 发条橙: 莫扎特与狼群
Feidu 废都
Fei shichang xingwei 非市场行为
feitian jiang 飞天奖
Fengrufeitun 丰乳肥臀
feng ru song shudian 风入松书店
Fengtou zhengjian nüzi congshu 风头正健女子丛书
Fenling yizu qinggan xilie congshu 粉领一族情感系列丛书
Foshan wenyi 佛山文艺
Fu chu haimian 浮出海面
Furong 芙蓉
Fuxi fuxi 伏羲伏羲
gai ban 改版
Gansu renmin chubanshe 甘肃人民人民社
gao fei 稿费
geren xiezuo 个人写作
gongzhuo shi 工作室
Guan Bo 关波
Guanchang xiaoshuo 官场小说
guanggao xiaoying 广告效应
Gu Cheng 顾城
Guohua 国画
Guo lin feng tushu zhongxin 国林风图书中心

Gushi hui   故事会

Hafo nühai Liu Yiting   哈佛女孩刘亦婷

Haidian tushu cheng   海淀图书城

Haima gewuting   海马歌舞厅

Haima yingshi chuangzuoshi   海马影视创作室

Hai Nan   海南

Hai Yan   海岩

Han Dong   韩东

Han Han   韩寒

Han Renjun   韩仁均

Han Shaogong   韩少功

Hanta gongsi   旱獭公司

haokan xiaoshuo   好看小说

Haoshu julebu   好书俱乐部

Hebei jiaoyu chubanshe   河北教育出版社

Heima congshu   黑马丛书

Helin langman xiaoshuo   禾林浪漫小说

hetong zuojia   合同作家

He Xiongfei   贺雄飞

Hong lajiao congshu   红辣椒丛书

Hong yingsu congshu   红婴粟丛书

Hong Zicheng   洪子诚

Hua cheng   花城

Huacheng chubanshe   花城出版社

Huang Beijia   黄蓓佳

Huanghe   黄河

Huanghuang youyou   晃晃悠悠

Huang Jiwei   黄集伟

Huangnijie shushi   黄泥街书市

Huangwu zhi lü   荒芜之旅

Huaxia chubanshe   华夏出版社

Huayi chubanshe   华艺出版社

Hunan wenxue   湖南文学

Huo Da   霍达

Huo zhe   活着

Hu Shouwen   胡守文

Hu Yanhua   呼延华

jiandao jia jianghu   剪刀加浆糊

jiang cheng zhi   奖惩制

Jiangsu renmin chubanshe   江蘇人民出版社

Jiangsu wenyi chubanshe   江苏文艺出版社

Jiangxiban   讲习班

Jiang Zidan   蒋子丹

Jia Pingwa   贾平凹

Jiating   家庭

Jiefang jun wenyi   解放军文艺

jigou gaige   机构改革

jihua jingji   计划经济

jingji datai, wenxue changxi   经济搭台,文学唱戏

Jingji ren   经纪人

jingji xiaoyi   经济效益

jing pin   精品

jingshen wuran   精神污染

Jin gu chuanqi   今古传奇

jingying yishi   经营意识

Jin Hezai   今何在

Jin Ti   金蜓

Jin Yong   金庸

Ji ri zuojia wang   今日作家网

Jishi wenxue   紀實文學

Judou   菊豆

ju jiang   巨奖

Juzi hong le   桔子红了

Kang Xiaoyu gongzuoshi   康笑宇工作室

Kanshangqu hen mei   看上去很美

Kewang   渴望

Kewang jiqing   渴望激情

Kongzhong xiaojie   空中小姐

Kouhong   口红

Kunlun   昆仑

Lailai wangwang   来来往往

Langqiao yi meng   廊桥遗梦

Lan hua bao   蓝花豹

Lan Lizhi   蓝栎之

Laoshe wenxuejiang   老舍文学奖

Leixing xiaoshuo   类型小说

Liang Xiaosheng   梁晓声

Liang Yusheng   梁羽生

Liansuo shudian   连锁书店

lianyin wenxue   联姻文学

Li Dawei   李大卫

Li Feng   李冯

Li Jingduan   李景端

Li Jingze   李敬泽

Lin Bai   林白

Linglei congshu   另类丛书

lishi hui   理事会

lishi yanyi   历史演义

Liu Fang   刘方

Liu Heng   刘恒

liuxing wenhua   流行文化

Lu Xingsheng   陆幸生

Lu Xun wenxuejiang   鲁迅文学奖
Maimai shuhao   买卖书号
Maodun wenxuejiang   茅盾文学奖
Mao wenti   毛文体
Ma yu zhe   马语者
Mei Jia   梅嘉
Meinü zuojia   美女作家
Meiren zeng wo menghanyao   美人赠我蒙汗药
mei su   媚俗
Meng Jinghui   孟京辉
Mengya   萌芽
Mian Mian   棉棉
Miao Hong   苗洪
minjian touzi   民间投资
minjian yuwen   民间语文
minying shudian   民营书店
Mo Luo   摩罗
Mo Yan   莫言
Muyu   母语
Nanfang wentan   南方文坛
Nanfang zhoumo   南方週末
Nanhai chuban gongsi   南海出版公司
Neimenggu renmin chubanshe   内蒙古人民出版社
Nian lun   年轮
Nie Zhenning   聂震宁
Niluohe shang de can'an   尼罗河上的惨案
Ni Ping   倪萍
Niu fanzhi shandao   牛贩子山道
nongmin zuojia   农民作家
Nü daijia   女带家
Nüxing xiezuo   女性写作
Nüxing zhuyi zuojia   女性主义作家
Nü you   女友
pin pai   品牌
Pinpai xiaoying   品牌效应
pin ren zhi   聘任制
Pi Pi   皮皮
pizi zuojia   痞子作家
Qian nian yi tan   千年一叹
Qianshou   牵手
Qianwan bie ba wo dang ren   千万别把我当人
Qianyue zuojia   签约作家
Qing ai hua lang   情爱画廊
Qingchun   青春
Qinhuang fuzi   秦皇父子
Qiong Yao   琼瑶

Qi qie cheng qun　妻妾成群

Qiuju da guansi　秋菊打官司

qiye wenxue　企业文学

Quanguo baogaowenxue jiang　全国报告文学奖

Quanguo duanpianxiaoshuo jiang　全国短篇小说奖

Quanguo shige jiang　全国诗歌奖

Quanguo tushu jiang　全国图书奖

quanguo tushu jiaoyihui　全国图书交易会

Quanguo wangluo yuanchuang wenxue da sai　全国网络原创文学大赛

Quanguo youxiu changxiaoshu　全国优秀畅销书

Quanguo zhongpianxiaoshuo jiang　全国中篇小说奖

Qunzhong chubanshe　群众出版社

Renmin wenxue　人民文学

Renmin wenxue chubanshe　人民文学出版社

Ren yao zhi jian　人妖之间

Ren mo yu du　人莫予毒

Rizi　日子

Rongshu xia　榕树下

ruan guanggao　软广告

San chong men　三重门

San Lian shudian　三联书店

San Mao　三毛

San shen zhi　三审制

Sao huang da fei　扫黄打非

Shanghai baobei　上海宝贝

Shanghai de fenghuaxueyue　上海的风花雪月

Shanghai renmin chubanshe　上海人民出版社

Shanghai wenhua chubanshe　上海文化出版社

Shanghai wenxue　上海文学

Shanghai yiwen chubanshe　上海译文出版社

Shanghen　伤痕

shangpin hua　商品化

shangye xiezuo　商业写作

Shan hua　山花

shehui xiaoyi　社会效益

Shen Changwen　沈昌文

shen pi zhi　审批制

shenti xiezuo　身体写作

Shenzhen youxiu wengao gongkai jingjia　深圳优秀文稿公开竞价

shichang hua　市场化

shichang jingji　市场经济

shichang yishi　市场意识

Shidai wenyi chubanshe　時代文藝出版社

shi fu hui　世妇会

Shifu yue lai yue youmo　师傅越来越幽默

Shiji duihua　世纪对话

Shijie wenxue   世界文学

Shijie zhishi chubanshe   世界知识出版社

Shi Kang   石康

Shishi wenhua zixun gongsi   时事文化咨询公司

Shi Tao   石涛

Shiyan xiju dang'an   实验戏剧档案

shiye danwei   事业单位

Shiyue   十月

Shouhuo   收获

shuang gui zhi   双轨制

Shuang leng changhe   霜冷长河

shu hao   书号

shu huang   书荒

shu shang   书商

shu tanr   书摊儿

Sichuan wenyi chubanshe   四川文藝出版社

Sichuan zuoxie   四川作协

Siren shenghuo   私人生活

Suiyue qingyuan   岁月情缘

Su Tong   苏童

Tamen   他们

Tamen congshu   她们丛书

Tanbai: Xue Mili zhenxiang jiemi   坦白：雪米莉真相揭秘

Tang   糖

Tan Li   谭力

tejia shudian   特价书店

teyue bianji   特约编辑

Tiandi tushu   天地图书

Tianjin wenxue   天津文学

Tianya   天涯

Tian Yanning   田雁宁

Tie Ning   铁凝

Tie wu zhong de nahan   铁屋中的呐喊

tizhi gaige   体制改革

tongsu wenxue   通俗文学

tuo gou   脱钩

tushu shichang   图书市场

Waiguo wenyi   外国文艺

Wang Anyi   王安忆

wang ba   网吧

Wang Hailing   王海羚

wangluo wenxue   网络文学

Wang Meng   王蒙

Wang ran bu gong   枉然不供

Wang Shuli   王淑丽

Wang Shuo   王朔

Wangshuo wenji 王朔文集

Wang Xiaobo 王小波

Wang Xiaoming 王晓明

Wang Yi 网易

Wanjia susong 万家诉讼

Wanr de jiu shi xintiao 玩儿的就是心跳

wan sheng dai 晚生代

Wan sheng shuyuan 万圣书园

Wan zhu 顽主

Wei Hui 卫慧

wen chang 文娼

wenhua chanye 文化产业

wenhua gongsi 文化公司

wenhua gongzuo shi 文化工作室

wenhua gongzuozhe 文化工作者

wenhua ju 文化局

Wenhua yuekan 文化月刊

Wenhui dushu zhoubao 文汇读书周报

Wen Jieruo 文洁若

wenlian 文联

wen qi lian yin 文企联姻

Wen Xi 文夕

Wenxue bao 文学报

wenxue chanpin 文学产品

wenxue qingnian 文学青年

wenxue shengchan 文学生产

wenxue tizhi 文学体制

Wenyi bao 文艺报

wenyi geti hu 文艺个体户

Wo de qingren men 我的情人们

Wo shi Wangshuo 我是王朔

Wu ge yi gongcheng jiang 五个一工程奖

Wukong zhuan 悟空传

Wulitou 无厘头

wuxing ziben 无形资产

Wu zhi zhe wu wei 无知者无畏

Xia Guozhong 夏国忠

xia hai 下海

Xiangyue xingqi'er 相约星期二

Xiao Qian 萧乾

Xiaoshuo xuankan 小说选刊

Xiaoshuo yuebao 小说月报

Xiao yanzi: nüsheng Zhao Wei 小燕子女生赵薇

xie ban 协办

Xin gainian zuowen da sai 新概念作文大赛

Xing An 兴安

Xinhua shudian　新华书店
Xin Jiping　辛继平
Xin Lang Wang　新浪网
xin shimin xiaoshuo　新市民小说
xin tiyan xiaoshuo　新体验小说
xinwen chuban bao　新闻出版报
xinwen chuban zong shu　新闻出版总署
xinwen xiaoshuo　新闻小说
xin xin renlei　新新人类
Xin zhoukan　新周刊
xin zhuangtai wenxue　新状态文学
Xi Shu　席殊
Xi Shu shuwu　席殊书屋
Xue Mili　雪米莉
Xu Kun　徐坤
Xu Sanguan maixue ji　徐三观卖血记
Yang de men　羊的门
Yang Zhijun　杨志军
Ya su gong shang　雅俗共赏
Ye Yonglie　叶永烈
yi ge dongtian de tong hua　一个冬天的童话
Yi ge ren de zhanzheng　一个人的战争
Yilin　译林
Yilin chubanshe　译林出版社
Ying er　英儿
ying shi wenxue　影视文学
ying xiao　营销
yingzi chubanshe　影子出版社
Yinse youhuo　银色诱惑
Yinsi wenxue　隐私文学
Yishu guan　艺术馆
Yi ta hu tu　一塌糊涂
yi wen yang wen　以文养文
Yongzheng huangdi　雍正皇帝
Yongzheng wangchao　雍正王朝
You li xi si　尤利西斯
Yue se liao ren　月色撩人
Yu hua　雨花
Yu Hua　余华
Yu Jie　余杰
yule wenxue　娱乐文学
Yu Luojin　遇罗锦
Yunnan renmin chubanshe　云南人民出版社
Yu Qiuyu　余秋雨
zanzhu zhe　赞助者

ze bian zeren zhi   责编责任制

Zhang Kangkang   张抗抗

Zhang Shengyou   张胜友

Zhang Yigong   张一弓

Zhang Yimou   张艺谋

Zhang Yiwu   张颐武

Zhao bu zhao bei   找不着北

Zhao Suping   赵素平

Zhao Zhongxiang   赵忠祥

Zhejiang wenyi chubanshe   浙江文藝出版社

Zhengyuan tushu   正源图书

Zhiheng celüe   制衡策略

Zhi li po sui   支离破碎

Zhisheng Dongfang Shuo   智圣东方硕

Zhiye: yi ge ren de zhanzheng   汁液：一个人的战争

Zhongchan zhe jieceng   中产者阶层

Zhongguo banquan daili gongsi   中国版权代理公司

Zhongguo chuban nianjian   中國出版年鑒

Zhongguo dangdai wenxue shi   中国当代文学史

Zhongguo dianying chubanshe   中國電影出版社

Zhongguo qingnian chubanshe   中國青年出版社

Zhongguo shehui ge jieceng de fenxi   中国社会各阶层的分析

Zhongguo shehui kexue yuan   中国社会科学院

Zhongguo shushing   中国书商

Zhongguo tushu shang bao   中国图书商报

Zhongguo xiju chubanshe   中國戲劇出版社

Zhonghua dushu bao   中华读书报

Zhongpian xiaoshuo xuankan   中篇小说选刊

Zhongshan   钟山

Zhou Hong   周洪

Zhou Xingchi   周星驰

Zhou Yikuai   周一快

Zhuang Zhidie   庄之蝶

zhuanye zuojia   专业作家

Zhuiyi shishui nianhua   追忆逝水年华

zhu qudao   主渠道

zhun huangse   准黄色

Zhuo mu niao   啄木鸟

Zhu xuanlü wenxue   主旋律文学

Zhu Weilian   朱威廉

Zhu Wen   朱文

zi ban faxing   自办发行

zi fu ying kui   自负盈亏

ziyou zuojia   自由作家

Zong Renfa   宗仁发

Zuojia　作家
Zuojia chubanshe　作家出版社
Zuojiang wenyi　左江文艺
zuo xie　作协

Ah, Zheng. "Changxiao shu" (Best Sellers; interview with Zhang Shengyou and An Boshun). In *Shiji duihua: wenhua shanbian yu zhongguo mingyun* (Centennial Dialogue: Cultural Evolution and the Destiny of China). Beijing: Zhongguo Shehui kexue chubanshe, 2000.

An, Boshun. "Chuangzao pinpai de san ge yaosu" (Three Elements of Making Brand Name Products). *Chuban guangjiao* 4 (2000).

———. "Bu laohu de chuangzuo linian yu zhuiqiu" (The Creative Idea and Pursuit of Cloth Tiger). *Nanfang wentan* 4 (1997).

Barmé, Geremie. *In the Red: On Contemporary Chinese Culture*. New York: Columbia University Press, 1999.

Cai, Zhiheng. *Diyici de qinmi jiechu* (The First Intimate Contact). Beijing: Zhishi chubanshe, 1999.

Chen, Ding. "Gongzuoshi fenfen guabai, dui chuantong chuban moshi zaocheng chongji" (Studios Springing Up to Challenge Traditional Model of Publishing). *Zhonghua dushu bao*, January 14, 1998.

Chen, Hua. "Dianying ban 'Wukong zhuan' bu tan aiqing" (Film Version of *Monkey's Biography* Won't Deal With Love). *Xinwen chenbao*, August 22, 2002.

Cheng, Mingshu, ed. *Ershi shiji zhongguo wenxue dadian 1966–1994* (Encyclopedia of Chinese Literature in the Twentieth Century: 1966–1994). Shanghai: Shanghai jiaoyu chubanshe, 1996.

Chen, Shu. "Chuangxin youmo, miaoqu hengsheng, zenyang du youlixisi" (Innovative, Humorous, and Witty: How to Read *Ulysses*). *Wenxue bao*, August 11, 1994.

Chen, Xiaoming, and Zhang Yiwu. "Shichanghua shidai: wenxue de kunjing yu kenengxing" (The Era of the Market: Literature's Dilemma and Possibilities). *Dajia* 2 (2002).

Chi Li. *Kouhong* (Lipstick). Nanjing: Jiangsu wenyi chubanshe, 2000.

Chi, Zijian. "Yi ben mianmuquanfei de shu: chenzhong xiang ce huanghun chuban de qianqianhouhou" (A Distorted Book: A Complete Account of the Publishing of *Morning Bell Rings Through Evening*). *Wenxue bao*, August 24, 1995.

Crevel, Maghiel van. "The Horror of Being Ignored and the Pleasure of Being Left Alone: Notes on the Chinese Poetry Scene." Modern Chinese Literature and Culture Resource Center, 2003 (mclc.osu.edu/rc/pubs/vancrevel.html).

Dai, Jinhua. "Introduction," in Dai Jinhua, ed., *Shiji zhi men: Nuxing xiaoshuo juan* (Turn of Century: Women's Fiction). Beijing: Shehui kexue chubanshe, 1998.

"Dangjin wentan qihaoduo" (Today's Literature Promotes a Profusion of New Schools). *Wenxue bao,* July 6, 1995.

Ding, Guoqiang. "'Lianyin wenxue' yinggai zenme xie" (How to Write Corporate Alliance Literature). *Zhonghua dushu bao,* June 17, 1998.

Driver, Nicholas. "Publishing." In *Doing Business in China,* ed. Freshfields Bruckhaus Deringer. New York: Juris Publishing, 2001.

Dou, Shicha. "Zhuan xiang tongsu bing fei lingdanmiaoyao, yi fu yang wen jianchi ban kan yuanze: Mengya zazhi she nuli fazhan sanchan jiji fuye wenxue xinren" (Becoming Popular Is Not a Panacea: Supporting Literature with Business Activities and Maintaining Publication Principles: *First Growth* Makes Effort to Develop a Service Industry). *Wenxue bao,* December 24, 1992.

Duo, Duo. "Bei maizang de zhongguo shiren 1972–1978" (Chinese Poets Buried: 1972–1978), in Liao Yiwu, ed., *Chenlun de shengdian: Zhongguo ershi shiji qishi niandai dixia shige yizhao* (Sunken Cathedral: Commemorative Pictures of Underground Poetry from 1970s China). Wulumuqi: Xinjiang qingshaonian chubanshe, 1999.

Eryue, He. *Yongzheng huangdi* (The Emperor Yongzheng). Wuhan: Changjiang wenyi chubanshe, 1991.

Fang, Wenyu. "Zhisheng Dongfang Shuo zai piping zhong re xiao shi qi wan" (The Wise Sage Dongfang Shuo Sold 170,000 Copies Despite Criticism). *Zhonghua dushu bao,* April 19, 2000.

Feng, Yidai. "Youlixisi zhongyi ben bijiao" (A Comparison Between the Two Chinese Translations of *Ulysses*). *Zhonghua dushu bao,* August 3, 1994.

Gao, Xingjian. *Xiandai xiaoshuo jiqiao chu tan* (Preliminary Exploration on the Techniques of Modern Fiction). Guangzhou: Huacheng chubanshe, 1981.

Ge, Xiaoli. "Soviet Songs and Us." *Beijing Wenxue* 8 (1999).

Gu, Lieming. "Jingti daitu zuoan wentan" (Watch the Cheats Who Fool Around in the Literary Field). *Wenxue Bao,* October 28, 1993.

Guo, Yujie. "Huhuan yizhong shengming de muyu: Tie Ning fangtan lu" (Crying Out for a Life Bath: Interview with Tie Ning), *Zhongguo tushushangbao shuping zhoukan,* April 25, 2000.

Guo, Xiaoli. "Wenxue qikan de shengcun yu chulu: jiuba quanguo wenxue qikan zhubian yantaohui ceji" (The Survival and Future of Literary Journals: Report on the 1998 National Literary Periodicals Editors in Chief Symposium). *Zhongshan* 5 (1998).

Hai, Nan. *Wo de qingrenmen* (My Lovers) Beijing: Zhongguo wenlian chuban gongsi, 1994.

Han, Dong. "Beiwang: youguan duanlie xingwei de wenti huida"(Memorandum: Answers for the Act of Breaking Away). *Beijing Wenxue* 10 (1998).

Han, Renjun. *Erzi Han Han* (My Son Han Han). Shanghai: Shanghai renmin chubanshe, 2000.

Han, Shishan. "Xiangkuang nanmian jia cheng zhen" (False Madness Turns into Real Madness). *Wenxue ziyou tan* 5 (1999).

Han, Xiaohui. "Chiluoluo de chumai ziji, yinsi wenxue yinqi feiyi" (Selling Oneself Naked: Privacy Literature Causes Controversy). *Wenxue bao,* September 22, 1994.

"Harry Potter Sales Break 1.3 Million in China." *People's Daily* (English), May 29, 2001.

He, Dun. *Huangwu zhi lü* (Road to Ruin). Beijing: Zhongguo qingnian chubanse, 2001.

He, Guimei, "Shijimo de ziwo jiushu zhi lu: Dui yijiujiubanian yu fanyou xiangguan shuji de wenhua fenxi" (Self-Redemption at the End of the Century: Cultural Analysis of the Year 1998 and Books on the Anti-Rightist Movement), in Dai Jinhua, ed., *Shuxie wenhua yingxiong: shiji zhi jiao de wenhua yanjiu* (Writing Cultural Heroes: Cultural Studies at the Turn of the 21st Century). Nanjing: Jiangsu renmin chubanshe, 2000.

He, Long. "Meizhong wenxue qikan pingjun zhiyou shige duzhe" (On Average There Are Only 10 Readers for Each Literary Journal). *Zhonghua dushu bao*, October 28, 1998.

He, Xiangchu, and Wu Guimei. "Shujia: gaochu bu sheng han" (Book Prices Reaching Chilling Heights). *Chuban guangjiao* 5 (2001).

Hong, Fei. "Ba aiqing yu langman songgei duzhe" (Bringing Readers Love and Romance). *Xinwen chuban bao*, May 24, 2002.

Hong, Zicheng. *Zhongguo dangdai wenxue shi* (History of Contemporary Chinese Literature). Beijing: Beijing daxue chubanshe, 1999.

Huang Jiwei. "1997 nian shi da chuban xianxiang" (Top Ten Phenomena in the Publishing Industry During 1997). *Zhongguo tushu shangbao*, January 9, 1998.

Huot, Claire. *China's New Cultural Scene: A Handbook of Changes*. Durham and London: Duke University Press, 2000.

Jiang, Zhenxin. "Wukenaihe beipo zhangjia, kuxin jingying jianshou jingtu" (Literary Journals Forced to Raise Prices, Editors Try Hard to 'Guard the Pure Land' of Literature). *Wenxue bao*, September 2, 1993.

———. "Touru juezhan, yingde huihuang: huigu he zhanwang zhongguo qikan ye" (Entering the Decisive Battle and Winning Glory: The Past and Prospects of Chinese Periodicals). *Wenxue Bao*, October 28, 1993.

Jiang, Xun. "Yi ju jie kun, chuang yiliu" (Philanthropy in Difficult Times). *Wenxue bao*, April 8, 1993.

Jin, Hezai. *Wukong zhuang* (Monkey's Biography). Beijing: Guangming ribao chubanshe, 2001.

Jing, Wang. "Wang Shuo: Pop Goes the Culture?" In *High Culture Fever: Politics, Aesthetics, and Ideology in Deng's China*. Berkeley: University of California Press, 1996.

Kaikkonen, Marja. "Stories and Legends: China's Largest Contemporary Popular Literary Journals." In Michel Hoxx, ed., *The Literary Field of Twentieth Century China*. Honolulu: University of Hawaii Press, 1999.

———. "From Knights to Nudes: Chinese Popular Literature Since Mao." *Stockholm Journal of East Asian Studies* 5 (1995).

Kong, Shuyu. "Journey Within: The Inward Turn of the Contemporary Chinese Novel" Ph.D. diss., University of British Columbia, 1997.

———. "For Reference Only: Restricted Publication and Distribution of Foreign Literature During the Cultural Revolution." *Yishu: Journal of Contemporary Chinese Art* 1(2) (Summer 2002).

Lan, Lizhi. Preface to *Qiujin: nüxing xing'ai wenxue* (Imprisoned: Women's Literature on Sex and Love). Shenyang: Chunfeng wenyi chubanshe, 1995.

Lee, Leo Ou-fan. *Shanghai Modern: The Flowering of a New Urban Culture in China 1930–1945*. Cambridge, Mass.: Harvard University Press, 1999.

Lei, Ben. "Shuye heima xi shuo shengyi jing: Huayi chubanshe de louxiang chuanqi" (Business Tips from the Black Horse in the Book Market: The Legend of Huayi Publishing House). *Wenhua yuekan* 1 & 2 (2000).

Li, Jingduan. *Botao shang de zhiji:Yilin bianji shengya ershi nian* (Walking on the Waves: Twenty Years as an Editor at Yilin). Chongqing: Chongqing chubanshe, 1999.

———. "Fanyi 'huai xiang' liu zhong" (Six Kinds of Unprofessional Phenomena in Translation). *Chuban guangjiao* (3) 2002.

———. "Dakai chuangkou chu kaifang: Yilin er shi nian huigu" (Open the Window to Accelerate Reform: Reflections on Yilin's Twenty-Year History). *Chuban guangjiao* 12 (1999).

Li, Xiaolan, and Tang Jian. "Zhang Shengyou tan chuban gaige zhong de pingheng zhanlue," *Chuban guangjiao* 3 (2001).

Liang, Xiaosheng. *Zhongguo shehui ge jieceng de fenxi* (An Analysis of the Different Social Groups in China). Beijing: Jingji ribao chubanshe, 1997.

Liao, Yiwu, ed. *Chenlun de shengdian: zhongguo ershi shiji qishi niandai dixia shige yizhao* (Sunken Cathedral: Commemorative Pictures of Underground Poetry from 1970s China). Wulumuqi: Xinjiang qingshaonian chubanshe, 1999.

"Liaokai banshui fu chou de miansha" (Unmasking the Myth of Royalty Payments). *Zhonghua dushu bao*, August 16, 1997.

Liebman, Benjamin. "Reluctant Ruffians: Language, Authority, and Alienation in Wang Shuo's Fiction" (senior essay). Yale University, 1991.

Lin, Bai. *Yi ge ren de zhanzheng* (A War with Oneself). Wuhan: Changjiang Art and Literature Publishing House, 1999.

———. "Guanyu yi ge ren de zhanzheng" (About *A War with Oneself*), in *Xiang gui yiyang miren* (As Charming as a Ghost). Taiyuan: Shanxi shifan daxue chubanshe, 1998.

———. *Zhiye: yi ge ren de zhanzheng* (Body Fluid: A War with Oneself). Lanzhou: Gansu renmin chubanshe, 1994.

Lin, Shaoting, and Wu Yiyi. "Beijing Cracks Down on 'Politically Incorrect' Publishers," *CND*, July 18, 2000.

Link, Perry. *The Uses of Literature: Life in the Socialist Chinese Literary System*. Princeton: Princeton University Press, 2000.

Liu Cuiping. "Biange zhong de zhengyuan" (Alpha Books in Transition). *Xin shu bao*, November 14, 2000.

Liu, Junping. "Youlixisi lianzhong yiben de bijiao yanjiu" (Comparative Study of the Two Translations of *Ulysses*). *Zhongguo fanyi* (3) 1997.

Liu, Nan. "Jingqi zhu ri hua Xi Shu" (Xishu and his Jingqi.com). *Wenhua yuekan* 9 (2000).

Liu, Ying. "Renmin wenxue xuanbu duannai yinfa zhengdong" (Announcement That *People's Literature* Must Be 'Weaned' has Caused Turmoil). *Wenxue bao*, April 1, 1999.

Liu, Yongjun. "Cong changxiaoshu paihangbang kan shichang zhoushi, 2000 nian tongji fenxi" (Predicting Market Trends from the Best Seller Lists: An Analysis of the Year 2000). *Chuban guangjiao* 4 (2001).

———. "Cong changxiaoshu paihangbang kan shichang zhoushi, 1999 nian tongji fenxi" (Predicting Market Trends from the Best Seller Lists: An Analysis of the Year 1999). *Chuban guangjiao* 4 (2000).

Long, Yin. *Zhisheng Dongfang Shuo* (The Wise Sage Dongfang Shuo). Beijing: zuo-jia chubanshe, 2000.

Lu, Sheldon H. *China, Transnational Visuality, Global Postmodernity*. Stanford, Calif.: Stanford University Press, 2001.

Lu, Xingsheng. *Yinse youhuo* (Tempted by Silver). Beijing: Zhishi chubanshe, 1999.

Lynch, Daniel C. *After the Propaganda State: Media, Politics, and "Thought Work" in Reformed China*. Stanford, Calif.: Stanford University Press, 1999.

McDougall, Bonnie S., and Kam Louie. *The Literature of China in the Twentieth Century*. New York: Columbia University Press, 1997.

Meng, Ye. "Renwen she yu hali bote you yici qinmi jiechu" (Another Close Contact between People's Literature and Harry Potter). *Zhongguo tushu shang bao*, May 3, 2001.

Mo, Luo. *Chiruzhe shouji: yige minjian sixiangzhe de shengming tiyan* (Notes from the Humiliated: A Folk Philosopher's Life Experience). Huhehaote: Neimenggu jiaoyu chubanshe, 1998.

Moran, Thomas. "True Stories: Contemporary Chinese Reportage and Its Ideology and Asthetic." Ph.D. diss. Ithaca: Cornell University, 1994.

Niu, Suqin. "Hong ying su, lan wazi, jin zhizhu: Hebei jiaoyu chubanshe san tao daxing nuxing wenxue congshu" (Red Poppy, Blue Stockings, Golden Spider: Three Major Women's Literary Series from Hebei Education Press). *Chuban guangjiao* 5 (1995).

O'Neil, Mark. "Film Maker Jittery as Hollywood Comes Calling." *South China Morning Post* (English), October 9, 2000.

Pei, Minxin. *From Reform to Revolution: The Demise of Communism in China and the Soviet Union*. Cambridge and London: Harvard University Press, 1994.

Propaganda Department and Press and Publications Administration. "Guanyu dangqian chubanshe gaige de ruogan yijian" (Several Opinions Regarding Current Reforms to Publishing Houses) and "Guanyu dangqian tushu faxing tizhi gaige de ruogan yijian" (Several Opinions Regarding Current Reforms to the Book Distribution System), April 1988. *Zhongguo chuban nianjian*, May 6, 1989.

Qie, Shi. "Muyu ying feng, weiran cheng lin: Yilin zazhi bu pingfan de ershi nian" (Growing in Wind and Rain: Yilin's Unusual Twenty Years). *Chuban guangjiao* 6 (1999).

Ragvald, Lars. "Professionalism and Amateur Tendencies in Post-Revolutionary Chinese Literature," in Goran Malmqvist, ed., *Modern Chinese Literature and its Social Context*. Stockholm: Nobel Symposium 32, 1975.

Rosenthal, Elisabeth. "New Gray Market in China Loosens Grip on Publishing." *New York Times*, June 27, 1999.

Sang, Ye. "Wulitou.com." *Xin zhoukan* (special edition introducing Wulitou.com), July 2000.

Schwartz, Benjamin. *In Search of Wealth and Power: Yan Fu and the West*. Cambridge, Mass.: Harvard University Press, 1964.

Shen, Changwen. "Yingzi chubanshe: dalu chubanjie xin ziyuan" (Shadow Publishing Houses: The New Publishing Resource in China). *Mingbao Yuekan* (Ming Pao Monthly) 7 (1999).

Shi, Kang. *Zhiliposui* (Fragmented). Changchun: Changchun chubanshe, 1999.

———. Preface to *Huanghuangyouyou (Swaying and Staggering)*. Kunming: Yunnan renmin chubanshe, 2001.

Shi, Yuanlou. "Chi Zijian wei chenzhong taohui shuofa" (Why Chi Zijian Wants Justice for *Morning Bell*). *Wenxue bao*, July 11, 1996.

Shih, Shu-mei. *Lure of Modernity: Writing Modernism in Semicolonial China 1917–1937.* Berkeley: University of California Press, 2001.

Song, Wenjing, and Zhou Xiaohua. "Wenxue qikan: da bian, xiao bian yu bu bian" (Literary Journal: Big Change, Small Change and No Change). *Zhongguo tushu shang bao*, June 5, 2001.

Standaert, Michael. "Interview with Yu Hua (August 30, 2003)." MCLC Resource Center (mclc.osu.edu/rc/pubs/yuhua.htm).

"State Bureau Examines Internet Cafés." *People's Daily* (English), August 20, 2001 (english.peopledaily.com.cn/200108/20/eng20010820_75430.html).

"The State Council's Announcement on Full Financial Self-Responsibility for the Publication of Periodicals" (December 29, 1984), in Institute of Law, Chinese Academy of Social Science, ed., *Collection of Chinese Laws on Economic Management*, Vol. 2. Changchun: Jilin renmin chubanshe, 1985.

Su Jinyu, "Jin bulaohu baiwanyuan zhenggao huodong weihe yanqi" (Why the Deadline for Golden Cloth Tiger Manuscripts Has Been Extended), in *Zhonghua dushu bao*, December 29, 1999.

———. "Guowai changxiao, guonei weibi neng changxiao: guanyu yinjinban changxiaoshu de caifang riji" (Foreign Best Sellers Will Not Necessarily Sell Well in China: Notes on Imported Best Sellers). *Zhonghua dushu bao*, January 23, 2001.

———. "Yingshi hong, tushu huo, chuban zhuizhe y anyuan pao" (Film / and Literature: Publishers Chasing Actors). *Zhonghua dushu bao*, March 7, 2001.

Sun, Wenqi. "Chuangye zhi xing jin fengliu: ji changchun yiqi chesen fushu diyi fenchang changzhang Guo Xuecai (A Creative Star Shines Its Heart Out: A Report on Factory Manager Guo Xuecai of the Changchun No. 1 Autoworks Affiliated Autobody Branch Factory). *Beijing wenxue* 8 (1999).

"Tamen ping shenme zai wentan jueqi" (For What Did They Become Prominent in the Literary Field). *Wenxue Bao*, September 3, 1998.

Tian, Yanning, and Tan Li. *Tanbai: Xue Mili zhenxiang jiemi* (Confession: The Truth about Xue Mili). Changchun: Shidai wenyi chubanshe, 1999.

Waiguo wenxue tushu mulu (1951–1990) (Catalogue of Foreign Literature, 1951–1990). Beijing: Renmin wenxue chubanshe.

Wang, Haijuan. "Wangluo wenxue luodi: Quan shi diyi" (Internet Literature Is Born: Everything Is New). *Beijing qingnian bao*, May 17, 2000.

Wang, Hailing. *Qianshou* (Holding Hands). Beijing: Renmin wenxue chubanshe, 1999.

Wang, Hong, and Chen Jie. "Zhiye zuojia shengcun zhuangtai baogao" (Report on the Living Conditions of Professional Writers). *Zhonghua dushu bao*, July 29, 1998.

Wang, Jifang. *Duanlie: shiji mo de wenxue shigu* (Breaking Away: A Literary Incident at the Turn of the Century). Nanjing: Jiangsu wenyi chubanshe, 2000.

Wang, Lei. "Huozhe zaoyu liangzhong shichang mingyun" (To Live Experienced Two Different Fates in the Market). *Zhonghua dushu bao*, September 1, 1999.

———. "Yingshi yu tushu hudong de dianxing gean: ji jiangsu wenyi chubanshe Yuese liaoren de cehua" (A typical case of the synergy of books and TV/films: The project of *Moonstruck* from Jiangsu Art and Literature Publishing House). *Chuban guangjiao* 2 (2002).

Wang, Linhzhen. "Retheorizing the Personal: Identity, Writing, and Gender in Yu Luojin's Autobiographical Act." *Positions: East Asia Cultures Critique* 6:2 (1998).

Wang, Meng. "Duobi chonggao" (Shunning the Sublime). *Dushu* 1 (1993).

———. Preface to *Zhongguo wangluo yuanchuang zuopin jingxuan* (Selection of the Best Internet Literature), ed. Wang Meng and Zhong Renfa. Changchun: Shidai wenyi chubanshe, 2000.

Wang, Shuo. *Wang Shuo wenji* (Wang Shuo's Collected Works). Beijing: Huayi chubanshe, 1992.

———. *Woshi Wang Shuo* (I am Wang Shuo). Beijing: Guoji wenhua chuban gongsi, 1997.

———. *Wuzhi zhe wuwei* (The Ignorant Fear Nothing). Shenyang: Chunfeng wenyi chubanshe, 2000.

———. *Kanshangqu hen mei* (Looking Beautiful). Beijing: Huayi chubanshe, 1999.

———. "Zhe zhihou yiqie jiang bian" (Everything Will Be Different from Now On), in Chen Cun, ed., *Wo ai shang na ge zuo huai bu luan zhong de nuzi* (Falling in Love with that Sedentary Woman). Guangzhou: Huacheng chubanshe, 2000, 291.

Wang, Shuo, and Lao Xia. *Meiren zeng wo menghanyao* (She Put Me to Sleep with a Potion). Wuhan: Changjiang wenyi chubanshe, 2000.

Wang, Xiaoming. "Kuangye shang de feixu" (Ruins in the Wilderness), in Meng Fanhua, ed., *Jiushi niandai wencun* (Collections of Writings on Literature from the 1990s), Vol. 1. Beijing: Zhongguo shehui kexue chubanshe, 2001.

———. "Fanyi de zhengzi" (The Politics of Translation), in *Ban zhang lian de shenhua* (The Myth of the Half-Hidden Face). Guangzhou: Nafang ribao chubanshe, 2000.

Wang, Ying, and Zhao Wuping, "Yilin ban Youlixisi yuan he changxiao" (Why Yilin's edition of *Ulysses* Sold So Well). *Zhonghua dushu bao*, May 10, 1995.

———. "Renwen ban Youlixisi jie mi" (Deciphering the People's Literature Edition of *Ulysses*). *Zhonghua dushu bao*, May 10, 1995.

Wang, Yun. "Helin xiaoshuo qishi lu" (The Lesson of Harlequin). *Zhongguo tushu shang bao*, January 3, 2002.

Wang, Zhenping. "Lun fanyi zhi dao, shuo youlixisi Jin Ti jiaoshou fangtanlu" (On Translation and *Ulysses*: Interview with Jin Ti). *Zhongguo fanyi* 1 (2001).

Wei, Hui. *Shanghai baobei*. Shenyang: Chunfeng wenyi chubanshe, 1999.

Wen, Jieruo. "Guanyu youlixisi liang zhong yiben de wo jian" (My View on the Two Translations of *Ulysses*). *Fanyi Yanjiu* 3 (2000).

"Woguo xikan jishen quanqiu faxing baiming qianwei" (Chinese Journals Top the Global Circulation Rankings). *Zhonghua dushu bao*, December 30, 1998.

"Writers Bank a Million for Novel Lives." *China Daily* (English), January 7, 2002 (www1.chinadaily.com.cn/cndy/2002-0-07/50769.html).

Wu, Peihua. "Minying shudian" (Private Bookstores). *Chuban guangjiao* 5 (2001).

Wu, Xusheng. *Da Hongdong: Zhong wai changxiaoshu jiemi* (Sensation: Revealing the Secrets of Best Sellers Chinese and Foreign). Guangzhou: Guangzhou chubanshe, 1993.

Xi, Dalang. "Xi Shu cidian" (Dictionary of Xishu). *Furong* 6 (1999).

Xiao, Qian. "Wo yu Youlixisi" (*Ulysses* and I). *Wenxue bao*, June 9, 1994.

Xiao Qian, Wen Jieruo, and Xu Jun. "Fanyi zhe men xuewen huo yishu chuangzao shi meiyou zhijing de" (There Is No Limit to Translation in Terms of Scholarship or Artistic Creativity). *Yilin* 1 (1999).

Xiao, Xiao. "Shu de guidao, yi bu jingshen yuedu shi" (Trajectory of Books: A History of Spiritual Reading), in Liao Yiwu, ed., *Chenlun de shengdian: zhongguo ershi shiji qishi niandai dixia shige yizhao* (Sunken Cathedral: Commemorative Pictures of Underground Poetry from 1970s China). Wulumuqi: Xinjiang qingshaonian chubanshe, 1999.

Xiao, Yuan. "Fazhan caishi ying daoli" (Change Is the Only Way Out). *Chuban guangjiao* 5 (2000).

Xie, Haiyang. "Qingchun jiujing zenme le" (What's Wrong with *Youth*). *Wenxue bao*, January 20, 1994.

Xu, Kun. "Cong ci yue lai yue mingliang" (Brighter and Brighter from Now On). *Beijing wenxue* 11 (1995).

———. *Shuangdiao yexing chuan* (Two-Toned Night Boat). Taiyuan: Shanxi jiaoyu chubanshe, 1999.

Xu, Lifang, et al. *Zhongguo bainian changxiaoshu* (Chinese Best Sellers in the Twentieth Century). Xi'an: Shanxi shifan daxue chubanshe, 2001.

Xu, Linzheng. *Wenhua tuwei: Shiji mo zhi zheng de Yu Qiuyu* (Breaking out of the Cultural Circle: Yu Qiuyu at the Turn of the Century). Hangzhou: Zhejiang wenyi chubanshe, 2000.

Ya, Shan. "Yipi wengao zuo shouci jingjia" (First Manuscripts Auctioned Off Yesterday). *Xinmin Wanbao*, October 29, 1993.

Yang, Aixiang. "Guanyu xiezuo chuban de fansi" (Reflections on Cooperative Publishing Arrangements), in Vol. 7 of Song Yingli et al., eds., *Zhongguo dangdai chuban shiliao* (Collection of Historical Materials on Publishing in China). Zhengzhou: Daxiang chubanshe, 1999.

Yang, Jing. "Hali bote, xinshu shangshi san ba huo" (Harry Potter Comes to the book Market with Force). *Zhongguo chuban* 12 (2000).

Yang, Xueping. "Zhuijiu linglei" (Investigating the Alternative). *Xin shu bao*, March 3, 2000.

Yang, Zhijun. *Zhongguo shushang* (Chinese Book Dealer), Yinchuan: Dunhuang wenyi chubanshe, 1996.

Ye, Yonglie. "Shenzhen wengao jingjia qin li ji" (Witness to The Shenzhen Manuscript Auction). *Zuojia* 9 (2000).

Yu, Haibo. "Youlixisi: Nanbei dazhan qing wei liao" (*Ulysses*: A Civil War Between the South and the North). *Zhonghua dushu bao*, May 11, 1994.

Yu, Jie. *Huo yu Bing: yi ge Beida guai jie de chouti wenxue* (Fire and Ice: Writing Locked Away in the Drawer by a Peking University Prodigy). Beijing: Jingji ribao chubanshe, 1998.

Zha, Jianying. *China Pop: How Soap Operas, Tabloids and Bestsellers Are Transforming a Culture*. New York: New Press, 1995.

Zhang, Changming. Speech at the 2000 Asian Entertainment and Media Conference. *Dianshi yanjiu* 6 (2000).

Zhang, Fu. "'No' xiaoshuo yu linglei yuedu" ("No" Fiction and Alternative Reading). *Jingpin gouwu zhinan*, December 24, 1999.

Zhang, Fuhai. "Zhua zhu meng de shou: liangqiao yi meng he yi feng mi zhongguo" (Holding Hands with Dreams: Why Bridges of Madison County Captured Chinese Hearts) (www.booktide.com/news/20000627/200006270050.html).

Zhang, Hongwei. "Xinzhongguo wushi nian chuban dashi ji" (Chronicle of Publishing Events in the Fifty Years of the People's Republic of China). *Chuban guangjiao* 10 (1999).

Zhang, Jun. "Duanlie: jingshen lichang yu xiezuo zitai" (Breaking Away: Spiritual Perspective and Creative Writing Attitude). *Huanghe* 4 (1999).

Zhang, Kangkang. *Qing'ai hualang* (Gallery of Love and Passion). Shenyang: Chunfeng wenyi chubanshe, 1996.

Zhang, Langlang. "The Legend of the Sun Brigade and Others," in Liao Yiwu, ed., *Chenlun de shengdian: Zhongguo ershi shiji qishi niandai dixia shige yizhao* (Sunken Cathedral: Commemorative Pictures of Underground Poetry from 1970s China). Wulumuqi: Xinjiang qingshaonian chubanshe, 1999.

Zhang, Li. "Wo ye zai zhao bei: ji zuojia chubanshe bianji tushu cehua ren Liufang" (I Too Am Looking for the Right Direction: Interview with Writers Publishing House Editor Liu Fang). *Zhongguo tushu shang bao,* April 3, 1998.

Zhang, Shengyou. "Tushu chubanye gaige zhong de zhiheng zhanlue" (A Balanced Strategy in the Reform of the Publishing Industry). *Wenxue bao*, June 7, 2001,

Zhang, Yigong. "Wo zai xunzhao qiyejia" (I Am Searching for Entrepreneurs). *Wenxue bao,* February 15, 1996.

Zhang, Yiwu. "Yige tonghua de zhongjie: Gu Cheng zhi si yu dangdai wenhua" (End of a Fairytale: The Death of Gu Cheng and Contemporary Culture). *Dangdai zuojia pinglun* 2 (1994).

Zhang, Yizhen. "Rongshu xia: ba suoyou lirun chi tou" (Under the Banyan Tree: Maximizing the Profit) (www3.rongshu.com/publish/readArticle).

Zhang, Zhiqiang. *Feifa chuban huodong yanjiu* (Studies on Illegal Publishing Activities). Guiyang: Guizhou renmin chubanshe, 1998.

Zhao, Chengyu, and Jiang Shuyuan. "Wangluo wenxue: xin wenming de haojiao haishi xin ping zhuang jiu jiu" (Internet Literature: A Clarion Call for a New Civilization or Old Wine in New Bottle). *Zhonghua dushu bao*, December 1, 1999.

Zhao, Wuping. "Shashibiya yizhu da zhuangche" (Clash of Translations of Shakespeare). *Zhonghua dushu bao*, February 7, 1996.

Zhao, Yuezhi. *Media, Market and Democracy in China: Between the Party Line and the Bottom Line*. Urbana and Chicago: University of Illinois Press, 1998.

Zhao, Yunfang. "Jin bubaohu yinlai zhongduo yingzhengzhe" (Golden Cloth Tiger Attracts Many Competitors). *Zhonghua dushu bao*, March 1, 1998.

Zhongguo banben tushuguan, ed. *Quanguo neibu faxing tushu zongmu (1949–1979)*. Beijing: Zhonghua shuju, 1980.

Zhongguo chuban nianjian 1989. Beijing: Zhongguo chuban nianjian.

Zhongguo chuban nianjian 1984. Beijing: Zhongguo chuban nianjian.

Zhongguo chuban nianjian 1981. Beijing: Zhongguo chuban nianjian.

Zhou, Baiyi. "Yao ding Qingshan bu fangsong: 'Yongzheng huangdi' yi shu yingxiao tihui" (Biting and Not Letting Go: Our Experience Marketing *Emperor Yongzheng*). *Chuban guangjiao* 2 (2002).

Zhou, Huimin. "Zhang Shengyou: Chuban gaige pingheng zhanlue di yi ren" (Zhang Shengyou: The First to Approach Publishing Reform with a Balanced Strategy). *Zhongguo qiye bao*, May 28, 2001.

Zhou, Yan. "Beijing wentan sha chu yipi yijia zuojia" (Writers Asking for Market Prices Appear in Beijing). *Wenxue bao*, July 16, 1992.

Zhou, Zan. "Dangdai wenhua yingxiong de chuyan yu jiangluo: Zhongguo shige yu shitan lunzheng yanjiu" (The Emergence and Decline of Contemporary Cultural Heroes: Studies of Chinese Poetry and Polemics in Poetry Circles), in Dai Jinhua, ed., *Shuxie wenhua yingxiong: shiji zhi jiao de wenhua yanjiu* (Writing Cultural Heroes: Cultural Studies at the Turn of Twenty-First Century). Nanjing: Jiangsu renmin chubanshe, 2000.

Zhu, Xiaoru. "Chun wenxue qikan ruhe zou chu kunjing: quan guo wenxue qikan shezhang zhubian huiyi zongshu zhi yi" (How Can Pure Literature Journals Escape Their Predicament: Comprehensive Report on the Meeting of Presidents and Chief-editors of National Literary Journals). *Wenxue bao*, October 30, 1997.

Zi, Sha. "Chubanshe goumai zuojia, dangfou; zuojia gan lun baoshengong, zhi fou" (Is It Proper for Publishers to Purchase Writers, Is It Worthy for Writers to Become Contracted Workers). *Wenxue Bao*, October 14, 1993.

WITHDRAWN
from
STIRLING UNIVERSITY LIBRARY